GRACE
UNDER PRESSURE

THE ROLES OF WOMEN
—THEN AND NOW—
IN THE CATHOLIC CHURCH

BARBARA A. O'REILLY

WestBow
PRESS
A DIVISION OF THOMAS NELSON

WestBow Press books may be ordered through booksellers or by contacting:

WestBow Press
A Division of Thomas Nelson
1663 Liberty Drive
Bloomington, IN 47403
www.westbowpress.com
1-(866) 928-1240

Because of the dynamic nature of the Internet, any web addresses or links contained in
this book may have changed since publication and may no longer be valid. The views
expressed in this work are solely those of the author and do not necessarily reflect the
views of the publisher, and the publisher hereby disclaims any responsibility for them.

Any people depicted in stock imagery provided by Thinkstock are models,
and such images are being used for illustrative purposes only.

Certain stock imagery © Thinkstock.

ISBN: 978-1-4497-2938-7 (sc)
ISBN: 978-1-4497-2939-4 (hc)
ISBN: 978-1-4497-2937-0 (e)

Library of Congress Control Number: 2011918762

Printed in the United States of America

WestBow Press rev. date: 4/30/2012

CONTENTS

For my late mother, Mary Jo Morris O'Reilly, whose love and devotion to my sister, Sheila, and I taught me about the unconditional love of God, and for my late father, Joseph J. O'Reilly, whose strong faith was an example to model.

"The presence and the role of women in the life and mission of the Church . . . remain absolutely necessary and irreplaceable." Pope John Paul II

"Some people claim there's a woman to blame . . . but I know it's my own damn fault." *Margarettaville* by Jimmy Buffet

"When you reach the end of your rope, you will touch the hem of His garment." Circulated on the Internet

"It all happened in a most remarkable moment . . . a moment like no other . . . . God became man. Divinity arrived. Heaven opened herself and placed her most precious one in a human womb. The omnipotent, in one instant, became flesh and blood. The one who was larger than the universe became a microscopic embryo. And he, who sustains the world with a word, chose to be dependent upon the nourishment of a young girl. From *God had come near*—Max Lucado, *Grace for the Moment*, December 25.

Foreword

By **Jack Falvey**, *business writer and educator, graduate of and adjunct professor at Boston College and professor at U. Mass, Boston; author of 14 books; and daily communicant at Catholic Eucharist.*

The wonderful stories of woman's contributions to the Catholic Church were hiding in plain sight all along. Barbara O'Reilly brings them alive for us in this well-written book. These stories involve more than women's washing and ironing of altar cloths. In true reporter style, she shows us that women in the church did much more than you ever imagined.

She takes us back through the ages, to see the relationship of women to the Catholic Church in a new and brighter light. Her first discovery was that her comprehensive Catholic education somehow missed all of the key points where women played a pivotal role in the growth and development of the ministry of Jesus. That's both while He was with us on earth and up to the present day. Her research remedies that defect for us all.

She does not find fault with Leonardo DaVinci in his depiction of the Last Supper, she just wonders who on earth cooked the big lamb dinner? There were a number of women named in the gospel stories who were a part of our Savior's close followers. Why would He leave them out of the night He would first celebrate and institute the Holy Eucharist? Most likely it was a shortage of canvas and oils in later centuries rather than a divine oversight on that holiest of Thursday nights.

Just what was the liturgical significance of pinning a Kleenex® tissue to the top of a woman's head for her to be present in church? Was there any? Once and for all, this practice is analyzed here in depth and significance. Were women throughout church history restricted from a more formal and full participation in God's work on earth for want of a tissue and a hair pin?

This book made me wonder is there a difference between a male and a female soul. There is not. Everything else about males and females is on the table in this text. Remarkably, there is no female bias in the writing. Trained as a reporter, the author is comfortable in letting the facts, once discovered, speak for themselves. Discovering and footnoting sources leaves little doubt to the authenticity of the practices presented. There is some humor in many of the things which previously were accepted as "gospel truth."

I believe this is the first time the cumulative case has been made for the absurdity of all that has gone before with its resultant, residual, modern day gender divisions in our church. How could this be? Readers will find out in clear prose just how all this has come to pass.

We are all called to service. Reading this book will make you wonder—is the service rendered by the Bishop preaching to his flock greater than the first grade teacher explaining God to her charges for the first time? Are either of these gender roles greater in God's eyes? Which appears to be the more difficult task? Which receives the greater earthly recognition and reward? Where does giving birth to a future Bishop rank? How about changing his diapers for a year or two? Where do women fit in the great plan of the life of the church?

You will think all these thoughts, and many more, as a result of this book. It raises some great questions, provides some great observations, and in so doing, raises even more questions as a result. Provocative is the best word for this process. I hope your thinking process will be as provoked as much as mine was as you go through the following pages. It's an awesome read, beautifully done.

Preface

I started this book in another time and place both in my life and in the world of women in the Church. It was the end of the 1970's. I was working as a reporter for a daily newspaper in Toms River, New Jersey, and had done a freelance story on the Catholic Charismatic Renewal in Ireland for *Logos Journal,* a monthly Christian magazine. While attending a Catholic conference as a reporter, I saw Dan Malachuk, publisher of the *Journal* and Logos Books, Plainfield, NJ, and introduced myself.

He asked me what I thought about the changing role of women in the Catholic Church. I said it seemed there was a great dichotomy between women who were learning about headship and submission— where a man is the head of the household—and with women who were seeking ordination to the Catholic priesthood. The latter idea was exploding in the media and in the world with the then very controversial ordination of women to the Episcopal priesthood.

The Catholic Charismatic Renewal members were a significant part of Logos' book audience. Catholic women were learning about headship and submission from their sisters in non-denominational or Pentecostal churches, where it was prevalent. Some women thought it was great and others did not.

Western society's ideas of religion descended from paganism with its many deities—including females!—through Jewish monotheism, into Christianity. Actually, headship and submission existed in the Catholic Church, and in most European cultures without the title, because of the common "ancestry" of the church. Until 1517 with Martin Luther's *95 Theses,* it was one Christian church. Arising out of the Judaic and ancient Roman and Greek societies, headship, anyway, became the model for family structure: the father/husband was the head of the family.

The Catholic Church was and still is patriarchal. Societal influences are ingrained in that. In the Catholic Church the remnant of it was women wearing a hat into church before Vatican II and the male dominated clergy and hierarchy. The Protestant Pentecostal movement in the United States first started in the early 1900's and included a strong emphasis on reading the Bible and the practices of headship and submission.

Mr. Malachuk asked me to write the book. That's how it began. I was and am a journalist, not a theologian. I was not an expert on women's issues; I just happened to be female. A "cradle Catholic," I was neutral on the question of women's ordination in the Catholic Church, not knowing a lot about it, nor why it was prevented. It just was. I thought there had to be some very serious reason why not. To find out that answer—well, you have to read the rest of this book.

I had a contract and did *a lot* of research. I learned a lot about women in many circumstances in and around the world and in the church. When I submitted the manuscript, the editors at Logos really liked my chapters. However, previously, Logos had published a daily Christian newspaper but it never took off and, sadly, bankrupted the company. Logos went out of business; I was released from my contract. In the meantime, life happened. I had to earn a living. I had and was healed of malignant melanoma. I've been living with Multiple Sclerosis (MS) for 40+ years. Through it all, the book never ended for me.

Some things evolved in time in the Church; some did not. I added things, subtracted others. Now, in a new millennium, new chapters were added, changes made to existing one. Only the information about how Jesus treated women—the book's core—can never change. Every one of His episodes with women was a miracle for His time and place and still are today for their examples for modern women.

I've tried very diligently to be factually accurate. If there are any factual errors, I apologize. I grew in many ways from "doing" this book, and hopefully, readers will grow, too, from its reading. Join me in my legacy!

Acknowledgements

Many people helped me through this endeavor—hundreds of women sharing their ideas, stories and aspirations; praying for me; encouraging me. The women and men who lent me books and tapes, including Fr. Jim Borstleman, Cathy Campisi, Claire-Marie Heesaker-Kahn; and Kathleen Egan Bittner, J.D., L.L.M, who gave me her research papers from the Diocese of Trenton's Institute of Lay Ecclesial Ministry (ILEM) course.

Thanks to song writers Mary Daly for allowing me to quote her song, *Touch the Hem of His Cloak,* from her album, *Day of the Lord;* and to Kathryn Christian for allowing me to quote from her CD, *Ascension.* Thanks to Therese Boucher for allowing me to use her material about the Christmas Carol Festivals. Thanks to Dan Malachuk who started me on this journey, and his wife, Viola, who wouldn't let the male editors at Logos change *any* language about the blood-taboos or church misogamy. I appreciate each of you.

I especially want to thank my good friends Bonnie LaFleur; Eileen Vander Meer, Claudia Pena, and the late Claire Dinard, for their love and prayers. Thanks to my long-time friend, Annie Darrow, for standing with me through it all and for all her prayers, wisdom, and insight. House sitting at Eileen's one summer while her family was on vacation, and taking care of her garden and the children's dog, "Screwball," is where I wrote many chapters. Also, thanks to the women from the Toms River Women's Aglow Fellowship, Toms River, NJ, in the late 1970's and early 1980's for all your prayer support. Thanks to Laura Turbini for encouragement.

Appreciation goes to my typists and word processors over time: Harriet Moses, who first told me about the Jewish tradition of G-D;

Iola Steinhoff (formerly Blaska); and Barbara Taranto. I knew the book was blessed in many ways from the get-go but I didn't know at the time, and subsequently learned, that the Lord used even the typing for good. For Iola and her children, it was Iola's only income at the time since her ex-husband was delinquent in child support.

Special thanks to a New Jersey pastoral associate who helped me a lot, pointing me forward, advising me about the important Emerging Models Project. She asked that her name not be mentioned—but she, I, and the Lord know who she is!

To a long-time colleague in Journalism and Public Relations, Ralph Hammock, who happens now to be a Deacon, for his professional encouragement and friendship; to Mary Ann Lacey, of the former House of Peace, Bronx, NY, who shared her experiences working as a lay woman in the Healing Ministry with a priest, the late Fr. Peter McCall, OFM Cap; and to Editor Emeritus of *The Monitor* newspaper, Deacon Joe Donadieu, for his knowledge, friendship and 30 years of writing assignments! Thanks, too, to author, educator and friend, Dr. Myna German Schleifer of Delaware State University, who happens to be Jewish and a published author, who encouraged its publication. Many thanks for invaluable help to my personal computer wizard, Lorie Glass, a friend since high school days. And endless thanks to my cousin, Theresa O'Reilly Pisacreta, who helped get the continuous file of all the individual chapters in order for Westbow. You are all angels in disguise.

Merci bien a Michelle Mally pour votre l'assistance re Jouarre en francais and for finding out about Regina Laudis in Connecticut.

To Debbie Tobias, thanks for your wise words, support, encouragement, and sharing the wisdom "Living in Holland," which gently details life with a chronic illness or the ups and downs of regular life: A traveler planned a journey to Italy to see the treasures, museums, coastal villages, cities, learn the language, and then live there. For unknown reasons, the traveler instead ended up in Holland and had to stay—with its different climate, different language, and different culture. It was quite disappointing to end up *anywhere else*, when everything had been planned for Italy. But, in time, Holland wasn't horrid as originally thought—there were tulips, windmills, the sea, and other delights, or learning to accept life where you are. I've landed "in Holland" frequently. The story helps pull me through.

They say a book is forever. All of you are part of this one, eternally. I couldn't have done it without you. With love, Barbara

CHAPTER 1

Proclaim Liberty to the Unfree

Jesus' public ministry was filled with examples of how people should act—toward God, toward others, and toward the unloved. His message was revolutionary in its simplicity, and in how different it was then—and now—from usual human activity. His entire earthly mission was about us.

In the language of the 21st century, his ministry was inclusive, interactive, and what today we call "politically correct." Religious and political leaders of his day radically disagreed—they thought Jesus *was anything* but correct. In fact, they despised him because he taught with authority and knowledge and because the people listened to and believed in him.

Jesus departed from the usual standards of His day with His enlightened attitude toward many aspects of Jewish life, not just His relationships with women. He panned the Pharisees, calling them "hypocrites and vipers" (Matthew 23).[1] He had a personal relationship with God—the God of Abraham, Moses and David, who was also the God of Sarah, Miriam and Deborah—and spoke of God with familiarity in any age where 'religious' people didn't even speak the word "God." Devout and Orthodox Jews today still spell the word, G-d, or GD, since they considered it too holy a word to be spelled out. Nor do they say God's name in the Old Testament, Yahweh, because it's too sacred.

Jesus even had the "audacity" to call God, "Abba," an endearment. It was the equivalent of calling Father-God "Daddy" or "Papa." Abba

---

[1]   See also Luke 11: 37-44, 12: 1-2.

is a term signifying relationship, rather than genus or gender, said noted Scripture scholar, Fr. George Tavard.[2] "God is beyond all genuses for Divine Fatherhood is an analogy that allows us to speak of the unspeakable," he wrote.[3]

> The human term of the fatherhood analogy is not human fatherhood as lived by human fathers; it is the experience of human persons, women as well as men, of relating to a human father in love, gratitude and obedience. The point for comparison of Divine Fatherhood is not human fatherhood, but human filiation. My experience of human filiation helps me to understand Jesus' relationship to his Divine Father.[4]

With all these non-conformities you would think Jesus' attitude toward women would have been anticipated rather than a surprise. It wasn't. However, His treatment of women just didn't pop up out of the blue. At significant times in the Old Testament women were treated less as inferiors than in the time of Christ. "Misogyny is not as pervasive in early Israelite society as it is in Paul's[5] or that of the authors of the present declaration,"[6] said Thomas L. Thompson in his article, "The Divine Plan of Creation: 1 Cor. 11:7 and Gen. 2:18-24."[7]

---

[2]   Tavard, George, Fr. "Sexist Language in Theology," *Woman: New Dimensions: Theological Studies*, (New York: Paulist Press, 1975) 140.

[3]   Ibid., 140.

[4]   Ibid., 141.

[5]   Although usually thought of as a contemporary of Jesus and the disciples, Paul was born in 10 A.D., a decade after Jesus' death, and executed as a martyr in 67 A.D. He was educated as a Pharisee in Jerusalem, and then converted to belief in Christ around 34 A.D. His letters probably date from 50 to 65 A.D. (*Jerusalem Bible, New Testament*, 194).

[6]   "The Declaration on the Question of the Admission of Women to the Ministerial Priesthood," The Sacred Congregation for the Doctrine of the Faith, October 15, 1976.

[7]   Thomas L. Thompson. "The Divine Plan of Creation: 1 Cor. 11:7 and Gen. 2:18-24," *Women-Priests: A Catholic Commentary*, (New York: Paulist Press, 1977) 211.

Jesus was well-versed in Scripture, so He was very much aware of the earlier contributions of women. Unlike His contemporaries, He didn't ignore the contributions. Not all the times He quoted scripture concerned women, but those times were significant.

In the desert before His ministry began, Jesus used His knowledge of Scripture to confront and rebut the devil's temptations and the latter's out-of-context Scripture passages (Matt. 4: 1-11, Luke 4: 1-13). As a child He questioned and conversed with the Scripture scholars in the temple (Luke 2: 41-52). After the question of divorce was raised, He spoke of marriage as a positive factor and not the negative, divorce. (Matt. 19: 3-12; Mark 10: 2-13)

Jesus went to his hometown synagogue and read the prophetic verse written about him in Isaiah 61: 1-2:

> ***The Spirit of the Lord has been given to me, for He has appointed me. He has sent me to bring the good news to the poor, to proclaim liberty to captives and to give the blind new sight, to set the downtrodden free, to proclaim the Lord's year of favor.*** (Luke 4: 8-19)

That verse is Jesus' mission statement. His audience in the synagogue listened to Him with rapt attention: Jesus spoke with authority and power. The people knew they were hearing a message from God—they just didn't realize it was about Jesus and His ministry.

If that quote was aimed at a particular audience it was women. They were only allowed in worship services at specified times of the year, or in specific areas of the synagogue or temple; women were not even considered a true part of the congregation—whose sign of inclusion was circumcision. Even today in Jewish Orthodox ceremonies, a 'quorum' of 10 men, called a *minyan,* is needed for a congregational service, no matter how many women are present. The Jewish Orthodox still separate the men and women by a wall or curtain called *mechitzah.*[8]

---

[8]   The Role of Women, Intermediate, Judaism. Accessed on-line, 2010.

Women were poor, owning no property, and 'poor in spirit,' knowing no salvation. They were unfree, being chattel—that is the property of a father or husband—or if a slave, the property of a master, called "Lord." (Or in the Hebrew, called "Ba'al," also the name of the Canaanite deity.) Women were tied to rigorous housekeeping chores. They were uneducated and spent most of their child-bearing years as "ritually unclean," leaving deep psychological scars. They had no civil rights, could not inherit or bear witness. They were not counted as citizens, not in the census, not even in the Scriptural accounts of the multiplication of the loaves and fishes. (Mark 6: 44, 8-9; Luke 9: 14; John 6: 10; Matt. 5: 38, 16: 9)[9] Women were blinded by society's patriarchal and cultural mores; they were bound by "The Sin of Eve," and surely, they were downtrodden.

If Jesus came to bring the Lord's favor for any one group, it was/ is women. The whole point of "the subordinate position of women in society was a fact illustrative of human alienation (from God) and hardly good or desirable," Thompson said.[10]

How Jesus treated women and how that affects the woman of today is the focus of this book. What role, function, or position do women in the Roman Catholic Church hold today? What role-changes are occurring?

While this book will confine itself to the topic of women in the Catholic Church, it is not exclusively for a Catholic audience. After all, the culture from which Christianity sprang was Jewish. Jesus was a Jewish man who treated Jewish women differently. It is His attitude we need to recapture.

---

[9] These biblical passages show there were definitely females and children present, as well as the 5,000 males. These multiplication stories are a reference to Moses feeding the people in the desert as well as a forerunner of the Eucharist where—as one of the Medieval Mystics, Julian of Norwich, said: "He fills us with Himself." So, it's altogether appropriate that the entire community of Jews were present, men, women and children. Maybe the total audience that day was closer to 8,000-10,000, or more, but we'll never know because only the men were counted, which was the custom of the time.

[10] Thompson, 210.

Until the 16th century, 1517, there was only one Christian Church so there is a common tradition for all Christian denominations. With increasing ecumenism between the denominations, the impact of one on the other is immeasurable. Besides, in Heaven, everyone loses his or her denominational label.

There are three primary questions this book will attempt to answer. How did we get here, where are women now, and where are we going?

CHAPTER 2

Jesus the Non-Conformist

Remember the Baltimore Catechism? If you are a "Baby Boomer" or older and Catholic, you certainly should. The Catechism was the standard text used for educating Catholic children in the faith from the late 1800's to the 1960's. It said, "Jesus Christ was born more than 1,900 years ago." It never said how different those times were from the 20th century when the catechism was current, or how different those days were from now, the 21st century. It never said—but should have—that the way Jesus treated women *was different radically* from the cultural mores of His day.

He broke all the taboos. Jesus was brazenly non-conformist and it shocked his male-disciples, the Jewish Pharisees, and other leaders of His time. Sometimes it even shocked the women. "What? You are a Jew and you ask me, a Samaritan, for drink? (John 4:9, *Jerusalem Bible)*[11] The Confraternity (Catholic/pre-Vatican II), King James and New American Standard (NAS) versions all include the fact that she was female in their translations. "How is it that you, being a Jew, ask me for a drink since I am a Samaritan woman?" asked the NAS edition.[12]

---

[11]   Unless specified otherwise, all quotes are from Jones, Alexander, Ed., *The Jerusalem Bible, Reader's Edition* (Garden City: Doubleday, 1966)

[12]   NAS, John 4:9

JOHN 4:7

Jesus at the well with the woman of Samaria.

The Samaritans were traditionally at enmity with the Jewish people. Samaria had been overtaken so many times by warring tribes—all with the pillage, rape and ravage mentality—that its bloodline was not pure. Thus, unlike the Jews, the Samaritans were of mixed blood. So, the Jews considered the Samaritans to be an abomination and unholy, even though they, like the Jews, worshipped Yahweh. That's why the Samaritans were despised by the Jews; their women were especially hated, or in current hip terminology, "disrespected."

In this encounter, it was even more shocking that He spoke to a *woman* in public than to a Samaritan. John 4:10 says, "Jews, in fact, do not associate with Samaritans." This is evident by the disciples' reaction to the situation and conversation: "At this point His disciples returned, and were surprised to find Him speaking to a woman, though none of them asked, 'What do you want from her?' Or 'why are you talking to her?'" (John 4: 27-28)

Why was it shocking? As a rabbi, a teacher, a man . . . He was forbidden by the Law from speaking to a woman in the street. Let alone to touch a woman or treat her as an intellectual and spiritual equal—all of which He did.

Jesus' demeanor with women—obvious in any reading of the Gospel accounts of the New Testament—was radically different from the way His male-disciples reacted to and treated women. Despite His example, they were bound by societal strictures. Jesus' way was radically different from the way women have been treated in the institutional church for two thousand plus years. Even considered now, Jesus' methods were, and are radically different from that of society.

CHAPTER 3

Overview:
Women's Roles—Then and Now

Where are we now? Believe it or not, women in the Catholic Church today are experiencing more widespread influence and real responsibility, as well as liturgical participation, than ever before. Few times in its history has the church allowed women to have so much clout. Never before did women have such diversity of ministry. The woman in the church today is radically different from how she was viewed through history, 20 years ago, even yesterday. The problem is: few people realize it.

These statements are not just a nominal and paternalistic pat-on-the-back. They are true. Several things are sure: today, woman's role, position, status in the Church is better than ever. She is no longer limited to one or two tasks, as in the former days of only washing altar cloths or teaching religious education in school, formerly called CCD (Confraternity of Christian Doctrine).

Probably most important is that many women active in the church today have a renewed spirituality in their own lives. They want to serve in ministry out of love for the Lord and willingness to help others. Women today are impacting more on various aspects of church life—through work in chancery officialdom, participation in liturgical functions, and under Canon Law, running parishes where there is no resident priest.

Pope John Paul II wrote in his "Letter to Women" in 1995 that women are *"absolutely necessary and irreplaceable"* in the

church. [13] That has to become the mantra for women serving in the church in the 21st century. The church cannot exist without women and our contributions. Make no mistake: it never did, nor could.

Realizing women's contribution and roles today ease somewhat centuries of blatant misogyny in the male-dominated church. Misogyny is defined as "hatred of women." Misogynous attitudes in the Church have been both overt and surreptitiously covered. Although often it was a reflection of male leaders' times or training, in no way is it "an imitation of Christ." Misogyny is prevalent in the world as well as church history. Those are facts. They cannot be ignored, yet it is being overcome, in most Western cultures anyway. That's as true for the church as it is for society.

Instead of being the leader and formulator of world opinion—which should be the church's rightful place in a perfect world—in many ways today, the church mirrors society. As society and its perspectives change, so do those of the people who comprise the body of believers; in turn, the church changes as these perspectives are incorporated. Unfortunately, the church, especially its hierarchy, is usually a slow mirror.

Overcoming long-entrenched misogyny is one problem for women today. Another is overcoming defining God solely in male terms, such as He, His, Father and Son. Such word usage has given us a distorted picture. Not only about God, whom we cannot begin to describe or understand in Divine completeness, but about women. In reality, God "The Father," is our "spiritual *parent*," encompassing elements of fatherhood *and* motherhood.

If God is masculine, or male, in human thinking, it follows that feminine, female, is "less best." So, in this illogical sequence, it continues that God's "better" gifts must be reserved for men. Unfortunately, that was the model of church and society for millennia. Fortunately, it isn't true.

So, why is the church always described in female terms as "Mother Church" or the "ecclesia?" It isn't because of the male clergy. It was started to show the departure from pagan practices which were

---

[13]   Pope John Paul II. "Letter of Pope John Paul II to Women," June 29, 1995.

necessary to worship the Loving God. Noted Scripture theologian Fr. George H. Tavard in his book *Women in Christian Tradition,* explains:

> When the main layer of Chapter 1 in Genesis was composed, the Temple was already built and a regular weekly liturgy followed the lunar calendar. The lunar calendar is also the female calendar. That is to say, the Female cycle has been taken as a pattern for temple worship and, accordingly, the life of worship. Thus the entire People, as represented at the Temple, became feminine in relation to Yahweh. The adoption of the lunar—feminine period as a pattern for both liturgical piety and the creation myth was meant to draw in the Hebrews toward authentic feminism, away from the siren songs of Canaanite female worship.[14]

If the entire people are feminine in relation to Yahweh, than *all people* are "daughters" and not "sons of God." How come no one ever preaches about that? The church, though always described in female terms, is neither male nor female. It contains both elements. It is, after all, God's church, made in Divine Image.

Does it surprise you that the Church, for centuries, was guilty of the sin of discrimination? We are surprised only because we expect the "Body of Christ on earth" to be different in its attitudes from society. Regarding women, it hasn't been. In His dealing with women in Scripture, Jesus said "no way" to this prevalent discrimination and treating women as inferiors. He treated women as equals, with respect for their individuality, intelligence, and faith. He treated women with dignity—all attributes unheard of in His day. His behavior, and its transforming grace, is the subject of several detailed chapters, the core of this book.

---

[14] George H. Tavard. *Women in Christian Tradition,* (Notre Dame, IN: University of Notre Dame Press, 1973), 11.

Catholic writer Arlene Swidler wrote a book entitled *Woman in a Man's Church*.[15] While this is mostly still true of the hierarchal structure, and often about women in Latino cultures,[16] it is not a precise statement about the body of believers. The majority of people who practice their faith within organized religious bodies, especially in Christian denominations, are women. That comes as no surprise; it was ever so.

Historically, women have been the mainstay both in attendance and contributions, as well as the moving force in getting others, namely, husbands and children, to attend services. "For too many years women kept the churches going. Without women we would have lost the church long ago," Ernie Raynor, then president of a Toms River, NJ chapter of Full Gospel Business Men's Fellowship International, said in a newspaper article about the men's non-denominational Christian group.[17]

Conditioning is still strong. Most people, when they heard the topic for this book, asked "What role?" That's just the point. Too often the lack of a role has been the stereotypical image and place of women in the church because the activities in which women were involved were not officially recognized as "ministry."

The dignity of the human person is a central theme in Catholic Social Teaching. In America since the Civil Rights era of the 1960's, discrimination against people because of their skin color or ethnic origin is illegal and, religiously, discrimination is considered the sin of racism. The U.S. Conference of Catholic Bishops (USCCB), previously called the National Conference of Catholic Bishops (NCCB), approved its *third* pastoral letter condemning the sin of racism in 1979. The pastoral said it was not sufficient to recognize that racism still exists in our society, but that specific things had to

---

[15] Arlene Swidler, *Woman in a Man's Church: From Role to Person.* (New York: Paulist Press, 1972).

[16] See Silvana Paternostro, *In the Land of God and Man.* (New York: Plume, a Division of Penguin Books, 1998).

[17] As quoted in Barbara O'Reilly, "Christian Businessmen Gather to Worship and Fellowship," *The Asbury Park Press,* Vol. 100, No. 124 (May 25, 1979), A19.

be done to eliminate it, to change individual attitudes, to prevent its perpetration on future generations.[18]

There is also the sin of sexism, discrimination because of sex. It is more pervasive than any other kind of discrimination, but up to 1979, the bishops never issued a pastoral condemning sexism.

The Bishops started drafting such a pastoral in the early 1980's. After four drafts, three previous defeats and many years, it was defeated again. The bishops finally released its women's pastoral, "Strengthening the Bonds of Peace: A Pastoral Reflection on Women in the Church and in Society," in 1995. That was 16 years after the racism pastoral of 1979. It welcomed women's gifts, affirmed the fundamental equality of women, acknowledged that sexism still exists in the church, and pledged renewed efforts to guard against it in church teaching and practices.[19]

Why was it so difficult for the Bishops to write about women? I think, wanting to offend no one, the Bishops chose to delay indefinitely rather than have something which was both topical and controversial. As with the sin of racism, specific things must be done to eliminate sexism. Future generations must be shielded against sexism. Individual attitudes still need to change.

What's coming in following chapters? We start with Eve in Paradise and go through pagan times. Then we follow women in the Old and New Testaments. Further chapters show women's contributions through 2,000 plus years of church. Then we continue with Catholic women of faith in various ministries in our own time. This includes forecasts for the future of the church in America from the ongoing Emerging Models Project, making this book as current as possible. Obviously, the book deals with women's roles—then and now.

The facts are that women did more in the church than wash altar cloths. This is gradually becoming more well-known, but,

[18] Barbara O'Reilly. "Bishops Recommend Catholic Institutions Take Steps to Eliminate 'Sin of Racism' and Bishops Attack 'Sin of Racism' but Fail in Assault on 'Sexism'." *Religious News Service*, New York, NY, Nov.15, 1979, 6-8.
[19] NCCB. "Strengthening the Bonds of Peace: A Pastoral Reflection on Women in the Church and in Society," 1995. The Bishops also released "Follow the Ways of Love," a pastoral on family in 1994.

unfortunately, the majority of Christians have no idea whatsoever about all the significant roles women held. Since Christianity's roots are in Judaism, we start there. We will look at all these aspects of women in the church in closer detail. These are a few:

IN THE OLD TESTAMENT:

- Women were the symbolic and literal "Mothers of the Church."
- Women held positions of responsibility in the religious life of the Israelites, including the God-appointed position of "Prophet." The prophet's word was the final authority and it was obeyed by the people, the priests, and the monarchy.
- Women led worship services at the Red Sea; before the Ark of the Covenant; and in the Temple.
- Women were an integral part of the praise ministry of their day.
- Women were eligible to take the sacred, priestly and consecrated, vow of the *Nazarite*.

IN THE FOUR GOSPELS:

- Women were disciples of Jesus, traveled in ministry with Him, and were his personal friends.
- Women were the recipients of major truths about His messianic ministry.
- Women discussed spiritual and intellectual matters with Jesus, despite the facts that women were generally uneducated and specifically forbidden from studying the Torah.
- Jesus broke the blood taboos and other cultural stereotypes regarding women and ritual uncleanness.
- Jesus' mother, Mary, was the first believer in the New Testament. Her role, then and now, is to bring us to Jesus.
- Women helped Jesus grow in his ministry.

- Women did not abandon Jesus as the men did during His crucifixion.
- Women were the first to discover Jesus was risen on Easter morning. Not just one woman but several.
- Women, including Mary Magdalene, were the first to see the Risen Christ. She was first to speak with Him.
- Mary Magdalene was the first to proclaim and preach the message of His resurrection and to meet the criteria of Apostleship.

IN THE ACTS OF THE APOSTLES, THE PASTORAL LETTERS OF THE NEW TESTAMENT AND IN THE EARLY CHURCH:

- Women were present at the outpouring of the Holy Spirit on Pentecost, considered to be the "birthday" of the church, and received the same gifts of the spirit as did the male disciples.
- Women were instrumental in the formation of the new Judaism, later known as Christianity. In fact, the initial meetings of the formative church were held in women's homes.
- Women held the position of prophetess in the early church, a position of great spiritual esteem and ranking importance. In writings contemporary to New Testament times, prophets and prophetesses were known as the leaders of worship.
- Women preached and taught the "Good News" and had many important converts.
- Women were "elect in the church," comparable to today's position of elder, and were "episcopa," that is overseers, the feminine root word for our term, "bishop."[20]

---

[20] Joan Morris. *The Lady Was A Bishop: The Hidden History of Women with Clerical Ordination and the Jurisdiction of Bishops.* (New York: Macmillan Co., 1973), 57.

IN CONTINUITY AND PERHAPS LEAST KNOWN:

- Women were deacons in both the Eastern and Roman rites: some as late as the 10th or 13th centuries.
- Mary Magdalene was maligned deliberately by a pope giving her an imaginary and negative life-style, unsubstantiated by Scripture.
- Women were ordained to the ecclesiastical hierarchical position of abbess and yielded quasi-Episcopal power with spiritual and civil jurisdiction over both men and women in medieval times. In rank, the abbesses were lower than a bishop and higher than a priest. The authority of the Abbess was fostered, recognized and preserved by Papal Bulls until 1874, a mere 138 years ago. The record was "deliberately falsified," said Joan Morris in *The Lady was a Bishop.*[21] "All these things have become hidden history. Nobody ever hears anything about it. It is hushed up, and the Christian tradition is presented as an all-male right of authority as though it had been so always."[22]
- In the Dark Ages in Western Europe, women were spiritual mystics, helping to preserve the Faith itself—and the faith of believers. Two of these mystics are now both canonized saints and Doctors of the Church, Saints Catherine of Siena and Teresa of Avila. There were named in 1970. Saint Therese of Liseux was named a Doctor of the Church in 1977. Mystic and medieval abbess, Hildegard of Bingen, will be made Doctor in Oct. 2012.

CURRENTLY:

- Today, women serve in every type of parish ministry except the ordained ministries, including the important Lay Ecclesial

---

[21]   Morris, xi-xii, 99-100.
[22]   Morris, 57.

Ministry (LEM), and outnumber men serving in LEM positions.

- Today, women currently serve in all levels of diocesan chancery offices, including as high positions as chancellor and vice-chancellor of the diocese. Women comprise one-quarter of all chancellor positions nowadays. That is to allow priests, who previously always held these positions, more time for priestly ministry not just administrative jobs.[23]

- Female altar servers were allowed at the end of the 20th century—in 1994. However, before altar girl servers were allowed, some pastors got around the technical prohibition against "girls," by having women as altar servers. One pastor said about the women altar servers in his parish, "They do a beautiful job. Some of the parishioners, especially newcomers, were surprised by it initially, but they got over it. The women are dedicated and perform with the utmost reverence, as you would expect." (FYI, women altar servers were not allowed in that diocese at the time.)

- Women are currently serving as associate pastors, sometimes called pastoral assistants, and as pastoral administrators, where women run parishes as Pastoral Life Coordinators (PLC) in parishes without a resident priest, in accord with church law.

- Women serve as canon lawyers for the church, and as director of personnel for dioceses. Also a woman served 13 years as Associate General Secretary of the National Conference of Catholic Bishops (NCCB). This was *prior* to the Vatican saying women could not hold the actual General Secretary position or the Associate General position.[24]

- Women head social service agencies such as Catholic Charities; church media outlets, like newspapers or the latest modern media; head evangelizations efforts for dioceses, and more.

---

[23] Renee M. LaReau. "Church Ladies: Women in Leadership," *U.S Catholic*, online, Dec. 16, 2010, assessed Feb. 2011.

[24] Ibid.

Vatican II called for a full participatory church. With women's inclusions in various ministries, it's on its way. It is far from a man's church; it has to be. That's the point of Redemption—it is for everyone.

CHAPTER 4

All About Eve and Paradise Lost

It all began with Eve back there in Paradise.

Jesus referred to this when He quoted Scripture on the divorce question. His emphasis was on marriage and the insolubility, the fidelity, of it. "Have you not read that the creator from the beginning 'made them male and female' (Gen. 1:27) and that He said, 'This is why a man must leave his father and mother and cling to his wife, and the two become one body?' (Gen. 2:24) They are no longer two, therefore, but one body. So, then what God has united man must not divide," Jesus quoted (Matt. 19:5-6).

Jesus' quote is a combination of the two creation stories in Genesis, called the Yahwist and Priestly traditions.[25] Scripture scholars agree the second version, Genesis 2:18-25, is *older* than the first version, Genesis 1: 26-31. Together they form two episodes of one story, although the Yahwist—the older version in chapter two—is often viewed as an amplification of the Priestly version of chapter one.[26] The two versions are written from completely different perspectives, with divergent theological points to emphasize and originate in two completely different religious traditions.

Donald Goergen in *The Sexual Celibate* said, "The Yahwist writes of Yahweh as Creator, the Lord of sexuality who loves His People."[27] Yahweh is the true Lord of fertility who creates for man

---

[25] *Jerusalem Bible.* "Introduction to the Pentateuch," 3.

[26] Tavard, *Women in Christian Tradition,* 11.

[27] Donald Goergen, *The Sexual Celibate,* (New York: Seabury Press, 1974) 233.

a fertile garden in which to live. "God is concerned about man and aware he struggles with loneliness," Goergen said.[28] The creatures of the garden do not provide proper society for the man, *Ish*, and so God creates a woman, *Ishah*, someone like man and yet different from him, a sexually different person, the completion of creation.[29]

"Sexuality," according to philosopher Dietrich Bonhoeffer's work, *The Creation and The Fall,* "is nothing but the ultimate realization of our belonging to one another," Goergen quoted.[30] Woman, or *Ishah*, according to Goergen, "is a gift for man so man might live in fellowship and not be lonely."[31]

So, who is man? "Adam is literally 'humus,' the one from the soil, 'adamah,' a name of humility," Tavard said.[32] *Significantly, the woman is not directly related to it, but to the other name of man, Ish, by which she is called Ishah.* From his origin in the earth, man had received a name, Adam, translating the lowliness of his condition. For the name, in Hebrew philosophy, unveils the true meaning of the reality it designates.

> From his companionship with woman, man obtains his name of glory, that which expresses his condition as a 'being-in-relation.' Adam, in Hebrew, is a collective rather than a singular word: that is, it fits man as mankind rather than as an individual. It denotes a quality, that of being from dust, which belongs to all those who will eventually be called men. It has no connotation of sex. The sex name of man is his other name, Ish, by which he relates to woman, Ishah.[33]

---

[28] Goergen, 15.
[29] Tavard, *Women in Christian Tradition,* 13.
[30] As quoted in Goergen, 232.
[31] Goergen, 15-16.
[32] Tavard, *WCT,* 6.
[33] Ibid.

Adam and Eve/Ish and Ishah

For man, "Fellowship is finally achieved. Woman is the expression of God's creativity through which loneliness is overcome," Goergen said. The undertone of the passage is one of fellowship and unity. The basic message is God's love: for God so loves mankind that He does not want man to be alone.[34]

There is no shame in the Yahwist tradition regarding sexuality; it is the same vein which runs through the Song of Songs, also called the "Song of Solomon," which is quite different in tone and language from most other Old Testament writings. It's obviously a celebration between two lovers—whether they are symbolically Yahweh and Israel; Christ and the ecclesia; an individual and God; or two romantically involved persons, who are absolutely committed to one another.

---

[34] Goergen, 16.

The Yahwist tradition, Goergen said, sees woman with equal dignity to man. "She is man's partner. Thus the Yahwist theology is distinct from the Canaanite's fertility cults' degradation of women with its fertility cults for worship of Baal, infant sacrifice, and sacred prostitution."[35]

Genesis is a mixture of the two traditions of creation sexuality. Genesis contains mixed elements in chapters 1 through 11 of both Yahwist and Priestly. For instance, Genesis 1 through 2:3, is Priestly; Genesis 2:4 through 4, is Yahwist; Genesis 5 is Priestly; Genesis 6 is Yahwist.[36]

The Priestly account associates sexuality with propagation, "Be fruitful and multiply," (Gen. 1:28) and its writer is presumed to have been a priest writing around the Sixth Century B.C. The Yahwist tradition is the one most frequently quoted in the New Testament.[37] The New Testament is completely concerned with the love of Creator-God for His People. That's why Jesus came. God's chosen people become brethren with Christ, joint heirs through Baptism. (See Rom. 8:17). "Brethren" becomes a 'family,' which noted teacher, Dr. Robert Frost, said "is what God always wanted."[38]

"Sexuality," Goergen said, "must be understood in the context of the theology of creation and not only the theology of the Fall, which comes later."[39]

Goergen continues his explanation with a comparison of spiritual and sexual union. (That's also the theme of the Song of Songs and of the on-again, off-again relationship between Hosea and Gomer in the book of Hosea. Hosea marries the prostitute Gomer, who cannot be faithful. The latter represents the relationship between God and the people of Israel, who stray and worship false gods.)

"The union of the soul (spirit) with God is the unitive way of mystical theology. Erotic union is the symbol for spiritual union,"

---

[35] Goergen, 233.
[36] Goergen, 14.
[37] Goergen, 232.
[38] Dr. Robert Frost, "The Father Heart of God," (Eastern General Conference Cassettes, Box 617, Ann Arbor, MI 48107).
[39] Goergen, 16.

Goergen said.[40] This yearning of God to be one with us is beautifully expressed in the well-known hymn "Hosea," from the album, *Listen*, performed by the Monks of Western Priory, Weston, VT.

> Come back to me with all your heart. Don't let fear keep us apart. Trees do bend, though straight and tall. So must we to others' call.
> *Long have I waited for your coming home to Me and living deeply our new life. (Chorus)*
> The wilderness will lead you to your heart, where I will speak. Integrity and justice, with tenderness, you shall know. *(Chorus)*
> You shall sleep secure with peace. Faithfulness will be your joy. *(Chorus)*[41]

Our desire to be one with God is rewarded with rest in God's presence, unity with the divine. Jesus' quote on marriage and divorce (Matthew 19: 5-6) stresses unity, the kind of fidelity which comes with God's love.

> Jesus refers to the fact of sexual differentiation. In Hebrew Theology, the Priestly tradition emphasizes the male and female, and He switches to the Yahwist, reinforcing it with His own words. Emphasis on fidelity comes on strongly in the gospels. Divorce is frowned upon because it is a lax attitude toward fidelity. Love is as strong as death. The two people are no longer two but are one as a result of God's activity. Hence there is sacredness to this union. Once such a human relationship is created, it cannot be undone. Fidelity is the hallmark of true union.[42]

"Love is as strong as death," and "fidelity is the hallmark of true union," exemplify the way Jesus loves us. Like the paradisiacal

---

[40]   Goergen, 17.
[41]   "Hosea," BMI, Benedictine Foundation State of Vermont, Inc., 1973.
[42]   Goergen, 20.

union, once a personal relationship with Christ is begun, it can never be dissolved.

> Nothing, therefore, can come between us and the love of Christ, even if we are troubled or worried, or being persecuted, or lacking food or clothes, or being threatened, or even attacked. For I am certain of this: neither death nor life, no angel, no price, nothing that exists, nothing still to come, not any power, or height or dept, nor any created thing, can ever come between us and the love of God made visible in Jesus Christ our Lord. (Rom. 8: 35-36, 38-39).

Men and women are inevitably linked, in creation, in life, in marriage, and in the ecclesia. Woman, *Ishah,* was taken from man, *Ish*; she is part of Adam, the collective word, meaning mankind, or in today's terminology, humankind. So, literally, what Genesis 1: 26-27 says and (hopefully what future Bible translations will say) is this:

> *Let us (Elohim*—the plural Hebrew name of God, which shows community, relationship and union with Divine nature, and indicating the Trinity)[43] *make humankind in our image,* in the image of ourselves, and let *them* be masters of the fish of the sea, the birds of heaven, the cattle, all the wild beasts and all the reptiles that crawl upon the earth. *God created humankind in the image of the Divine, in the image of God, men and women were created; male and female God created them.*

Genesis 1:31 says, "God saw all he had made and indeed it is very good." It is only "very good" after mankind is distinguishable as men and women, not before. Prior to that, creation is "incomplete." Woman is the perfection of God's creation.[44] Fr. Tavard explains:

---

[43]   *Jerusalem Bible*, 3, Footnote, lE, 7.
[44]   Tavard, *WCT*, 13.

God looks at his work when it is half done and pronounces the verdict that the work should be brought to completion. Adam invents animals' names but finds no companion among them; he can establish no society with them. They answer his call; but nothing else happens. Adam himself is not transformed and completed by his experience. As far as mankind as a whole is concerned, there is only one creation, that of Adam. The next step does not come as a second process of creation but as a step within the total process or as a further development of what began with the fashioning of Adam. We should therefore understand woman not as an addition to the mankind that is the person of Adam; rather Adam himself; (in that part of him which was his rib) is built up into woman.

She (*Ishah*) proceeds from inside of Adam where she was already present as that to which mankind was destined, as the development that would bring it to perfection, as the identity with a difference which make society-building possible. 'This is bone of my bone and flesh of my flesh.' Mankind recognizes itself in Ishah. It speaks of itself as being present in women. Adam becomes a person, aware of himself, reaching consciousness as mankind at the unveiling of woman. For woman also is mankind: the differentiation of Adam into *Ish* and *Ishah*, of mankind into male and female.

She is no other than Adam; but she is Adam as bringing to perfection what has been imperfect. She is mankind as fully aware of its status, as the goal and perfection of man. She is not made as Adam's helpmate just because he is lonely. She is created as the perfecting element. Seeing each other, *Ish* and *Ishah* know each other to be one. They were not ashamed because they were not viewing each other as strangers, but saw each other as himself.[45]

---

[45]   Tavard, *WCT*, 7-8.

Together, man and woman are made in the likeness of God. Tavard explained:

> Adam is therefore made one and many, singular and plural. The singular is Adam, the collective term for mankind which in itself has no connotation of sex. The plural, with which Adam is identical, in the image of God, he created them male and female.

> Neither male nor female alone is in the likeness of Elohim, but both together. Man and woman are not only two, they are also one. Their oneness in distinction is the image and likeness of God. By multiplying, they will fulfill themselves as 'image' of Elohim, by becoming numerous like the Elohim in the heavens. By dominating the earth they will also become the image of the divine power.[46]

For centuries men have attributed the "Fall of Man," meaning mankind, to the "Fall of Eve," meaning one woman. Everything was blamed on her, since she believed the serpent's suggestion first and made the choice for the forbidden. New Jersey minister Malcolm Smith taught that the choice was the important thing; not whether or not it was to eat an apple or anything else, or whether to cross a bridge or climb a mountain.[47]

It's pretty apparent that to blame everything on the woman denies certain male responsibility in the whole situation. First, if you read and interpret Genesis literally, Eva, which means "mother of life," or *Ishah,* the woman, was not yet formed from the rib when *Ish,* the man, was warned about the choice-tree. The warning is in Genesis 2: 16-17; the mating-making verses are Genesis 2: 18-25. So, the man, apparently, was the one who told the woman. She heard the message second-hand (as in legal rules of evidence, it was "hearsay.") Perhaps

---

[46]   Tavard, *WCT,* 10-11.
[47]   Rev. Malcolm Smith, "Jesus—Lord of the Mind," From *"Your Thought Life, I,"* MS217, Logos Tapes, Hazlet, NJ 07730.

the man did not stress its importance; or perhaps she just disregarded the message and its warning. It really doesn't matter since there is no denying she chose and 'ate' first.

Second, what is forgotten is *that her action did not cause the wrath of God.* It was only when the man 'ate'—he who was warned by God—that the sin resulted.

Third, presumably, the serpent is speaking to the woman in the presence of the man. The Bible doesn't say otherwise—that Adam was off walking elsewhere (all we know of what Adam and Eve "did" in the garden, was "walk and talk with God in the cool of the evening"). Adam never protested, never told Eve to "stop it," and, although *both of them* had authority over all the creatures (Gen. 1:26, 28), *neither* told the serpent to "get lost." If they had used their authority, the serpent would have had to do as they commanded. *Fini.* The fact that the story reports the animal talked and communicated with *Ish* and *Ishah* intellectually, shows the different level of existence which was, evidently, the norm in Paradise.

Eve cares about knowledge and sees the choice-tree as desirable to further her knowledge. J. Edgar Bruns in *God as Woman, Woman as God* said, "It is she whom the serpent approaches, implying that she would be more readily tempted by the promise of wisdom than her male spouse."[48] It was her desire to be wise, *to be God-like,* which was her undoing. The woman was tempted first, not because she was more susceptible—as the male population likes all women to believe—but according to Tavard, it was precisely because she was the perfection of creation.[49]

> What the serpent tells Eve is not false—but he speaks ambiguously to mislead her. In what way does the knowledge of good and evil bring about a likeness to Elohim? There is no question of becoming equal to Yahweh. Even the serpent could not suggest this since the woman knows she was built

---

[48] J. Edgar Bruns, *God as Woman, Woman as God*, (New York: Paulist Press, 1973), 20-21.

[49] Tavard, *WCT*, 13.

by Yahweh. She desires not the status of Elohim, but the ability to know.

> She desires to know the law, still a secret hidden in God, the Law which is the structure of her own future as the house of Adam. The woman wishes to know what touches her most intimately; in what way, through what means, by what episode will the house of mankind be built? Woman wishes to have a fore-knowledge of the structure and the history of man. This is the 'good and evil' question: that which is known only to Yahweh and to those to whom he reveals it.[50]

For Eve it was a spiritual search and an intellectual one. Women are more likely to seek spiritual answers before men do. Women still want to know the future. That's why women, innocently curious, throughout the ages have been influenced by or involved in the occult, especially horoscopes and charting the future.[51] The Lord's way is usually not the complete panorama but a step-by-step faith-walk.[52]

Ish, or the male, broke God's command because the man also sought to learn God's knowledge. Thirst for knowledge, especially about the course of the future, has been responsible for the development of all the sciences—from the wheel to the iPad®—it is an attempt to transform the earth and assure mankind's future.[53]

---

[50] Tavard, *WCT*, 13-15.

[51] Dealing with the occult is neither a joke, fun, nor unimportant to Satan. In seeking spiritual answers, i.e. the future, from a spiritual force that is not God, people are in effect "placing false idols before us," that is, breaking the First Commandment.

[52] I happened to be climbing alone during a trip to the Grand Canyon a number of years ago, although we weren't supposed to go alone in case of an accident; I had gotten separated from my small group. I didn't realize how far I had gone until I looked out over the edge of the cliff, seeing the river way below. It looked like a precipice! And I was terrified. I was pretty klutzy so I prayed frantically: "Lord how am I going to get down from here?" The clear answer in my spirit was, 'just the way you got here: one step at a time.' I trusted and got down in one piece.

[53] Tavard, *WCT*, 15.

Ish and *Ishah* both 'ate'; both received limited insight, not the total complexity of the wisdom of God. Their nakedness was now an embarrassment. Through God's wondrous plan—that the serpent never even suspected, thinking mankind was the ultimate plan of God, and never conceptualizing incarnate redemption—Eve, symbolically and literally, becomes the "mother of life." Her name becomes synonymous with shame and redemption: shame for the loss of innocence and immortality; and redemption, since Jesus, a human being, would bring "spiritual life" back to mankind. According to Tavard:

> The curse of women evokes a reversal of the order of the universe achieved in Eden. The higher aspect of mankind becomes enslaved, and the ruder aspect, the man, takes over the leadership. Man's relationship to the soil is also reversed. No longer in paradise, now he must labor and till, struggle with nature, and at the end, return to dust.[54]

The goal of the Messianic era will be to return to the Prelapsarian order, Tavard said, since "the primitive order had been lost and women had become little more than slaves.[55]

---

[54] Tavard, *WCT*, 15.
[55] Tavard, *WCT*, 17-18.

CHAPTER 5

Women's Passage:
From Being 'Paradigm'
to Being 'Paradox'

Women became little more than domestic slaves because of a change in the perception of their worth. Much of this is directly attributable to the writings and thinking by some of the greatest male minds on record, the three great theorists—Aristotle, Augustine and Thomas Aquinas. The latter two are known as "Doctors, or Fathers, of the Church" for their contributions to theological study.

After Paradise, as civilization was settling in, the nomadic tribes ruled the world. Women often had more influence in those periods of history than in later "more-civilized" times, such as during the Greek and Roman empires. Why? Women were vital contributors to the survival of the tribe. Who they were and what they did was necessary. Woman was seen by the ancients as the life-giver. She not only brought forth life from her body, she could nurture it as well. Frequently, women maintained the agricultural aspects of the transient society while the men hunted for an elusive prize, namely an animal for dinner; thus, she gave the tribe sustenance in times of scarcity.

Women were also considered important because of the chronological proximity of those times to the pagan eras of rampant goddess worship. However, as the value of women's contributions declined in the eyes of successive societies, so did women's influence. Woman as goddess was prevalent societal philosophy and not a curiosity or quirk. Woman, after all, was the life-giver, the bearer and nurturer of children, and she was mysteriously connected to the cycle of the moon. She bled and still lived.

Elizabeth Dobell in "God and Woman: The Hidden History" explained:

> It was the creative mystery of woman, the flow of a mothers' milk, her menstrual cycle—rhythmically in accord with the waxing and waning of the moon, the birth, increase, decline and 'death' of that celestial orb—was linked to the mystery of creation . . .

> In their desire to be linked to that all-encompassing power, the ancients began developing, at least as early as 30,000 B.C., a mythology of the naked goddess.[56]

From 30,000 B.C. to 2,000 B.C.—and in some places as late as 500 A.D.—*men were subordinate to their wives and mothers.*[57] The Supreme Being—worshipped in the temples—was known as the "Great Mother." She was worshipped in her own right and not as the wife or daughter of some male deity. Even the priests who lead the worship were female, "as astounding as all that may seem at present." Dobell said.[58]

The art of the period confirms the tradition. Statues of naked women, or a woman with a male child, predominate. Our "sophisticated" society views it as mythology and not reality.

Civilization, according to the ancients, was totally equated with woman and her intelligence, Bruns explained. Although it "was a major theme of ancient mythologies, even early Christian development, our own history and social development have not encouraged such a view," Bruns wrote.[59]

---

[56] Elizabeth Rodgers Dobell, "God and Woman: the Hidden History," *Redbook*, (March, 1978), 39.

[57] Dobell.

[58] Ibid.

[59] Bruns, 1.

Considering women's worth exclusively as a result of her breeding capabilities, despite Judeo-Christian influences to the contrary, our society still considers it more acceptable, even 'okay' for a man to 'sow his wild oats,' than for a woman to have a sexual encounter with anyone other than her husband.

The whole cultural phenomena of woman as pre-eminent in society was dramatically reversed in the writings of the Greek philosophers and many 'Doctors of the Church.' While both Augustine and Aquinas made significant contributions to theology, their offerings on women were based on the prevailing thought of the day and, generally, are not positive. Nevertheless, their ideas have *substantially influenced* Christian thinking throughout the ages.

"Contemporary Catholic thought operates with several models of womanhood in mind. All of them can be related to the theology of the Fathers in some ways. Overall, the impact of the thoughts of Thomas Aquinas has been devastating for the Christian concept of womanhood," Scripture scholar, Fr. George Tavard, said in *Women in Christian Tradition.*[60]

Aquinas' position on women was based on an inaccurate notion of fertilization and conception since the science of genetics was unknown. Even queens of England, including some wives of Henry VIII, allegedly were divorced or executed because they birthed female children instead of the desired male heir. The women were accused, whether true or not, of out of wedlock affairs, i.e. treason, "not of birthing daughters."

In the ignorance of their day, they didn't know it is the X or Y chromosomes in the male sperm, and not the female who contributes only X chromosomes, which determines the sex of a child. So, if you didn't get what you wanted in life—or in the birth of a child—blame it on the perfect scapegoat—'the defective female.'

Aquinas' now-fossilized notion was that man was the active force and woman merely a passive receptacle, in every interrelation, including sexual intercourse. Aquinas helped propagate the thinking—popularized by Aristotle—that womanhood is inferior, subordinate,

---

[60]   Tavard, *WCT,* 125, 127.

weak, and intuitively evil. We know today that is ridiculous, but their attitudes and viewpoints (Aquinas lived from 1225-1274) affected women's lives in every aspect of previous societies—and ours. The need for women's "liberation" movements, on-going since the 1800's, is an effect of this kind of writing and thinking about women.

Aquinas' major work, *Summa Theologica,* is a huge synthesis of Christian thought interpreted through Greek philosophy and science. In *Summa,* Aquinas called women "misbegotten males." He said female conception was due to a defective force—"either a defective mother or a humid, wet wind." The last resort causing female conception, and this was only a remote possibility, was that it might be caused by a defective, weak male.

Aquinas said there is only one purpose for women's existence—procreation. In that, she was man's indispensible partner (*Summa Theologica,* I. 92.1).[61] This was not inferred or hinted at in the passage but stated blatantly, "Woman was created only for the purpose of generation."[62] It's a blatant chauvinistic statement in our view centuries later, but in his time, it was the recognized belief.

Aquinas was male, priest, celibate, and secluded in his monastery. He had no need for women, so the fact that he said women were useful for something, anything, seems like a great concession. "The idea that there is only one thing that women need men for would never have occurred to him," Arlene Swidler remarked in *Woman in a Man's Church.*[63]

Tavard quoted Aquinas' belief that women were "misfits, freaks of nature."[64] In *Summa,* woman was described as:

> Something deficient or accidental. For the active power of the male seed intends to produce a perfect likeness of itself with male sex. If a female is conceived, this is due to a lack of

---

[61] Sr. Albertus Magnus McGrath, O.P., *Women and the Church,* (Garden City, NY: Doubleday & Co, 1976), 81.

[62] As quoted in Tavard, *WCT,* 132.

[63] Arlene Swidler, 12.

[64] As quoted in Tavard, *WCT,* 131.

strength in the active part, to a defect in the mother, or some external influence like that of a humid wind from the south.[65]

Aquinas' theories are based predominantly on those of Augustine and Aristotle. From Aristotle, whom Aquinas studied closely, came the ideas of woman's biological deficiencies and inherent evilness. "Aristotle justified the societal inferiority of women by their presumed biological deficiencies," Tavard noted.[66]

Plato and Socrates similarly endorsed the usual prejudices against women, Tavard explained, but noted that the Pythagoras school and the Stoics asserted the fundamental equality of men and women.[67] However, other Greek philosophers wrote about the inherent evilness of woman and that the 'fall of Eve' was due to her inclination to sin, because of her "weakness."

Other Christian thinkers who preceded Aquinas were as bad—or far worse; after all he was their pupil. Each imitated the philosophy of their mostly-pagan times, and not the Christian ideal they were supposed to follow. Tertullian called woman, "the gates of the devil,"[68] and Clement of Alexandria wrote, "Every woman ought to be overcome with shame at the thought that she is a woman."[69] That seems to be a reflection of the Jewish prayer recited daily by men, "Praised be God that he has not created me a gentile; praised be God that he has not created me a woman; praised be God that he has not created me an ignorant man." (Modern Jewish interpretations of this prayer said it means the man is thankful that he has more obligations and responsibility under God, and that it is not anti-female.)

Origen, Clement's successor in the School of Alexandria, thought the body was especially evil, and recommended castration so men might avoid the temptation which women represented.[70] Cyril of Alexandria, another of the church 'Fathers,' said, ever since Eve, every woman is

---

65   Ibid.
66   Ibid., 75.
67   Ibid.
68   As quoted in Tavard, 131, and Swidler, 13.
69   As quoted in McGrath, 80.
70   McGrath, 80.

"death's deaconess." He noted her sex is: "especially dishonored by God and man. On the other hand, the male sex is ever elect of God, because it is a warrior breed, because it is capable of coming to spiritual vigor, capable of sowing seed, of teaching the rest, of tracing its steps to the mature measure of the fullness of Christ."[71]

Augustine led a riotous and sin-filled life prior to his conversion; he acknowledged in his writings that he was—in current terminology—an unwed father. It apparently did not enhance his appreciation of women. Augustine did write that the soul was created in the image of God for both men and women—but since only men were in God's human image (that is, Jesus'), men were better.[72] For Augustine, Aquinas, and the others in the Hellenic-Scholastic tradition, perfection wasn't seen in the whole, only in its dominant part.[73] In their eyes, that was male.

Remember, all this, which often has been glossed over by men, is history not fiction; I didn't make it up. I'm just reiterating it since many people in authority today either choose not to remember it or won't admit it.

Over and over again, the male superiority was expressed in terms of sexual intercourse. In *Women and the Church,* Sister Albertus Magnus McGrath, O.P., wrote, "Augustine's own sexual profligacy and his early involvement with Manichaeism, gave him a morbidly negative view of sex which has tainted Christian thought ever since. For him sexuality was wholly in the animal domain and not properly human at all."[74] In Augustine's view, "marital intercourse is materially evil, and conjugal embraces," even for procreation, "was a venial

---

[71] As quoted in McGrath, 80.

[72] Since priests and popes long have been trained and inculcated with these church doctors as being the preeminent superlative thinkers of the Western world, it's no surprise that the same argument appears in the Vatican document on the *Question of the Admission of Women to the Ministerial Priesthood:* that is, women can't imitate the 'maleness of Christ.' I studied *Summa* in Political Theory class in college but, fortunately, those excerpts did not include the female passages. If it had, there might have been a riot! It was an all women's college. Besides, the female verses are not about politics and government.

[73] Tavard, *WCT,* 132.

[74] McGrath, 81.

sin."[75] The common notion was that the woman attracted and aroused the man sexually—thus *she* was the more guilty partner.[76] Aquinas wrote in *Summa*:

> Man's superiority is demonstrated in coitus because he bears the more active and, therefore nobler part, while woman is passive and submissive (*Summa Theologica.* 111, suppl. 66:5). The active power, as Aristotle said, is in the male semen. The woman provides the material element which has so far a vegetable kind of life. This material is transformed by the power in the male semen so as to bring into existence a sensitive being (*Summa* I, 118.1 and 4).[77]

McGrath mentions, "It was one of the more marvelous manifestations of the vice of self-centeredness, which accounted for the absence until the middle of the 20th century, of any understanding of female sexual arousal by the male.[78]

"Macho Man" was the name of a popular rock song in the 1970's. "I want to be a macho, macho, macho man," the lyrics said. That doesn't mean "I want to be the boss." McGrath says machismo, a term in Latin cultures, is literally "excessive male pride in the sowing of the seed, amounting to a kind of self-adulation."[79] The narcissistic macho men of today are not limited to Latin cultures, nor to professional athletes and Hollywood stars. They are everywhere from Hollywood to TV, even to Washington D.C. and state capitals. McGrath said machismo, and "mistaken Aristotelian notions of anthropology, genetics, and embryology, transmitted by Augustine and the medieval scholastics, have shaped church thought and church law in regard to women down to the present."[80]

---

[75]   Ibid.
[76]   Ibid.
[77]   Ibid., 81.
[78]   Ibid., 81.
[79]   Ibid, 80.
[80]   McGrath, 80-81.

Aquinas wasn't satisfied with classifying women as misfits. Her position in society, as well as nature, was inferior, he believed. Woman's singleness of purpose—where woman is subject to man—was "extended to civic and social order," Tavard quoted. "Nature has given man more intelligence" and "good order would not be preserved in human society if some were not governed by those who are wiser."[81]

Tavard noted that no matter what the philosophers said—medical science from the time of Hippocrates—taught that "women actively participated in conception of a child and wasn't just a passive recipient and nutritionist of the seed."[82]

This concept was defended by the Franciscan School of Theology and St. Bonaventure, Tavard explained, although the latter believed the male sex was more perfect than the female.[83] Tavard wrote:

> Thomistic opinion on women's participation in conception has been extended by some authors to the entire realm of feminine existence: woman's very nature is receptive. She gives herself only by receiving—no matter what she received: the male seed, or commands, or a husband, or children or God's inspiration or the church's sacraments. Her fulfillment is reached, not through self-development, but through self-opening to others. She sanctifies herself by making herself available to those in need. Simone de Beauvoir in *The Second Sex* believes this is an aberration that has been bred into woman by male dominance and is maintained by education.[84]

There is nowhere where that is truer than in the church. Unfortunately, man decides the standards for feminine behavior—both in the church and in the rest of our society.

---

[81] As quoted in Tavard, *WCT*, 132.
[82] Ibid.
[83] Ibid., 133.
[84] Ibid., 133.

Madonna Kolbenschlag in her book, *Kiss Sleeping Beauty Good-bye,* believes girls and women are taught passivity, to wait for something, preferably someone, "The Other," who will come along and activate her life. Most of the fairy tale characters we grew up with—Sleeping Beauty, Snow White, and Cinderella—personify exactly this. It is so imbued in our culture, women live it. Kolbenschlag calls this the 'formula female':

> The female child is destined from her earliest years to learn how to exist for others. Although every little girl is endowed with her own motive and psychic force, she is soon equipped with two kinds of persona, to be tried on, occasionally worn, held in readiness for the future. She will specialize in one of the roles, or perhaps interchange both, later, when she is a 'woman'.

> One persona is that of the desirable object. The second persona in the little girls' repertoire is that of the desire to live for another. This role will school her in self-forgetfulness, service and sacrifice, in nurturing rather than initiating behaviors. Above all, it will teach her to 'sleep'—to wait, forever if necessary, for the expected other who will make her life more meaningful and fulfilled. She will give up everything when the expected one comes, even the right of creating her own self. Whether it is husband, a religion or a revolution . . . she is ready to live outside of herself, to abdicate from responsibility for herself in favor of something or someone else.[85]

The church has caught women in a bind. Throughout its history the woman was told:

She had the same privileges as any believer in Jesus Christ—*but*

---

[85]   Madonna Kolbenschlag, *Kiss Sleeping Beauty Good-Bye: Breaking the Spells of Feminine Myths and Models,* (Garden City, NY: Doubleday and Co., Inc., 1979), 12.

✓ She is different.

✓ She cannot expect to do the same spiritual things as men.

✓ She cannot receive the seven sacraments promised through Baptism. She must accept that because "not everyone receives every sacrament."

✓ She is told reception of seven sacraments is not an automatic right, guaranteed by Baptism. (Although some men in the church can and do; some married men become priests after their wife dies or clerics who leave the priesthood can marry later). She's told, "That's different."

✓ She is told to give of herself completely, to do for others, to die to self. She is told: this is woman's role. But that contradicts scripture which says neither she nor he can be saved by good works alone.

✓ She is told her role is to be mother. Men are not told or raised that their role is being father. Celibate priests are not fathers either.

✓ Being mother doesn't account for the widows, never married, consecrated religious sister, little girls. If your sole purpose is to be mother, and for whatever circumstances you aren't, what are you?

✓ Women were also told that being married—the only church approved way to become a mother—was a less holy and less spiritual path than the single or religious life, i.e., celibacy. (No thought was given in the equation for clergy or religious who are not celibate . . . .)

✓ Women are told liturgical language which says "Christ died for all men," or "for us men and for our salvation," the latter in the Creed at Mass, is really "inclusive"—that *it means* everyone, male and female—and is the same as the words a few lines down, "for *our sake* He was crucified," or "*for our* salvation." Church teaching is that the use of the word men is different here than when it is used in the job-description directive, "only men" can be ordained to the deaconate or the priesthood, although it's the same word.

After more than 30 years of dealing with the inclusive language issue, and making some modifications, but not all, the USCCB and the Vatican insist the meanings are dissimilar, unalike, or like antonyms (the exact contrary of another word, such as start and stop), not synonyms (a word having the same meaning, as in car and automobile). For the past 20 years, the church hierarchy was redoing the prayers and wordings at Eucharist, but only in the Old Testament readings. The new Lectionary was released in early 2011 but it started to be used at Liturgy in November 2011, the start of the church calendar year with Advent. Allegedly, the effort was to make the wording closer to the original languages. To a lot of women observers, sadly, that often means less inclusive rather than more inclusive.[86]

It was Augustine who promulgated the thinking that celibacy was the better way to attain spiritual perfection. This, despite the fact that much of the superiority of the male was attributed to the act of sexual intercourse and man's presumed dominant position in it. Not a celibate analogy. Celibacy was finally mandated for the male clergy in the Roman church's Western Rite in the 12th century, after more than half of the life of the church had passed as non-celibate. In fact, in the early centuries of the church, one pope was the grandson of an earlier pope[87] and other papal relationships were familial as well.

For centuries, the church has subtly—and not-so-subtly—stated that celibacy was better than marriage. First in the line-up were the persons with so-called "religious vocations," namely the priesthood and then a step lower and sideways, women religious and religious brothers. Next were the people who chose the single life without a religious vocation. The married couple was on the bottom of the

---

[86] New Lectionary readings, or the readings read during liturgies, came out in December 2010, and the New American Bible, Revised Edition (NABRE) was released in March 2011. The latter took 100 biblical scholars, including non-Catholics, 20 years to complete. It includes a whole new translation of the Old Testament, even the Psalms. Its purpose: to have closer conformity with the original languages in the Old Testament readings. In examples on the web sites following the release of NABRE, it also seemed some of the language was clearer. There were no changes to the New Testament.

[87] See Pope Paul III, (Alexander Farness), Wikipedia, online, accessed 2010.

list. We were actually told that in Catholic grammar school in the 1950's and early 1960's. The fact that priests and women religious came from marriages and families was insignificant. The fact that every walk of life should be a religious vocation was overlooked. The inference was that you could not have a life dedicated to Christ, or be holy, unless you were a vowed religious.

Christianity arose from the Jewish culture where celibacy was clearly an oddity. Even in the priestly tribe of the Levites, the job of high priest was passed along through inheritance from father to son. Except for the monastic, desert-based Nazarite sect, the Essenes, being unmarried was unusual. Although the Bible does not say so directly, other literature from that period and from the Dead Sea Scrolls, indicate both Jesus and John the Baptist belonged to the Essene community at some time. Paul is also thought to have been an Essene.

Since marriage and its resulting conjugal union—even for procreation—was negated in church tradition, if not actual doctrine, there was a problem: what to do with young women. First of all, a young woman was her father's property and it was unseemly for her not to marry. However, to dedicate a woman's life to God by not marrying became a means to spiritual perfection for a woman—who was equal under the rite of Baptism and inferior under society's laws. It might have worked if, as the first Christians fervently believed, Jesus was coming again in that century.

These unmarried virgins were not the forerunner of religious communities for women. Rather, the forerunner was the Order of Widows; the unmarried woman was the exception. It was much later before women, banding together in church service, became known as a religious order which we would recognize today. Initially, most of the members opted to live together for convenience; they were independent and financially self-sustaining. Their role was one of church service—and they were ordained for this special purpose, Morris said.[88] That is, to care for the cathedrals and oversee the catechumens, or those preparing for Baptism. They led a life of service, not one of contemplative prayer.

---

[88]   Morris, 9.

The role of deaconess, according to Morris' *The Lady Was a Bishop,* was necessary whenever baptism was performed on female catechumens.[89] When deaconesses lived in community, they became known as canonesses, living under a rule, and the title deaconess became less frequently used.[90] Canonesses were both secular—those who lived in private apartments—and regular, those who lived in community.[91] Canonesses assumed the duties traditionally done in church service by the deaconesses; that is the teaching of religion to women, running schools, caring for the sick, and celebrating the Divine Office.[92] The contemplative-prayer-life-only nun resulted years later from a mandate by male ecclesial superiors.

When Vincent de Paul and the Daughters of Charity started ministering to the sick and poor of the slums of France in the 1700's, it was a direct aberration of this ecclesial-imposed mandate. By that time, nuns needed special permission from the bishop to teach—one of the canonesses' earliest services.

It is interesting to note that only after the imposition of celibacy for the male clergy in the 12th century—which many priests strenuously objected to at the time—women in church service communities were moved away from the actual cathedral to a distant secondary site.[93] The women were deliberately secluded in outlying monasteries, not the men.

According to priest-historians, scholars believe it was partially due to the problem of property squabbles which eventually caused the mandatory priestly celibacy requirement in the Western Rite. Since it wasn't imposed until the 12th century, it is considered 'fairly recent' regulation in church discipline. Although in the 21st century, the way celibacy is referred to by the hierarchy, is as if it had existed since Pentecost. It didn't.

In the Eastern Catholic Rite, priestly celibacy is still not mandatory except in two instances: candidates for ordination as a bishop must

---

[89]   Ibid., 4.
[90]   Ibid., 7.
[91]   Ibid.
[92]   Ibid., 10, 12.
[93]   Ibid., 15

be celibate, and priests ordained in the U.S. since 1955. If priests are ordained in the Eastern Rite outside the U.S., they may be married, even if they eventually minister in Western Rite parishes in the U.S. One Eastern Rite married priest served in a Bronx, NY, 'Roman' parish in at least one example.

The alleged property squabble resulted from the death of a married priest. According to a priest-historian, the question was: who inherited the dead priest's property, including land? Did it belong to his wife and family or to the church?

These changes in perception of women's worth within the church structure are directly attributable to the influence of Aquinas' thought. As his importance as a major theologian grew, women's status diminished. Not only did Aquinas call women "misfits," he loaded the whole burden of sin onto women's shoulders when he called women "enticers to lust," that is, that just being a woman was sinful. Aquinas believed if women must be in church at all, they should be seen and not heard. "The voice of a woman is an invitation to lust, and therefore, must not be heard in the church," he said in another section of *Summa Theologica.*[94]

"The Thomastic version is that women should not be allowed to preach less men's minds be enticed to lust. Women are evil, impure, unfit to minister because men find them sexually attractive," McGrath wrote.[95]

Noted anthropologist Ashley Montague blamed Aquinas and the Christian Church for centuries of bad example to society. "Women have been conditioned to believe that they are inferior to men and they have assumed—that what everyone assumes—is a fact of nature," Montague said.[96] When Montague published his book, *The Natural Superiority of Women* in 1953, it was considered revolutionary for its time. At its release, Aquinas must have "turned over in his grave" at the very title—let alone the thought!

---

[94] As quoted in McGrath, 137.
[95] Ibid., 137-8.
[96] Ashley Montague, *The Natural Superiority Women,* (New York: MacMillan Co., 1953), 23.

The idea of the natural inferiority of women, of women not being "good enough," of being impure, unclean and sinful, especially not good enough to enter the Sanctuary or to touch the Consecrated Host (until Communion in the Hand was permitted after Vatican II) is the underlying cultural argument. It is the same argument which kept women from liturgical service in the church practically from its formation. Women's self-worth has been systematically diminished in and by the church.

Yet, the *Summa Theologica* is considered a brilliant theological masterpiece. By whose standards? It's some legacy to the women of the church. So much so that Pope John Paul II wrote two documents affirming the value of women in the church. These are "On the Dignity and Vocation of Women" *(Mutieris Dignitatum)*, issued Oct 6, 1988, and "Letter of Pope John Paul II to Women," June 29, 1995.[97]

"The presence and the role of women in the life and mission of the church . . . remain absolutely necessary and irreplaceable," he said.

The world readily adapts aspects of Judeo-Christian thought only if and when it suits the world's purpose. The world readily accepted the tradition of both Jewish and Christian cultures which said women were different—meaning inferior—and that women must accept the "role" God and nature intended, meaning what men "preferred."[98]

It seems to me, Aquinas' theory that women were created "only for procreation" eliminates a major dogma of Christian belief—that people are created for salvation, that we were created to fellowship with God. It isn't even suggested in Aquinas' theory. The Christian life, according to Kolbenschlag, calls everyone to a higher existence, to a faith that promised personal growth and transcendence, and at the same time, demands the acceptance of suffering and diminishment. It is the enemy of complacency; it requires continuous conversion.

---

[97] John Paul II, "On the Dignity and Vocation of Women", *Origins*, Vol. 18, No. 17, Oct. 6, 1988, 261-263 ff. and "Letter of Pope John Paul II to Women," June 29, 1995.

[98] Kolbenschlag, 13.

Christianity's ultimate laws contradict the image of the formula female, a mode of behavior encouraged by the church's response to its women members. "Love your neighbor as yourself." "Let us not love in word or speech, but in deed and in truth." Psychologists tell us a person cannot love another until he or she properly loves his or her own self. Similarly, a person cannot love others or God unless he or she has the individual power to choose and act. A sense of self-worth and a sense of self-creation are fundamental to spiritual maturity.[99]

It's difficult for us to realize that centuries ago women were worshipped for their very sexuality. Science today tells us that in the fetus it is the female sex organs which develop first and from that, there is the derivation into male organs. Yes, women have come a long way in the two millennia plus of Christianity, but it's still a far cry from women as paradigm of life, the perfection of creation, and representative of God the creator—to being a misbegotten creature, a mistake, the paradox of humanity. But what Aquinas and the others forgot is this: God created woman in the divine image and God doesn't make mistakes. Jesus brought salvation to the lowly and despised—even if that was only in men's minds regarding women.

---

[99]   Kolbenschlag, 30-31.

CHAPTER 6

Old Testament Women in Ministry: From Sarah, the First Woman of the Old Covenant, To Miriam, the First Woman Prophetess

It is a mistake to believe women played no role in the religious life in the Old Testament. Often women were used as the instrument for fostering God's designs, and not just in a passive way as the mother of a patriarch or hero, although that was true in some early situations, of course. These women were in "ministry" even then. Who were they and what did they do?

<u>Sarah</u> is Abraham's wife. She gave birth to Isaac, (Gen. 17: 15-20, 21-22, and 21: 1-7) so she is a crucial to salvation history.[100] She is a woman of faith, as are all of these women, and is a forerunner of Mary's cousin, Elizabeth, in the New Testament. Like Sarah, Elizabeth also had a baby (John the Baptist) in advanced age—a baby who would proceed the coming of the covenant. Isaac was the promise of the eternal covenant with Abraham; Jesus is the promise of the new and everlasting covenant with God. Just bearing Abraham's child, as the slave girl Hagar also did, was not sufficient to the salvific plan. Sarah was chosen specifically to "have nations come out of her, Kings of peoples shall descend from her," (Gen. 17: 19-20, 16-17). It was the son of Abraham's wife who counted with

---

[100] Bruns, 42. See also Isaiah 66: 7-9, Rom. 9: 7-13.

God. McGrath quoted Father George Tavard's book, *The People of God:*

> Through the wife, God builds the House of His People. On the human level, the People is neither the outcome of a passing or a dominating association, nor a testimony to the virility of the father. The People is the fruit of a permanent association of equals.[101]

Rebekah (or Rebecca) is Isaac's wife, specifically chosen by God to be so. (Gen. 24). Her sons are Jacob—an ancestor of David, the earthly king, and Jesus, the heavenly king—and Esau, an ancestor of the Arabs. Both Jacob and Esau are Semites. The enmity and eventual peace among the Jewish people and the Arabs proceeds, in biblical prophecy, the second coming of Christ. The Bible says no one knows the time or the hour except the Father. In the early part of the 21st century, watching most evening newscasts' reports about the continued violence and animosity between Israel and Palestine, we know we're not there yet!

Rachael and Leah are sisters and the wives of Jacob. Jacob agreed to work for seven years to win Rachael's hand in marriage. After seven years of labor, the father-in-law gives his older, homely daughter, Leah, instead, and gets away with his scheme due to heavy bridal veil covering. Jacob also gets to marry Rachael after the wedding week, but has to work an additional seven years in payment. He actually labored 14 years to pay for his marriage contract for Rachael. (Gen 29: 15-35, 30: 1-25). Jacob's work, which was tending sheep to win Rachael, foreshadows Christ, the Good Shepherd, and the Church for which He had to suffer.[102] The Twelve Tribes of Israel sprang from the 12 sons borne to Jacob by his two wives, and the rivalry between them for his attention and his male children. It is

---

[101]   As quoted in McGrath, 21.
[102]   Thierry Martens, O.S.B, *Bible Themes, A Source Book,* Vol. 11, (Notre Dame, IN: Fedes Publishers, Inc., 1964), 401.

Joseph—the child of Jacob's great love, Rachael—who saves his family from the famine by leading them to Egypt. The Twelve Tribes are paralleled by the 12 closest disciples of Jesus, generally called apostles, although that was not a term used during their life-times; it was conditional on seeing the risen Christ and preaching the good news of the Resurrection.[103] Obviously, not all of "The Twelve" did that; Judas didn't. Scripture scholars generally believe the Twelve Disciples, representing the Twelve Tribes, represent all humanity.

Miriam was a Prophetess, holding the office of Prophet. She was the sister of Moses and Aaron; she helped lead the Chosen People into the Promised Land along with her brothers (Micah 6:4). Her parents were Jochebed and Amram and they belonged to the priestly tribe of Levi (Numbers 26: 58-59). It was she who told the Egyptian princess of a good nurse maid (their Mom) for the child, Moses, found in the swamp basket. (Exodus 2: 1-10)

In ministry, she led the music singers and dancers of the freed Israel of God (Numbers 15:1, 21-22). She was the director, perhaps the orchestrator, of worship on one of the most glorious days after safely crossing the Red Sea, the day of Baptism into the Cloud (1 Cor. 10:1). The Cloud, majestic and luminous, hovered over and preceded the people of Israel on their wilderness journey. It settled onto the Ark of the Covenant and the Temple. Called the Shekinah, or glory, it was the actual presence of the Lord. (Heb. 1:3, James 2:1) Miriam's exultant song, "Sing ye the Lord for He hath triumphed gloriously, the horse and rider has been thrown into the sea" (Exodus 15: 20-21) is still proclaimed in song and worship, more than 3,400 years later.

Psalm 68: 24-25 shows that women in that worship-parade played the tumbrel and danced among singers and other instrument players,[104] as they also did in David's day. Today, women are taking an active part in the music ministry in their local parishes, as cantors

---

[103]   Raymond E. Brown, S.S., "Roles of Women in the Fourth Gospel." *Women: New Dimension,* 116.

[104]   Muriel Evans, *Ministries for Women: Old and New Testament Examples of Women in Ministry.* Aglow Bible Studies, (Edmonds, WA: Aglow Publications, 1975), 7.

or Leaders of song for Mass and other liturgical celebrations, and in prayer groups. Women and men are learning to dance "in the spirit," as David did as an expression of praise. (2 Sam.6: 5, 14-15, 21-22; 1Chron. 15: 28-29). This is a return to worship patterns of the Old Testament.

A Prophet in the Old Testament, "nebiah" in Miriam's case, (the feminine of nabhi) is one who proclaims, actively announces, or pours forth the declarations of God. The words have their source in God. He places them in the mouth of the prophet or prophetess and they, in turn, declare them to the people as God's mouthpiece.[105]

The Spirit of God empowered the prophet or prophetess to speak and, in those times, the gift of prophesy appeared only occasionally. The fact that Miriam, a woman, is a Prophet is "of no small significance." [106] Miriam was stricken with leprosy for seven days for desiring (along with brother Aaron) a greater share in the responsibility of managing the wondering Israelites (Num. 12: 1-15). Neither got it, but significantly, the company of more than two million did not break camp and move forward until she was restored.[107] Since they followed the Cloud of the glory of the Lord (Exodus 13: 21-22, 40: 36-38), that meant Yahweh did not move the Cloud until her chastisement was over, her healing complete.

Despite Miriam's one mistake, she was not only held in high esteem by the People of Israel, but also in God's sight. She made one mistake in a life of grace, compared to two much more serious ones committed by Moses: not circumcising his son and in striking the rock at Meribah. Before the Egyptian years, Moses wrested with God and almost died for failing to circumcise his son. His wife, Zipporah, had to do it for him (Exodus 4: 24-31). At Meribah, Moses struck the rock with the branch instead of merely commanding the water to gush forth, as Yahweh directed (Numbers 20: 2-12). For their lack of faith, Moses and Aaron were prohibited from entering the Promised Land; the Bible does not say if Miriam was prevented from entering.

---

[105] Ibid.
[106] Ibid.
[107] Ibid.

The gift of Prophesy is still used in the church. Women and men, especially in the Charismatic Renewal within the Catholic Church, and other Christian churches, are prophesying. They are empowered by the Holy Spirit to share the message of the Lord mentioned in Joel 2: 28-29, "I will pour out my spirit on all mankind. Your sons and daughters shall prophesy, your old men shall dream dreams, and your young men see visions." Prophesy was also a recognized ministry for women in the early church. Paul wrote, "All should desire and covet the gift" (1 Cor. 14:1, 39). It is neither fortune telling, nor predicting the future. It is not scary but a spoken message from God to exhort, or encourage the people of God. It is a message spoken through the person's spirit, which is in tune with God's Spirit, filtered through the person's physical mind and language. It should have an independent confirmation. Prophesy is one of the gifts of the Holy Spirit (1Cor.12: 10) which are received at sacramental Confirmation. Unfortunately, many Baby Boomers received confirmation as children in the 4th or 5th grades, or today they receive the sacrament as young teens, and do not realize how important these gifts are for living a Christian life. Christians often don't know the function of the gifts and don't utilize them. The disciples of Jesus had private tutoring on how to be Jesus-like for three years. In the crunch, the male disciples betrayed Him, denied him, abandoned Him in the garden and at the foot of the Cross. Afterwards, they hid; desperately afraid they too would be captured and murdered. The only faithful ones at the Cross were the females and one teenage boy, John.

After receiving the power of the Holy Spirit on Pentecost, the disciples preached the world upside down for Jesus the Christ (it is His title, not His last name). All the disciples—both men and women—boldly proclaimed to the horror of the establishment, "We don't follow how Caesar tells us to think anymore; we have another King, Jesus. We follow His example." That was the reason the disciples were persecuted for their belief. It wasn't because other people were against a new religion, but because the Christians threatened the governmental status quo. What if everyone stopped thinking that Caesar was lord of their lives—mutiny!

If the male-disciples with all their tutoring needed the power of the Holy Spirit to change their lives and to proclaim Jesus as Lord, how much more do we need the gifts and power of the spirit, 2,000+ years removed from Jesus' earthly walk?

The word charismatic is taken from the Greek "charismata," which means "gifts of God's Love." The greatest gift is Jesus, and through the power of the Holy Spirit, we are able to affirm Him. In confirmation, we acknowledge before the whole church that as individuals we believe Jesus is the Lord and Savior of our lives. Though Christians receive the Holy Spirit at sacramental Confirmation, and at Baptism, most of us do not live with the power of the spirit. Later on, we often realize we are empty and search for something that seems to be "missing." We were created to fellowship with God, to walk and talk with God in the garden. We are never satisfied, Augustine said, until we are filled with God.[108]

---

[108] Each person individually must accept Christ as the Lord and Savior of his or her own life. It is a personal choice and not because we were raised as Catholic, Lutheran, Presbyterian, or any other denomination, nor because our parents or grandparents were a particular religion. Noted evangelical teacher, the late David Du Plessis, who was known as "Mr. Pentecost," often taught, "God has no grandsons." That is, God has male sons and female sons, children of the promise. It requires an individualized decision to accept and receive salvation. You can't do it for your children or parents. Asking Jesus to live through you and fill you with the power of His Holy Spirit is called the "Baptism in the Holy Spirit." Those who received the sacrament of Confirmation as youngsters need adult recommitment. Jesus Christ is in the business of being Savior; salvation is His responsibility. Believe. He hears and answers prayers.

CHAPTER 7

From Rahab, the First Woman of the Promised Land to Anna, the Link Between the Old and New Testaments

Other ministries for Old Testament women included hospitality to spies, victory for a defeated army and success through weakness. If they don't sound like ministries, elaboration of the methods used to achieve these ends certainly is.

Rahab, the prostitute or harlot, is the first woman of importance in the Promised Land. In Joshua 2, she saved the lives of the "spies" sent by Joshua to reconnoiter the territory, held by the King of Jericho, but promised by God to the Jews. In return, her family was saved when Israelites slaughtered the people of the territory. Rehab understood that God had ordained the chosen People to possess the land and was not about to deny God just to foster the territorial ambitions of an earthly kingdom.

"The welcome which the harlot Rahab reserved for the messengers became the model of the Church of the Gentiles which welcomed the faith of the Living Christ," according to Thierry Maertens.[109] The gospel of Matthew also lists Rahab as the mother of Boaz, the grandfather of David (Matt. 1:5). "She is one of the progenitors of the Messiah," said Bruns,[110] as is Ruth, Boaz's wife and David's grandmother (Book of Ruth).

---

[109]   Maertens, 401.
[110]   Bruns, 43.

Deborah was one of the Judges of Israel for at least 20 years (Judges 4). The judges were chosen by God (Deut. 16:18) and they "ruled in all the gates."[111] Deborah was one of 13 Judges who ruled Israel for more than 450 years (Acts 13:20). Additionally, Eli the Priest (1 Sam 8: 1-5); Samuel the prophet (1 Sam 7:16, 15-17); and the sons of Samuel (1 Sam. 8: 1-5) also may be considered Judges.[112] Another term used to describe the judges was "saviors" (Nehemiah 9:27)—for with the power of God they were raised up to save their nation. Deborah saved the nation literally as well.

The Judges were on par with the Levites. Their authority was final; disobedience resulted in death. (Deut. 17: 8-13) They were commanded by Yahweh to "feed" his people (1 Chron. 17: 6, 10), another forerunner of Jesus and the Multiplication stories. They discerned, regulated and directed the Hebrew republic from Moses' day to the time of King Saul. They managed the government with spiritual enlightenment. (We need some of that in government today . . . .)

Deborah was also a prophetess and the wife of Lapidoth (Judges 4:4), combining both "career" and marriage. She was a judge with authority over both men and women. Deborah is the only Judge, except for Samuel, with the title, 'prophet,' an honor indeed. She also possessed the gifts of wisdom and knowledge (1 Cor. 12:8) since she could not have known by intuition that God would deliver Israel by the hand of a woman (Judges 4:9-10). Israel was in crisis, the enemy was attacking, and the commanding general of the army refused to go into battle unless Deborah was there (Judges 4: 8-9). She said yes. The women of the Bible always do.

Deborah showed responsibility, obedience, absolute trust in God, self-confidence and determination. She led the country with wisdom and equality, saved her people in the hour of danger, and recorded her achievement in Judges 5. According to Rick Yohn in his book, *Discover Your Spiritual Gift and Use It*, writing is an extension of the gift of prophecy. Deborah was both a prophetess and a writer, recording the magnificence of victory through Yahweh.

---

[111] Evans, 11.
[112] Ibid.

Other women's inspired messages are also recorded in the Bible. They are **Hannah** (1 Sam 2:1-10); and **Elizabeth** and **Mary** (Luke 1:41-45; 46-55). Scripture scholars believe the Letter to the Hebrews—which they know was not written by Paul but is closely influenced by his thought—was written by **Priscilla**, one of the leaders of the early church. It is only one of the pastoral letters which is not personally signed by Paul.

Then there is **Bathsheba.** No one ever mentions her among the prominent women of the Old Testament—she didn't save the nation or memorialize her spiritual insights. However, she is very important to the genealogy of Jesus, because she was David's mistress (2 Sam. 111, 12), and later, his wife. David certainly loved Yahweh and was the anointed king of God's chosen people, but in his humanness, he sinned. David saw this beautiful woman bathing—actually taking her purifying bath after her menstrual period (2 Sam 11:4), called *mikvah* (or *mikveh*)—he lusted and had her brought to him.

A Jewish woman was considered "unclean" for seven days following her period, called the "courses" in many Bible translations, as well as during it. In effect this made her "clean to touch"—and have sex with—just around the time of ovulation. So, it's no surprise women in that society spent most of their lives ritually unclean or pregnant.

David is the king—young, handsome, a mighty warrior. Bathsheba was faithful to her husband, Uriah, the Hittite, a mercenary solder in King David's army, but how do you refuse the king's command? She submits to his advances. There is intercourse, adultery, conception. After he finds out Bathsheba is pregnant, David's sin intensifies. He had Uriah brought home from the front on leave—hopeful Uriah would have sex with his wife to cover up the illicit pregnancy. David is foiled when the man innocently refuses to sleep with his wife. There was a prevalent belief at the time that sexual intercourse was debilitating, especially for soldiers; Uriah does not have sex with Bathsheba believing he needs his strength and energy in battle.

David is now in a real bind. He had Uriah murdered—by deliberately sending him to the front line of combat, where he is killed. David marries Bathsheba after the appropriate mourning period. Nathan, the prophet, confronts David with the awfulness of his actions. David repents, anguishing in body and spirit for his sins, but the child, whom David loved, dies. David consoles Bathsheba and she conceives again. Bathsheba' role was essential and the Lord turned the evil into good. Her second child was Solomon (2 Sam 11:24-25,) who will be David' successor as king. This child is dearly loved by Yahweh.

The gospel of Matthew lists Bathsheba in its genealogy of Jesus, recalling, Maertens said, "The names of sinners and foreigners."[113] Matt. 1:6 says, "David was the father of Solomon, whose mother had been Uriah's wife."

With **Jahel (or Jael)** (Judges 4: 17-22) and **Esther, Judith** symbolized weakness. But God works through the weak and gave these women victory. (Books of Judith and Esther)[114] It had been alleged the books of Judith and Esther are fictitious and do not correlate with the known facts of history. Neither are they pure fantasy, said Bruns, but emerge from real people and real situations. "They are parables of how God protects His people," he said.[115]

David and Judith are God's instruments while Esther's story parallels the story of David and Goliath. "Protection of Yahweh is the same theme in Esther. The story of Esther is the root for the Scheherazade of the Persian legend," according to Bruns.[116] These heroines, like their male colleagues, Saul and David, are also substitutes for God himself, having quasi-divine characteristics.[117] **Susanna** in Daniel 12: 1-64 is also a figure of the poor justified.[118]

Another instance when the Lord uses women to speak to men is **Huldah** (2 Kings 22: 14, 2 Chron. 34:22), a contemporary of the prophet Jeremiah. Even the High Priest trusted the words of her prophesy and she was the instrument for reform in a period of great spiritual decline. Her prophecy to King Josiah, concerning

---

[113]   Maertens, 402.
[114]   Ibid.
[115]   Bruns, 47.
[116]   Bruns, 50-51.
[117]   Ibid., 54-55.
[118]   Maertens, 402.

the destruction of Jerusalem came true, as did her warning that he would be spared because he had humbled himself before God. By her prophecy, she influences governmental policies and was held in high esteem by all.[119]

Another woman who prophesied in the New Testament was **Anna**, the old woman of the temple, present at Jesus' circumcision (Luke 2: 36-38). She, along with Simeon, and not John the Baptist, were the first to announce the redemption of the Messiah, Christ, was at hand. Muriel Evans wrote:

> Anna's ancestry is of great interest. She was not a daughter of Judah, but was a descendant of one of the dispersed tribes of Israel. That Anna, of the tribe of Asher, was associated with the Temple at the time of the advent of the messiah, is truly amazing. Under Jeroboam, the 10 tribes had defected, had refused to worship at the Temple in Jerusalem, and had set up their own idolatrous worship centers.

> Significantly, Anna appeared to salute the Savior, 'who had come to seek and to save that which was lost.' It was not accidental that Anna should be living at the time of the first advent of the Lord Jesus Christ. Anna stood as a last link between the prophetesses whom the spirit prompted under the Old Covenant, and the women into whom the spirit was to be poured copiously under the new.[120]

Her audience in the Temple likely was large, since it was the hour of prayer.[121] Prophetic voices inspired of God had been silent from the time of Malachi to the events in Matthew's gospel. The temple built by Herod was begun in 17 B.C., and within its precincts—shortly after God sent His Son to be born of a woman—Anna was

[119] Evans, 23-24.
[120] Ibid. 28-29.
[121] Ibid.

recognized as a prophetess.[122] So, the people listened when she spoke. (Luke 2: 36-38)

There are several other attributes of women in the Old Testament which we rarely hear about—women worshipped before the Ark of the Covenant, with no veil of separation; women were part of the established singing ministry which praised daily in the Temple and were supported by "all Israel" for this ministry; women were allowed, as well as men, to take the vow of the Nazarite, the most sacred vow of dedication to God. "All of the House of Israel" brought up the Ark of the Lord, including men, women, maidservants and male servants (2 Sam. 6: 14-23), and 1 Chron. 15: 1-3, 25, 29 and Psalm 68:25). Ms. Evans related:

> During David's reign, the daughters of the Lord played and danced before the Ark of the Covenant, which symbolized the presence of the Lord, when the king brought it up to Jerusalem. In David's day, the people came before the presence of the Lord openly to praise and worship Him, with no veil separating them from the Ark which was simply set up inside curtains (1 Chron. 17:1). The women were included in this worship as well as the men.[123]

The sons and daughters of Heman "sang in the House of the Lord for the service of the House of God," according to 1 Chron. 25:6. Later when the Temple was constructed, women continued in their music ministry within the court of the Temple. The Temple had two courts—one for the priests and the great court, where all the people gathered to worship. (2 Chron. 4:9). There was no division of males and females, only between the Levitical genealogical priests and the people.[124]

The Temple erected under Zerubbabel, after the Babylonian exile, Ms. Evans related, had a choir of men and women who were

---

[122]   Ibid., 27.
[123]   Evans, 31.
[124]   Ibid., 32.

instrumental in daily temple worship. Ezra 2:65, 3:10-13 says there were "200 singing men and women," and Nehemiah 7:67, 12:40-47, says "240 singing men and women." Whatever the number, women were an integral part of the worship choir in the Temple. All Israel helped support the ministry by providing food for the singers and temple porters (Nehemiah 12:47). Ms. Evans noted a gradual change:

> By the time of Herod's Temple, however, the scribes and Pharisees had multiple rules and regulations. Worship of Jehovah had become dry and exceedingly formal under rabbinic law, which the Lord denounced in Matthew 23. Not only were the women excluded from singing in the service, with their places being assumed by Levite boys, but the worshippers as a whole were restricted from taking part in the praise, except for responsive 'amens.'

> Stemming from misconceptions of God's commandments, religious traditions were instituted and maintained by Jewish leaders. In the temple Herod built, one such tradition was evident in there being a court set aside for women and beyond which women were seldom allowed to pass. Due to this temple plan, traditionally, Jewish women have been seated separately from men in synagogues and given an inferior place. What a departure from the perfect plan of God in which women were a vital and vocal part of the worship of Jehovah! Even from ancient times women were encouraged by the Lord to share in the most sacred vow of consecration available to His people—the vow of the Nazarite. (Num. 6:2)[125]

There are three Nazarites named in the Bible: Samson (Judges 3: 7, 24), Samuel (1 Sam. 1: 11, 20), and John the Baptist (Luke 1: 13-15). Luke, the author of the Acts of the Apostles, tells of Paul making a vow and shaving his head as part of it (Acts 18:18, 21, 23). No women

---

[125]   Ibid., 32-33.

are mentioned in the Bible as being Nazarites, but that they were eligible, from the very inception of the sacred vow, is unquestionable (Numbers 6: 1-21, especially Numbers 6:2).

"Speak unto the children of Israel, and unto them, when either man or woman shall separate themselves to vow a vow of the Nazarites, to separate themselves unto the Lord." (KJV)

"Say this to the sons of Israel, 'If a man or woman wishes to make a vow, the vow of the Nazarites by which he is pledged to Yahweh, he shall abstain from wine and strong drink, and neither drink the juice of grapes nor eat grapes, fresh or dried,'" (Numbers 6: 1-4) (*Jerusalem Bible*).

Women are included without reservation in both translations. Women are included in the "children of Israel" in the King James Version; and are included in the "sons of Israel" in the Jerusalem Bible. Women were neither secluded nor separated from men in the sight of God. Every time these two identifying phrases are used throughout the scriptures, women were included whether they are specifically mentioned in each reference or not.

The Jerusalem Bible notes the Nazarites vow was taken by one specially pledged to Yahweh. It wasn't just for males. That was a deviation from the tradition of the Levitical priesthood and, of course, the ordained deacons and priests in the Roman Catholic Church today.

The fact that this vow was for both male and female is of vital significance. By making no distinction between men and women in this solemn ministry, the Lord was prophetically pointing forward to, and typifying, the day when there would be 'neither male nor female but one in Jesus Christ' and we would all, without distinction of sex, be 'kings and priests unto our God.'

The three obligations upon the Nazarite were also similar, and even superior, to those incumbent upon the high priest. The Nazarite was a priest in an "extra-intense" way since he or she became such by personal consecration instead of by genealogical descent. While the priest had to abstain from wine during his actual ministration in the sanctuary, the Nazarite had to refrain from all that pertained to the fruit of the vine during the entire period of his/her vow. The priest was to avoid defilement from the dead, except for his nearest relatives, but the Nazarite had to ignore the dead bodies of even his/her father and mother, brothers and sisters. Also, while the high priest wore the holy "nezer" upon the mitre, the Nazarite's own hair was a halo of glory, the "nezer" of God upon his or her head.

Anna, who was certainly set apart to the service of God, was in the court of women of the Temple to which she as restricted by the prohibitions of her day. This court obtained its name, not from its exclusive use by women, but because they were not allowed to proceed further except for sacrificial purposes. The court was a large area, over 200 feet square (approximately the length of two football fields), and was the common meeting place for men also. According to Jewish tradition, women occupied a raised gallery along three sides of the court during worship.

The division, then, between men and women were merely a token one, for in essence they worshipped together. It is of supreme importance to remember that when Jesus Christ came to set all things in their proper perspective, the early church gathered together, male and female, 'all with one accord in one place.'[126]

As Jesus died on Calvary, the Temple curtain was split in two (Luke 23: 45-46). No longer was there any separation between humans and the Holy of Holies of God. Christ had bridged the gap (Ezekiel 22:30). All could come to the mercy seat. Men and women could directly enter the presence of Yahweh; there was no division any more. All could enter eternal life; all could come equally, and as equals, before the throne of God.

---

[126] Evans, 33-4.

CHAPTER 8

The New Covenant Starts with Mary

The bulk, or weight as it is called, of the Bible shows women in positions of responsibility in relation to God. It shows women filled with the joy of the Lord, with personal knowledge of God, of equality in God's eyes. There is nowhere in Scripture that demonstrates this better than Jesus' own dealings with women, especially His own mother.

Matthew begins his gospel account with the genealogy of Jesus; Mark with the preparatory ministry of John the Baptist; Luke with the birth of John the Baptist followed by the birth of Jesus; and John, with the eternal principle of the everlasting Logos, the word, the creator-God who became incarnate man.

Both Mary and Joseph were of the House of David (Luke 2:4). Matthew's family tree lists the progenitors of Jesus from Abraham to "Joseph, the husband of Mary, of whom was born Jesus, who is called Christ." (Matt. 1:16, KJV) That is because Joseph is considered to be the legal father of Jesus.[127] For those of us who learned about the doctrine of the Virgin Birth of Jesus at a young age, it's still a little surprising, since Jesus' humanity came through Mary as a result of her female body. However, it was in keeping with the custom of that time.

In our culture the lineage is passed along through the father, but to the Jews, even today, nationality and religion are passed through the mother. The reason for this is simple and stems directly from their

---

127 Gospel of St. Matthew, *Confraternity Edition*, (New York: Apostolate of the Press, 1953) 8, footnote 1:16.

paternalistic culture: there could be no mistaking the child's mother. Paternity is less easy to ascertain. In ancient times when property began to be important economically and leaving that property became inheritance, it was obligatory that only the rightful heir be the recipient. Female chastity became essential. Male promiscuity was overlooked—as long as the female, and her legitimate offspring, were secure.

The late cartoonist Charles Schultz, who died in 2000, created a whole episode in the cartoon strip, "Peanuts" based on the old adage "a woman's handshake is not legally binding." That was a true legal fact until the end of the 20th century. (Actually men's handshakes weren't legal either but accepted as proof of the men's "contract.") Lucy shakes hands with Charlie Brown and promises she will not pull the football away as she holds it for his kick. She always pulls the ball away, sending Charlie sprawling.[128]

Lucy's remark is rooted in fact. In Biblical times, and still somewhat among Orthodox Jews, a woman was considered a "perpetually minor child," and as such, was incompetent to give evidence in court and could not defend herself.[129] According to the culture of her time, Mary, a woman, and worse, a teenager, could not make her own decisions—especially about life choices. God doesn't "buy into" any of this socially—induced discrimination. He treats women the same as He treats men.

The New Covenant starts here. It starts with Mary's yes. The new covenant is a whole revolutionary concept of thinking in love about other people. It's a new way of thinking about women in particular.

---

[128] For the record, according to a newspaper interview with Schultz in 1979, for 20 years Lucy pulled that ball away. In July and August 1979, she makes a 'deathbed promise' to Charlie, who is hospitalized with a mysterious illness, that she will not pull it away if he recovers. Her brother, Linus, is the witness. When Charlie gets out of the hospital—she does keep her promise—Charlie misses and instead kicks her hand! Good Grief! Schultz said in the interview, "Don't expect major personality changes." Now, since no artist continues the strip at Schultz' family's request, we never did see Charlie kick a football . . . . Was it ever even possible?

[129] McGrath, 19.

Mary holding baby Jesus

The angel, God's personal messenger, sought Mary directly and asked her if she would cooperate. There was no intermediary; she was not coerced but had free choice. Contrary to the paternalistic culture of the time, the angel neither went first to Mary's father, Joachim, nor to her fiancé, Joseph. They weren't even consulted. They might have refused as an initial reaction because the request was so unusual, so extreme, its consequences so frightening: she would be labeled an unwed mother and risked death. Nothing like this had ever happened before in the history of the world; there was no guideline.

Stoning, the Jewish method of execution—which could have prolonged agony and be very painful—was the penalty for an unwed pregnancy. In their society, the unwed mother was a bad reflection on the man's household. His property had been violated and her economic worth "as merchandise" was destroyed. It was the worst stigma women of that time could endure. We don't look at Mary that way.

Mary was engaged to Joseph and it wasn't even his baby. He was disgraced, too, and had every right, under their law, to have her stoned to death, or at least ostracized, that is put outside the town to fend on her own, which was extremely difficult to survive. Remember, he didn't believe her story at first either. It took an angelic dream to convince him. Everybody in small towns knows everyone else's business, so can you imagine if you had to explain away this pregnancy to your fiancé, your parents, the elders of the local synagogue and the neighbors?

How convincing does it sound to humans to say—"This is God's child?" I'm sure they thought it was bad enough that she was a teenager and pregnant—but now totally crazy, too, and her family and Joseph also—for going along with this amazing story. These people were expecting the Messiah—but they were not expecting extraordinary circumstances, nor expecting them in their own village.

Mary may not have understood the logistics of how the angelic request could happen since she was a virgin but she certainly understood she also was being asked to accept its unbelievable ramifications for her life. I'm sure she realized in that moment that if she and the baby lived, it would never be easy for them. I trust she believed God would somehow protect them or He wouldn't have asked her to do this. But it was all faith. There was no guarantee.

She said yes. Probably she said yes every day for the rest of her life. Certainly, she said yes every day for nine months, as the brilliance of the angelic vision faded, and the pressure mounted.

The punishment for adultery was death. The law forbade only the man from having adulterous relationships but both male and female were punishable, again by stoning. In practice it came to be that the woman was more readily, or actually the only one, punished. Again the reason was that the husband's property was damaged, his honor must be avenged. Monetary or social retribution was required. The woman's worth as a person did not enter into it at all. Equality in God's eyes did not follow through to equality in man's eyes.

Back to Mary. The covenant started literally, as well as figuratively, with her yes. She accepted God's offer. She also knew that the baby inside her was her Salvation, the Lord Messiah for whom all Israel waited. She was the vessel, the literal, "Ark of the Covenant."

Human beings have three components—the physical body, the soul which is the intellect, will, mind and emotions (which is often misinterpreted to mean the spirit); and the spirit. The latter is created in the image of God, an everlasting spirit. Mary recognized this distinction and mentions it in her "Magnificat," her hymn of praise to Yahweh, proclaimed to Elizabeth (Luke 1: 46-55). "My soul proclaims the greatness of the Lord and my spirit exults in God my savior" (Luke 1: 46-7). What she is really saying is, "My mind and emotions praise the Lord and my spirit rejoices in God, who is my salvation."

Intellectual praise becomes worship on the spiritual level. When Mary says, "Yes, from this day forward all generations will call me blessed, for the Almighty has done great things for me. Holy is His name, and His mercy reaches from age to age for those who fear Him" (Luke 1:48-50), she is speaking of her salvation ("has done great things for me") and worshipping Him in spirit ("Holy is His name").

Mary's society said she could not make life-choices. However, she said yes to salvation, the eternal life-choice. I believe Mary is the first spirit-filled Christian in the New Testament. John the Baptist is the second. Contrary to the cultural mores which stipulated men made the decisions, Mary said yes to God's question—would she turn her life upside down to achieve the Divine plan?

Sr. McGrath quotes from an apocryphal book of the early Christian era, *The Proto-Evangelium of James*, which details the life of Mary, her dedication to temple service at age three by her parents, Anna and Joachim, and her happy service there. "And when she was 12 years old (some manuscripts say 14) there was held a council of priests, saying, 'Behold, Mary has reached the age of 12 years in the temple of the Lord. What shall we do with her, lest perchance she defile the sanctuary of the Lord?'"[130]

McGrath explained: "The reference is, of course, to the onset of menstruation in the adolescent Mary. What they do with her is betroth her to Joseph, and she who would defile the Sanctuary of the Lord by being a normal physiologically mature female, carries the Lord himself in her womb for nine months."[131]

It is at Mary's request that Jesus performed the first miracle of His public ministry, during the marriage reception at Cana. (John 2: 1-11). He turned the water into wine as a personal favor to her and the young couple, but I don't believe he didn't anticipate the request. What we tend to forget in the Cana story is Jesus was acting on instructions from the Father; it wasn't chance. Since Jesus did everything the Father told Him, we can assume that "okay" preceded this miracle, as well as all the others including the multiplication of the loaves and fishes and the raising of Lazarus.

Almost everything Jesus said or did was symbolic of His fulfillment of the Scriptures or a referral back to the faith and prophesies in the Scriptures. (There wasn't a New Testament yet, of course.) The miracle at Cana was symbolic also. It foreshadowed the institution of the Eucharist, at the Passover supper banquet or feast, changing the wine into His Blood.

There is a popular Catholic tradition that Jesus cannot refuse His mother any request. While that is possibly true when she intercedes in prayer on our behalf, which is what she does, Mary does not act

---

[130]   McGrath, 17-18.
[131]   Ibid, 18.

through power of her own. However, few of us have her faith! She told the waiters at the wedding feast, "Do whatever He tells you." (John 2:5) Most of us don't do "whatever" Jesus says, let alone without a squabble.

Jesus does not single Mary out during His ministry as being better than others because she is His mother. Not even when a woman in the crowd yells out a compliment to them both. "Blessed are the breasts that nursed you and the womb that bore you." Rather, to the contrary, Jesus pointedly mentions, as recorded in the Synoptic Gospels,[132] that it isn't physical relationship which matters to Him, but the ones who do the will of God who are His brothers and sisters and mother.[133]

At the foot of the Cross, Mary's discipleship is made clear. So is that of the beloved disciple, John. It's the believer who is in true relationship to Jesus, rather than physical, generic affiliation, or earthly proximity, according to Fr. Raymond E. Brown in *"Roles of Women in the Fourth Gospel."*

> At the foot of the Cross are brought together the two great symbolic figures of the Fourth Gospel whose personal names are never used by the Evangelist, "the mother of Jesus" and "the Disciple whom Jesus loved." Both were historic personages, but they are not named by John since their primary (not sole) importance is in their symbolism or discipleship rather than in their historical careers. By stressing not only that his mother had become the mother of the Beloved Disciple, but also that this Disciple has become her son, the Johannine Jesus is logically claiming the Disciple as his true brother.[134]

---

[132] The Synoptic Gospels are those of Matthew, Mark and Luke. The word, synoptic, comes from the Greek, synopsis, or view, according to the Maryknoll Catholic Dictionary, (Albert J. Nevins, M.M., editor, Dimension Books, New York: Grosset and Dunlap, 1965, p. 556). The word Synoptic was first given to these three gospel accounts by J. Griesback in 1776, "since they can be arranged in three parallel columns and thus can be seen as one view."

[133] See also Matt. 12:46-50, Mark 3:31-35, Luke 8:19-21; and John 15:14.

[134] Fr. Raymond E. Brown, "Roles of Women in the Fourth Gospel," *Woman: New Dimensions*, 122.

Brown says the "Beloved Disciple" was the "ideal of Discipleship," but a woman was "intimately involved with the Disciple on an equal plane."[135] Brown says, "A woman and a man stood at the foot of the Cross as models for Jesus' 'own,' his true family of disciples."[136]

Mary is present also at the Ascension and on Pentecost with the male and female disciples for the outpouring of the Holy Spirit. It is her refilling. It is also very symbolic that on Pentecost the mother of the Messiah should be there—she who gave birth to the New Law. Pentecost is the Jewish feast of Shabuoth, which comes 50 days after the first day of Passover. Shabuoth is also called the "Feast of Weeks," and symbolized God's bounty in the wheat crop. Shabuoth commemorated the giving of the Ten Commandments, the old Law, to Moses on Mount Sinai. Jesus is the Paschal sacrifice, the Passover Lamb, slain to atone for mankind's sin. Wheat, of course, is what makes bread, the new Eucharistic body of Christ. The Ten Commandments were the beginning of the Law, the way of life under the Old Covenant. The Holy Spirit is the way of life under the New Covenant.

Mary is notable because she is the stereotype of all women—as disciples of Jesus. Mary is notable because she said yes—to salvation, as well as to being Jesus' Mom. She is considered holy and notable because she obeyed God.

---

[135] Ibid, 123.
[136] Ibid.

CHAPTER 9

The Incredible Encounter with the Samaritan Woman

Two of the most remarkable stories in the Bible are also two of Jesus' most startling encounters with women. These two are the discourse with the Samaritan woman at the well (John 4), the subject of this chapter, and the healing of the woman with the issue of blood, as recorded in the three Synoptic gospels, Matthew, Mark, and Luke (Matt. 9: 18-22, Mark 5: 25-34, Luke 8: 43-48), and detailed in the next chapter.

The discourse with the Samaritan woman comes shortly after the start of Jesus' public ministry, according to the Reference Passage Bible New Testament, which lists topics chronologically.[137] It is the 25th section out of 225 in the Gospels and out of 604 in the entire New Testament.[138]

After Jesus' background, there are the meetings with John the Baptist and choosing the first five disciples. The only other precedents to the story of the woman at the well are the marriage feast at Cana (§20); the first Passover and cleansing of the Temple (§21); the discourse with Nicodemus, which calls for spiritual rebirth (§22); John baptizing Jesus (§23); and the imprisonment of John (§24).

Jesus' whole ministry would be predicated on two discussions— the first, with Nicodemus, a Jewish religious leader, to whom Jesus

---

[137] *Reference Passage Bible, New Testament, With Old Testament References.* I.N. Johns, ed., (Plainfield, NJ: Logos International, 1978).
[138] Ibid., 142.

said we need spiritual renewal in our lives (John 3: 1-21), and the second, with the Samaritan woman, to whom Jesus told His identity and mission: I am Messiah, the Christ, the long-awaited Anointed One of God. (John 4: 25-6). His speaking to her, and telling her such a significant spiritual truth, also implies the gist and thrust of His ministry of love and forgiveness. He is saying in effect (and in its retelling, to a much wider audience) "Get rid of your outdated discrimination. Love your enemy. Treat others as you would be treated. The old taboos are over forever. The poor, downtrodden, and the unlovely—personified by women—are not to be despised, exploited and oppressed."

It's no wonder the male-disciples were flabbergasted!

The conversation with the Samaritan woman preceded His public ministry and its healings and teachings, the Sermon on the Mount, and even the selection of the other seven disciples. It was an *absolutely revolutionary* story for their culture and we have lost the full implication of it.

Leonard Swidler, in his now infamous article, "Jesus was a Feminist," which caused furor when first published in 1971, said Jesus was (is) a feminist because He fits the definition. "A feminist is a person who is in favor of, and who promotes the equality of women with men, a person who advocates and practices treating women primarily as human persons (as men are so treated) and willingly contravenes social customs in so acting."[139]

Jesus' greeting to the Samaritan woman was nothing short of extraordinary. In his article, Swidler quoted Scripture scholar, Peter Ketter, who explained, "A rabbi regarded it as beneath his dignity, as indeed positively disreputable, to speak to a woman in public."[140] The rabbi could not even speak to his own wife, daughter or sister, L. Swidler explained, and cites the warning from the ancient Proverbs of the (Church) Fathers, "One is not so much as to greet a woman."[141]

---

[139] Leonard Swidler. "Jesus was a Feminist," *The (New) Catholic World,* (Jan. 1971), 177.
[140] As quoted in L. Swidler, 178.
[141] Ibid.

That was the social climate of Jesus' time.

The setting is a hot, dusty day, around noon, the time of densest heat when no one goes to the well. Water is drawn only in the early morning or the cool of the evening. The well, itself, is significant in that it's considered a religious landmark—a miracle in the middle of the desert—and is the well from which Jacob provided water to his flocks and family. It is his son, Joseph, who saves the family from the famine by bringing them to Egypt. Besides that significance, water in the New Testament always represents the Holy Spirit and Baptism, and the cleansing of sin. The well was also the traditional wedding site in small villages.

Jesus is hot and thirsty. He is tired from the mornings' journey, over mountainous terrain and through desert by foot. As the late evangelist Kathryn Kuhlman used to teach, "Jesus was as human as if he had never been divine." He is resting, leaning against the well, waiting for the disciples to return from town with some food for lunch. There was no convenience store on the corner. There was no corner.

A woman comes along to draw water. She cannot come when the other women do because she has an unsavory reputation; "respectable" women are not seen in her company. Everyone knows everyone else's business in small towns, then and now. Her story: she's living with some guy to whom she isn't married and she has been married five times.[142] It is possible some of her husbands were brothers, since under Jewish tradition, the surviving brother was obligated to marry his brother's widow, but not likely. Then it wouldn't be an issue in the

---

[142] According to the Ignatius Catholic Study Bible, §4:18 and 4:6, "The woman's personal life parallels the historical experience of the Samaritan people. According to 2 Kings 17:24-31, five foreign tribes intermarried with the northern Israelites (Samaritans) and introduced five male deities into their religion. These were addressed as 'Baal,' a Hebrew word meaning Lord or husband. The prophets denounced the worship of these idols as infidelity to the true covenanted spouse, Yahweh. Hope was kept alive that God would become their everlasting husband in the new Covenant. This happens in the ministry of Jesus, the divine bridegroom, who has come to save the Samaritans from a lifetime of struggles with the five pagan 'husbands.' Jesus is the divine bridegroom in search of believers to be his covenanted bride."

story and it is. It's an integral part of what Jesus says to her. Perhaps she was widowed or more probably, divorced.

Women *could be divorced* if they no longer pleased their husbands, burned the dinner, were incompatible, had adulterous relationships, or for any other reason. Women *could not divorce their husbands, not even for adultery.* Talk about a double standard! Although divorce was permitted under Mosaic Law, a woman was considered a failure if divorced. This notorious woman had failed five times and she's in yet another questionable relationship. No one knew or cared anything about women's libido in those days.

Remember: 1) Jewish men, particularly rabbis, did not speak to women; 2) Jews despised Samaritans and did not speak to them; 3) Menstruating women were considered unclean, as well as anything they touched or sat upon; 4) The Jews considered Samaritans to be of mixed blood lines, because of so many wars and invasions of Samaria with their resulting rapes and intermarriages. To the Jews, that meant the Samaritans were impure. They thought that a Samaritan woman was *so impure*; it was as if she was menstruant from birth. This was both by rabbinical regulation and as the accepted and recognized view.[143] 5) Her spittle was considered to be especially contaminated.[144] A Samaritan woman was the scum of the earth to Jewish men.

So here's this total foreigner, and a Jewish man at that, obvious from his clothing, resting alongside the holy well. Suddenly He asks the woman, "Can I have a drink from your cup?" What! Not just any old jug or vessel but from *her cup!* And, it was not an accident; nothing Jesus did was accidental or done without prior prayer. Jesus knew she'd be coming in midday to the well. Whom do you expect to find living in a village or town but mostly natives of the place, in this case Samaritans? It's such an affront it's comparable to riding in the New York City subway today, or being in any other public place, and having an absolute stranger—especially one who is considered to be an enemy of your country—come up and ask if he could give you a kiss on the lips. Preposterous! It's shocking enough to make

---

[143]   McGrath, 30.
[144]   Ibid., 31.

the woman fall over in a faint or smash the cup into smithereens by dropping and breaking it on the hard ground, presumably like rock, which surrounded the well. It wasn't just desert sand.

She's incredulous and in effect responds, "What are you doing talking to me? Are you a lunatic?"

She's also wary, and perhaps, a bit snippy. She has a shady reputation anyway—what would the town's people or her current live-in male companion say if they saw her talking to a Jew! After all, the Jews are positively nasty to Samaritans. "What? You're a Jew and you ask me, a Samaritan woman, for a drink?" (John 4: 8-9). Maybe she thought this guy, whom she had never seen before, was "being fresh" as well as rude and crazy.

Jesus doesn't get aggravated; he probably expected her reaction. He continues to speak with her and immediately starts talking about spiritual matters. The terms "Living Waters," and "Gift from God," (both verse 10) are analogies and symbolic in their religion (both Jews and Samaritans worship Yahweh though the Jews think the Samaritans don't do so properly) and these are familiar terms to them. Their conversation shows she is scripturally knowledgeable and capable of intelligent thought to talk about these topics—another shocker.

Males of that era did not think women were capable of intelligent thought and discussion. Women were officially uneducated and particularly restrained from studying the Torah, because men believed women could not understand "higher" spiritual truths. Jesus apparently didn't know that was the "standard of His time" because look at what they discuss: "the most profound spiritual truths; the doctrine of grace, the true nature and service of God; His own mission as Christ the Messiah."[145]

Somewhere along the way of discussing the Living Water, she probably drew some water and He drank. After all, He asked for a drink to start the conversation. It seems like the only natural, hospitable thing to do for someone with whom you're chatting. Hospitality was a cultural mandate for Semitic people, a custom fostered by the Jewish religion.

---

[145]   McGrath, 30-31.

What the Bible account does not tell us but what was obvious, blatantly obvious, to the original readers of the Gospel account, who were familiar with local customs, is that it would be a *defilement for Him* to drink from her cup, or even to touch it. To do so would require subsequent purification in the temple or synagogue. Sr. McGrath explains further:

> The Samaritan woman, then, was not just an enemy of His people; she was also religiously anathema as being an unclean person. This uncleanness was, in Jewish thinking, conveyed to the vessel she held. If, as in this case seems highly likely, it was a vessel from which she herself was accustomed to drink, Jesus was very seriously offending against the laws of purity by drinking from it, too. The spittle of the menstruant was thought to be especially contaminated. Not defying, *but ignoring the taboos,* Jesus by His quiet matter-of-fact actions repudiates centuries of thought and legislation which would define woman in her specific mature womanliness as unclean and unfit for direct association not only with the divine, but even periodically with the human.[146]

When the disciples return, she hurries off into the town and tells everyone, "This man told me everything I've ever done. Is He not the Christ?" They come to see and listen to Him based on the woman's testimony. Upon hearing Jesus, the townspeople believe for themselves that He is the Messiah (verses 29-30, 39-42).

What she did was preach the "Good News" of salvation and, on the basis and strength of her witness, others came to believe in Him. It is the same kind of preaching the disciples, male primarily, would later use to make converts.

According to Fr. Brown, even the word in Greek used by the evangelist was the same in both situations. "The Evangelist can describe both a woman's witness and the (presumably male) disciples at the Last Supper as bearing witness to Jesus through preaching

---

[146] Ibid.

and thus bringing people to believe in Him on the strength of their word . . . That the Samaritan woman has a real missionary function is made clear."[147]

Rachael Conrad Wahlberg in *Jesus According to a Woman* said Jesus' self-revelation as Messiah was deliberate and His choice of a listener was hardly accidental.[148] Neither her sex, marital status, nor "state of grace" were important to a woman's spreading the gospel—or her effectiveness in doing so. "Jesus does not prevent her from proclaiming the gospel because she is woman," McGrath said.[149]

Wahlberg said the woman had a vocation to preach which was at odds with the cultural conditioning:

> Jesus gave the woman a message bombshell. He knew it would motivate her to preach. It acted as a spiritual 'call' within her. She went forth immediately to tell a message—and the message got through. She left her water-pot to go and tell. She left her woman-job for her preacher-job. Her culturally-assigned status gave way to her Jesus-assigned status—one who is worthy to go and tell.[150]

She was an unlikely messenger. Perhaps that's why she was effective. Which of the people Jesus ever chose was likely? John and Peter were rough, uneducated Galilean fishermen. Matthew was a despised employee working for the equivalent of the Internal Revenue Service of the hated Roman government, hounding the people for their exorbitant taxes. Before Paul met Jesus on the road to Damascus, he was a bounty hunter. His motto for killing the newfangled Christ-believers was, "Have zeal, will travel." Jesus' own mother was an unmarried teenager and her fiancé initially thought about putting her to death for what he humanly thought was an indiscretion, not

---

[147] Brown, 115.
[148] Rachael Conrad Wahlberg. *Jesus According to a Woman.* (New York: Paulist Press, 1975), 96.
[149] McGrath, 30.
[150] Wahlberg, 94.

knowing it was a miracle. He changed his mind when alerted by God through a dream, thus saving both Mary and Jesus.

"Jesus looked through the three negatives," Wahlberg said, "woman, Samaritan, and sinner—and saw a person useful for the kingdom."[151]

What are implications of this story?

1. Jesus deliberately addresses her. He initiates the conversation, disregarding the inferiority of women's status from the very beginning of His ministry.
2. He asks for a drink from her cup. The full impact of the blood taboos will be discussed in detail later in another chapter but it was a revolutionary gesture and their society knew it. Also, Jesus asked a woman to minister to His need. Wahlberg said that alone is significant.[152]
3. Jesus carries out an intellectual and spiritual discussion with a woman, who obviously is capable of understanding and discussing intelligently, something which was shocking to the men of their era.
4. Jesus' dialogue with the woman at the well is the longest conversation recorded in the gospels, so it increases with significance for that reason alone. Besides, Jesus obviously had to tell the male-disciples what had happened since they were in the town buying food during the entire conversation. When they came back, He said to them, "I have food you do not know about," meaning the spiritual food of His conversation and His healing outreach to her.
5. Jesus tells her He is Messiah, the redeemer (verses 24, 26) which is the first time He mentions it. Importantly, it is the strongest statement He makes about it in the course of His entire ministry, until His trial. She understands the implications of that message. Why didn't He confide this revelation to some lofty religious leader, even the High Priest?

---

[151] Ibid., 97.
[152] Ibid., 92.

Who knows? In John 3, Nicodemus, a religious leader, did not understand the implication of the revelation about spiritual re-birth. Perhaps Jesus' revelation to the Samaritan woman was just a confirmation to their society that He, the Christ, had not created the female half of His creatures (John 1: 1-3) less equally than the other half.

6. The ministry of Jesus was to save "the lost sheep of Israel." This is His first evangelization outreach to non-Jews, although the Samaritans believed and worshipped Yahweh, the God of Israel. Later, the Syro-Phoenician woman is His first outreach to the gentiles in His adult ministry. Of course, the Magi, or Wise Men, who came to give presents to baby King Jesus, are the first Gentiles to acknowledge the kingship of Jesus.

7. The Samaritan woman, who is never identified by name, nor allegedly heard from again during His ministry, *proclaims*, that is, preaches, the gospel message of salvation. *She is an evangelist.* People believe her testimony, her witness, in a patriarchal era when women were not valid witnesses in court.

8. She is one of the "harvest-reapers." The rest of John, Chapter 4, is all about reaping the harvest—that is, reaping the spiritual harvest of believers into the Kingdom—"the fields that are ripe for harvest." According to Brown, that "is a reference to the Samaritan villagers coming out to hear Him because of the woman's witness."[153] In the Biblical account, "the woman has sown the seed among the villagers," Brown explained, "thus preparing for the apostolic harvest . . . The woman's role is an essential component in the total mission."[154]

9. Since the well was the traditional wedding site, metaphorically, as she accepts his Messiah-ship, she becomes the 'Bride of Christ.' This appellation, 'Bride of Christ,' generally is reserved for the church itself, which we've seen is referred to in feminine terms. Since this is the very start of Jesus' ministry, it is before

---

153 Brown, 115.
154 Ibid., 116.

the church is established, when Jesus said to Peter, "You are Peter and upon this rock, I will build my church." (Matt 16: 18). Like Mary at the foot of the Cross, as pointed out in Chapter 8 above, the Samaritan woman becomes one of Jesus' "own" through her relationship with Him.

According to Jewish tradition, everything about the encounter between Jesus and the Samaritan woman was incredible and unbelievable. According to Jesus, it was the "modus operandi," his normal operating procedure.

CHAPTER 10

The Women of Faith in Sickness and in Death

The healing of the woman with the blood issue is almost as important in its impact as the discussion with the Samaritan woman (Matt 9: 19-22, Mark 5: 25-34, Luke 8: 43-48). Jesus is on the way to the home of Jarius, a synagogue official, to heal his daughter who is grievously ill. The crowds are crushing around Jesus, some out of faith in His message, many others from curiosity. They had heard the reports and came to see the lame walk, the deaf hear. It certainly was exciting and, of course, there was no television, or iPad®, to occupy the evenings.

This woman had a bleeding disease for 12 years. She had been to see many doctors, apparently, mostly charlatans, who took her money and ran, all to no avail. None of them could help her, not one could alleviate the blood issue, or hemorrhage. She was medically incurable.

In Jewish society, the woman during her menstrual periods, and for seven days after the cessation of the flow, was 'unclean.' So was any person who had a bodily discharge. Anything, or anyone, touched during the unclean time assumed the uncleanness. This poor woman had a bodily discharge of blood—a double defilement—in effect making her utterly, unspeakably and permanently unclean. The only difference between this woman and the despised lepers was that she was not forced totally outside of the community, as they were. Apparently, she was dreadfully ostracized, and her illness and its history were well-known in the neighborhood.

She, too, had heard about Jesus. Maybe she had seen others healed of various infirmities. Jesus was a celebrity and she was the dregs of society. She must have rationalized, "I'm not worthy enough to even talk to Him, let alone to ask Him to heal me, but if I just get close enough to reach out and touch Him as He walks by, then I will be healed. In the middle of such crowds, who would know? No one will notice me."

So she acts on her thought. Instantly, she is healed and she knows it. So does Jesus. He also knows that His saving, healing power has been tapped deliberately and not just in the crunch of folks around Him. The male-disciples scoff when he asks, "Who touched me?" Luke attributes the statement to Peter, never known for his finesse.

In "Just Let Me Touch the Hem of Your Cloak," from Mary B. Howard's album, *Day of the Lord: Songs of Scripture,* the dialogue goes like this. "Hey, who touched me? Jesus cried to all the people standing there. Of His Father's power leaving him, he was aware. 'It was no one," Peter said, 'just rude people crowding in.' Till the woman cried, 'you've healed me, Lord, of my suffering and my sin.'"[155]

The male-disciples certainly didn't know who touched Jesus, let alone that anyone had! Jesus knew not only that someone had been healed—but who it was, what she was healed from and, of course, why she did it surreptitiously. That's why He made her own up to it. Not for either of them, but for the others. Not to embarrass her but to prove a point.

The New American Standard Bible says in Mark 5: 32, "And He looked around to see the woman who had done this." Possibly the author and translators included the word "woman" in the sentence because of familiarity with the story or due to the fact that Jesus knew it was a woman who touched him.

The *Jerusalem Bible* says, "Then the woman came forward, frightened and trembling, because she knew what had happened to

---

[155] Lyric used with permission by Mary B. Howard, *Day of the Lord: Songs of Scripture,* a record album produced by the Family Life Bureau, FLB Productions, P.O. Box 339, East Brunswick, NJ 08816.

her and she fell at His feet and told him the whole truth." (Mark 9: 33-34) She was frightened and trembling, according to the footnote on the verse, because, "According to the law, she was unclean, and to be touched by her would be a defilement."

Jesus was very well aware of this. He doesn't rant and rave and scream at her saying, as the Pharisees might have, "Look what you've done! You have some nerve! Now I have to go to the temple and be purified—just because of you—and take all that time away from my important work." Probably he smiled and very gently listened as she explained the situation. A lot of people had crowded in brushing against Him but the woman with faith was the one who was healed. Jesus said to her, "My daughter, your faith has restored you to health. Go in peace and be free of your complaint."

The words "my daughter" show relationship between Jesus, the creator, and the woman, His creature. Her faith was in Him as Messiah. That's why she was healed, not because she happened to touch His cloak. The words, "Go in peace," are especially significant considering how ostracized she was for those 12 years and how fearful of discovery she was in the encounter.

The line in Mary Howard's song about being healed of suffering and sin is very appropriate. "Once established, the idea of female uncleanness persisted in Judaism. In the Old Testament, the terms to be unclean and to defile have always a moral connotation. While in pre-Mosaic times this may not always have been so, in post-Mosaic times the idea of moral transgression is never absent," according to McGrath.[156]

The purity laws affecting women are called "the Blood Taboos" by Biblical scholars. "The Blood Taboos were not just hygienic legislation," Joan Morris said in *The Lady Was a Bishop,* "but the idea of the woman being in contact with the evil one."[157] This is evident in any reference in the Bible to someone possessed. They were possessed by an "unclean spirit," as in Mark 5: 2, 9, and 12. Wahlberg calls the woman with the blood issue, "the audacious

---

[156] McGrath, 17.
[157] Morris, 106.

woman" because she reached out to touch Christ and be made clean.[158] The evangelists thought it was significant, also, otherwise three of them would not have mentioned it in such detail. The equivalent story in John's gospel, and of even greater significance, is the Samaritan woman.

Jesus does not reject the woman with the blood issue. He does not shrink from her touch. There is an ancient Catholic tradition that the woman was Veronica, the one who wiped the face of Jesus with her veil during His excruciating trek to Calvary. Her kind action resulted in an imprint of His anguished, bloody face on the cloth. It is a relic preserved in St. Peter's Basilica, Rome. There is very little known about the woman, Veronica. She is sometimes identified as the woman with the issue of blood.[159] If so, He does not shrink from her touch a second time.[160]

Again with the woman of the blood issue, whom Wahlberg called the woman of faith, as with the Samaritan woman, Jesus squashes the blood taboos. Jesus does not go to the temple to be purified—but onto Jarius' house to raise a little girl from the dead. Yes, a little girl.

There are three instances in the Gospels of Jesus raising dead persons and all of them closely involve women. The first is of Jarius' daughter (Luke 8: 40-42, 49-56; Mark 5: 21-24, 35-43, and Matthew 9: 18-19, 23-26). There is a slight discrepancy in the three synoptic accounts in timing. Matthew says she was already dead when Jesus started out and it happened before the healing of the woman of faith (formerly the woman with the issue of blood). If Jesus would just touch the child, she would live again.

Mark and Luke both say she is critically ill but alive. After the woman's healing, messengers announce the child died. Anyway, by

---

[158] Wahlberg, 31-41.

[159] Maryknoll Catholic Dictionary, 588.

[160] The Catholic Church established the prayer form, the Stations of the Cross, to remind Christians of Jesus' torture and death. Although it can be prayed at any time of the year, it is most often done in Liturgical celebrations during Lent. There are 14 stations—all incidents which happened during the Scourging and Crucifixion. Station Number Six is Veronica, or some other woman, wiping Jesus' face with her veil. Her kind action is memorialized forever.

the time Jesus gets to the house she is dead and the keeners (wailers, official mourners) are already there. He tells them to be quiet since the child is "only asleep." Naturally, they think His remark is extremely strange since the child seems still and lifeless to them. The child's parents believe Jesus and know differently. She is a young adolescent, maybe 13 or 14, and not a baby.

Jesus *takes the little girl by the hand* and commands her to get up and live, which, of course, she does. Then He gives her something to eat, which proves she is alive. Maybe He also realized she probably hadn't eaten for some time while ill and she probably would be hungry. Jesus is always considerate of our needs. Naturally, the keeners and mourners are astounded. Who ever saw such a thing!

The second raising is of a male youth—because Jesus is moved by the boy's mother's distress. He is the only son of the widow of Nain. (Luke 7: 11-17) Jesus' compassionate heart goes out to the woman and He said, "Do not weep." He *put his hand on the bier* and the bearers stood still (verses 13-16). "Then He told the boy to get up and He gave the son to the mother." A widow without a son to support her would be destitute very shortly; there was no one else to help her, no Social Security. Jesus knew this, of course. Again, touching the bier was defilement and he should have gone to the Temple to be purified. He doesn't because he knows true defilement, or sin, comes from the heart.

The most spectacular resurrection is that of Lazarus (John 11). In verse 11-15, Jesus said to the male-disciples, even before they arrived in Bethany, that Lazarus was resting and he would wake him. The disciples assumed Jesus meant Lazarus was resting from the effects of the illness and not dead. Jesus already knew what the Father had planned for this situation. He had been in the desert praying. Jesus finally arrives in Bethany a few days later and sees the anguish of the sisters, Mary and Martha, at the death of their brother. Lazarus was Jesus' dearly loved friend, and He weeps. The sisters don't understand. Both are friends of Jesus, each in her own right, and say with some recrimination: "If you had been here, Lazarus wouldn't have died." Even so, based on the faith of Mary and Martha, and as a result of their desire that Jesus "do something," that Lazarus is raised. It is particularly due to their belief in Jesus as the Resurrection.

Jesus reveals the central truth of Christianity to the homemaker, Martha, in verses 25-27. Belief in Him means eternal life, He explains. This is the second time Jesus makes a significant spiritual revelation to a woman. The first was about His Messiah-ship to the Samaritan woman. Again, this revelation is not to a doctor of theology, or a learned rabbi, but to an everyday woman, who comprehends, and believes.

Jesus says, "Lazarus, come on out here." Lazarus does and the Father is gloried. Lazarus was in the tomb about 4 days when he was raised. Due to the heat of the climate, the custom was immediate burial, so probably in chronological time, he was only dead about three full days. There is an obvious parallel between this resurrection and what would be Jesus' own. It was more than just a symbolic forerunner of Easter morning but proof of the truth of the message of Christianity—Jesus is the Resurrection.

L. Swidler in "Jesus Was a Feminist" said there is a significant difference in the raising of Jarius' daughter. It is the only resurrection account where Jesus touches the corpse—which made Him ritually unclean, as did touching the bier holding the dead body of the widow's son. Jesus doesn't touch the young man's body, He just says, "Young man arise." Finally, at the Bethany burial site, He calls, "Lazarus, come out."

This is the third time Jesus deliberately ignores the taboos against women being unclean because of Blood Taboos or death. As usual, He was operating on instructions from the Father. To Jesus, the only form of uncleanness worth noting came from the heart. It was not a person's physical condition; it was not the kosher or non-kosher food you ate, (Acts 10; 11: 1-18), which mattered. In God's sight, it is sin which makes you unclean. This is described well in Mark 7: 14-23, especially verses 21-23. "It is what comes out of a man than makes him unclean. For it is from within, from men's hearts, that evil intentions emerge: fornication, theft, murder, adultery, avarice, malice, deceit, indecency, envy, slander, pride, folly. All these evil things come from within and make a man unclean." That's why Jesus ignored the taboos.

He was trying to show the chosen people, especially the religious leaders, that circumstances were secondary. As He often told them, adhere to the spirit, rather than the letter of the Law. That lesson was the same one learned much later by Antoine de St. Exupery's Little Prince who learned from the fox "which has been tamed." The fox told the Little Prince, "What is essential is invisible to the eye. It is only with the heart that one can see rightly."

Sin is still the spiritual pollutant, showing "stain," an unclean spot, making us dirty.

The Myth of the Menses

To understand the implications of Jesus asking for a drink from the Samaritan woman's cup, being touched by the woman of faith (with the blood issue), and touching the dead girl, we must refer to the ingrained Blood Taboos. Scholars refer to them as the Blood Taboos because they resulted from deep-seated superstitious fears of the primitives and the restrictions of the Jews concerning the menstrual cycle. They are also called Family Purity Laws.

Blood to the Hebrews was the life-force. It was mysteriously sacred. That is why a blood sacrifice was required for redemption. When Yahweh established the covenant with Noah and his sons after the flood, (Gen. 9: 4-6) there was only one thing which God reserved to His own dominion, the blood. "I give you everything, with this exception: you must not eat flesh with life, that is to say blood, in it. I will demand an account of your lifeblood." What that means, explains the footnote in the *Catholic Bible's Confraternity Edition* is, "Since God reserves the disposition of life to Himself, man was forbidden to eat meat with blood in it. Moreover, dominion over human life belongs to God. Therefore, He demands an accounting when human life is taken unjustly."[161]

Blood, according to *Smith's Bible Dictionary*, has a double power—that of sacrificial atonement and that of becoming a curse when wantonly shed, unless duly expiated.[162] Abel's sacrifice,

---

[161] *Confraternity Edition Bible*, Old Testament, Footnote 9:4, 26.
[162] William Smith, LLD, *Smith's Bible Dictionary*, Spire books. (Old Tappan, NJ: Fleming H. Revell Co., 1976), 88-9.

according to Smith, was bloody. Both that, and Cain's sacrifice were Eucharistic, meaning to give thanks.[163] The blood sacrifice had the sweeter savor (Gen. 4: 1-6).

One of the first differentiations which separates worship of Yahweh from that of pagan idols, Abraham learns, is now there is no human sacrifice. Abraham didn't know this initially. His faith is tested—would he be willing to sacrifice his most cherished son? The son whom Yahweh promised would be the ancestor of kings and nations. "What kind of a covenant is this anyhow?" he must have wondered. The answer, incredulously, but unhesitatingly, is yes. Yes, even this, Lord. Abraham believes Yahweh can work it out even as the ax in his hand shakes with the heaviness of his faith on the hill of Moriah, traditionally considered as the site of the later Temple of Jerusalem.

The new sacrifice, the new temple, is all part of the New Covenant. Jesus is the blood sacrifice, the atoning offering for sin, and the Father's most cherished son. Believers, filled with the Holy Spirit, are the new living temples. Sin offerings and burnt offerings were the method of sacrifice for the Jews until the destruction of the Temple, around 70 A.D. Atonement for defilement, uncleanness, caused by sin, was necessary to remove its stain.

In other primitive cultures, men associated blood with life and death, good and evil. It was both dynamic and dangerous, and regarded with a mixture of awe, reverence, fear and dread. Most of all, its ill effects were thought to be contagious. McGrath wrote:

> The mere listing of the taboos of uncleanness shows the anxieties of the male. The female experience is alien and to be dreaded, because it is different from the experience of the male, who sets himself up (as he can in his dominant position as hunter and warrior) as normative human being. Menstruation he finds especially fearsome.
>
> Blood is everywhere in the primitive world regarded with extreme anxiety. Reverenced as the seed of life, it is never to

---

[163] Ibid., 159.

be spilled upon the ground. When the female loses blood in menstruation, she is losing the only thing which makes her of any value; the blood with which she nurtures the all-powerful male seed. This periodic loss must bespeak some inherent wickedness, some demonic quality in her. She is, therefore, attractive and repulsive, to be both loved and hated. The fear of menstrual blood was so great in folk societies that neither the husband nor anyone else could, without defilement, touch the woman or anything she had touched during her period. Demons, at work in all sorts of sickness, were thought to be especially active at the time of childbirth. These notions of defilement and danger can be found not only among primitives, but also in Buddhism, Shintoism, Islam and Hinduism.[164]

In some primitive cultures the men often had blood initiation rites to emulate the normal bleeding of the female. Among Jews, however, there was no question—the menstrual cycle was regarded as "unclean." Leviticus 15: 19-33 details the laws of isolation and purification required. Jewish uncleanness, ceremonial or not, allegedly cut off a person from social privileges and citizenship among God's people was held in abeyance, temporarily.[165] Incongruously, while women were 'able' to be unclean members of God's people, legalistically they were not able to be members of the covenanted people, whose sign was circumcision (Gen. 17: 10-14).

To the Jews there "was a sacredness attached to the human body which paralleled that invested in the Ark of the Covenant itself," almost a body-holiness, Smith said.[166] There were three stages of uncleanness:

1. Least significant was defilement until evening, which was removed by bathing and changing the clothes. Contact with dead animals was one cause.

---

[164] McGrath, 15-6.
[165] Smith, 716.
[166] Ibid.

2. Next in severity was defilement for seven days and it had to be removed "by the water of separation." This kind of defilement was caused by things like touching a human corpse. Allegorically, if not deliberately, the waters of Baptism are modeled on this. In Baptism, the defilement of sin, the separation from God, is removed from the Christian; the dead spirit is brought back to life in God.
3. The most severe defilement was morbid, perpetual or menstrual uncleanness, lasting as long as the state lasted— say for the duration of a woman's menstrual period, or in cases such as leprosy, defilement was for life.

Birth and death were states of uncleanness. This showed humanity's weakness, both the human's coming and the going was marked by pollution. The woman was doubly defiled, 80 days, if she gave birth to a daughter, and defiled only 40 days for the birth of a male child. Atoning sacrifices, as with sin atonement, had to be sacrificed at the Temple after the conclusion of seven-day, or durational defilements. To touch or be touched by someone who was defiled made the object of the touch unclean also.

Although discrimination against women and the affects of the blood taboos are underlying aspects of our society, at least in the Western World, they are not as overt as they were during Jesus' earthly life. Today their influence is subtle but there is no doubt they still impact on women. Throughout the history of religion, there was nothing even subtle about it. Rather, direct commands relegated women to outside positions—in the women's court in the Temple or synagogue, outside the Sanctuary in Christian churches, and even outside the church and removed from the Sacraments themselves in the Middle Ages.

In our society, there are three primary and obvious references to the blood taboos. The first is the hang-up many women have about menstruation and the pass-along problem of having to tell their daughters this fact of life. This is a direct result of the centuries old connotation of the menstrual cycle being, "the curse." The name, "the curse," possibly descended from the "Curse or Sin of Eve."

Somewhere along the way the curse became "My friend," probably when some woman—with a sigh of relief—whether married or not, was delighted to find she was not pregnant after all. Second, many couples refrain from sexual intercourse while the woman menstruates claiming it is "messy," but the unconscious, historical meaning is "do not touch." Third, commercial advertisements for "sanitary napkins" or tampon products often have the most blatant references to the blood taboos. The advertising copywriters instinctively seem to dwell on the negative connotations. The implications of these advertisements are directly related to the taboos, whether consciously directed or not. Regarding the advertisements, the very word sanitary means "related to the preservation of health; favorable to health, cleanly." It is an adjective derived from the word sanitation, meaning "the removal or neutralization of elements injurious to health.[167] There's nothing wrong with the words and their meanings except in relation to the Blood Taboos and the implied negativism. Both definitions suggest, "Woman—be clean, otherwise, we're all in for a lot of harmful effects." That's exactly what the Blood Taboos propagated and suggested: the woman was "unclean and possessed of evil" during this monthly time. Besides, all of this has nothing to do with preservation of health. Menstruation is normal, healthful; its absence or irregularity is the problem.

Even the word "tampon" (whose great success is its hidden secrecy) means "a plug of cotton or lint for insertion in a wound or body cavity; to plug up as a wound."[168] A wound is a tear, an unnatural rending of the body. There is nothing unnatural about menstruation—none of us would be around if it wasn't—but the connotation, the implication is that it is not natural but deviant. Why? Because men, not God, made the rules society adheres to, rules which often foster the male and denigrate the female.

The advertisements say, "Be secure," "Be confident," "Feel feminine, even on heavy days." Menstruating may not be soft and fuzzy but it probably is the most female thing there is, and what's the

---

[167] *Reader's Digest Great Encyclopedic Dictionary*, 1190.
[168] Ibid., 1367.

definition of feminine anyway? Not, "be clean," "you don't have to be embarrassed, ashamed, hide, or limit your activities in the slightest. Why you can even swim, horseback ride, do gymnastics, wear white, be with friends—even males—and no one will know!" "Our products take away the ignominy of a natural physiological function. Use them and there will be no differentiation excluding you, the menstruating female, from the rest of society." The products today are necessary, of course, the implications are not, and never were. Which sex are the copywriters of those ads, do you think?

Jesus' actions completely destroyed the concept of male supremacy and that's another reason why the religious leaders of His day were so skeptical and abusive toward Him. In their view, the Messiah would foster male superiority, not human equality.

The negative impact of the Blood Taboos is christened here as the "Myth of the Menses." This myth was blatantly obvious in the Catholic Church. Until the Protestant Reformation—which began in 1517 with the posting of Martin Luther's "95 Theses" on the door of the Wittenberg Cathedral to protest human foibles within the church structure—it was one church. The 'Myth of the Menses' traditions hold true for all Western Christian denominations today.

In *The Lady Was a Bishop,* Morris includes a special appendix, "The Taboo of Women during Pregnancy and Menstruation," because of their impact on the life of women in the church.[169] Menstruation implied impurity and the threat of contaminating others, Morris

---

[169] Ms. Morris, a linguist, documents all her extensive research from the original languages. The Medieval Abbesses, which Ms. Morris details extensively, are well-known to historians but not to the average churchgoer. The extent of the Abbesses authority was comparable to a male bishop, even if the abbesses never had the official bishop title! The closest to a woman actually acting as a bishop, Morris said, was St. Bridget of Ireland. For some odd reason, historians always neglect to mention the abbesses, or that they yielded such authority and ecclesiastical power and rank. I went through 16 years of Catholic school and never heard of them or their authority. I thought an abbess was like the Mother Superior of our high school . . . Wrong! During a trip to France, in one church, I saw the robes, mitre and crosier in gold of a Medieval Abbess—in a glass enclosed container—and it was the exact items as those of a bishop! It is the mitre (or headdress) and crosier (or staff) which symbolize the office.

said.[170] "This factor, more than any other, has been the cause of ostracizing of womankind—impeding them from participating in social, political and religious meetings.[171] For centuries, women were blatantly discriminated against by the church for the Myth of the Menses. Morris explained:

> Although eventually the Church in the West gave way to women's participation in the sacraments at all times, there is no doubt it was this prohibition in the early centuries of Christianity that had made it impossible for women to be ordained as priests or to serve at the altar. The clerical ministry of deaconess was only permitted to women at the age of 60, when women had passed the menopause and the possibility of the contagion of impurity.[172]

The menses myth was pervasive with the Zoroastrians from Iran to India, who believed the menses were caused by possession by the god of Evil, Ahriman.[173] The woman was kept apart and confined—to protect others. "Her very look, they thought," Morris said, "could injure and defile fire."[174] The Hindu Brahmans pray for a son, but the pregnancy itself is impure. Morris said the *Maitareya Samhita* manuscript ranks a pregnant woman as "inferior to a bad man and a major evil in human society."[175] Chinese Buddhists cannot burn incense during the menses and after pregnancy. However, for them, pregnancy is not impure. The woman must wait 100 days following pregnancy before approaching the altar of Buddha.[176]

In the Eastern and Russian Orthodox churches, and the Ethiopian Orthodox Church, many of the Old Testament injunctions are still

---

[170]   Ibid., 105.
[171]   Ibid., 111.
[172]   Ibid., 105.
[173]   Ibid.
[174]   Ibid., 106.
[175]   Ibid.
[176]   Ibid., 109.

adhered to, Morris said.[177] In the Eastern rite, however, there was some clarification of woman's cycle. *The Didascalia* and *Apostolic Constitutions* contain a clause which prohibits any imputation of sin during a woman's natural monthly discharge. While in the West, there were proscriptions in Canon Law until 1684 proscribing a woman from entering a church while menstruating.[178]

In 601 A.D. Pope Gregory (the Great) wrote a letter, Epistle 64, to St. Augustine of Canterbury in reply to a question posed by Augustine. Ahead of his time in this regard, Gregory insists a woman cannot be prohibited from entrance into the church or from receiving the sacraments during her periods or pregnancy. We think that's almost humorous, saying, "Of course!" but since Augustine had to query the pope on this subject, it wasn't obvious to him. Morris quotes the original Latin letter from Gregory preserved in the Vatican archives:

> Why should a pregnant woman not be baptized? It is ridiculous to see a contradiction between the gift of fertility and the gift of grace received at Baptism. She is not prohibited from entering the church after childbirth, during her periods of natural flux also. She is not to be prohibited from entering a church for the natural flux that she suffers cannot be imputed to her as a fault; therefore, it is right that she should not be deprived of the entrance into a church. If she goes to communion, she is not to be judged adversely. She has no sin. People see sin where there is none. We all eat when hungry and without sin in doing so, even though it is through the sin of the first woman that we are hungry. So women when menstrous have no sin; it is natural.[179]

Gregory's wise words were not taken "ex cathedra," that is, a statement by the pope on faith and morals, which is spoken with

---

[177] Ibid.
[178] Ibid.
[179] Morris, 110.

infallibility. In England and on the continent, women still were excluded during the menses.[180] Theodore of Tarsus (St. Paul's home town) was consecrated as English Bishop of Canterbury in 668 and during his episcopacy things reverted to the Eastern custom: women do not enter a church while menstruating nor communicate (receive Holy Communion). This injunction went both for nuns and laity; otherwise, a penance of three days of fasting was mandatory.[181] Fasting in those times meant no food or water—a rather strict punishment for being normal.

No one ever thought of excluding the men for having an erection or an ejaculation, activities that are usually more frequent than once a month. Both menstruation and ejaculation are necessary for eventual conception which in those days—and up until Vatican II—was the redeeming value of marriage.[182]

According to Morris, the synod of Mean (1493) said entrance into church by menstruating women could not be denied, "but it was better if they did not come." In 1572, there was a Canon Law against women going to communion after childbirth. As late as 1684, women were told to remain at the door and not to enter the church during her period.[183] The Jewish tradition was strong and pervasive in the Roman church. The Doctor of the Church, Augustine of Hippo, said defective children result from conception taking place during menses, Morris quoted.[184] Today, we know that is a serious misconception (no pun intended) since ovulation precedes the onset of the period by 14 days and it is only for 72 hours during ovulation that a woman can be fertilized by the sperm.

Another one of the great Doctors of the Church, St. Jerome, said, "Nothing is so unclean as a woman in her period, what she touches

---

[180]   Ibid.

[181]   Ibid., 111.

[182]   Vatican II said the primary purpose of marriage is the mutual satisfaction of the partners.

[183]   Morris, 109-111. (Gregory always wasn't so enlightened. See chapter on Mary Magdalene.)

[184]   Ibid., 109.

she causes to become unclean."[185] Sounds very old, right? Well that statement was made in 1517, the same year as Luther's "95 Theses," and not in pre-Christian Jewish days. It was the women and not a priest who should have revolted! (The Reformation didn't help women at all; Luther was very establishment in his ideas on women, although, at the same time, also very devoted to Mother Mary, Morris said.)

The Greco-Roman culture didn't help much either since that was a very patriarchal, discriminatory society. Phiny, one of the classical Greek Patriarchs, was just as bad as the Doctors of the Christian churches. He said the menstrual blood sours wine, withers crops, rusts iron and drives away hailstorms. (He should have been thankful for small favors!) Most of all, having sex during the menses meant death for the man, he believed.[186] Apparently, many risked it—none have lived to prove otherwise.

The thinking of those times is documented in the English Penitential Law book, *Liber Legum Ecclesiasticarum.* Women were restricted from approaching the altar during mass and had to remain in their places. The priest would go and receive any monetary obligation the women wished to offer to God. "The reason given," Morris explained, "is that women must remember their infirmity and weakness of their sex, and be careful not to render impure any of the things that pertain to the ministry of the church." She added, "The offering was accepted notwithstanding the risk of impurity."[187]

The Myth of the Menses or Blood Taboos are an example—the most base kind—of how society was not Christianized but how Christianity was socialized.

---

[185]   Ibid., 106.
[186]   Ibid., 112.
[187]   Morris. 112.

Jesus blessing the children and their mothers.

CHAPTER 12

Close Encounters of the Christ-Kind

Many other women in the gospels had "close-encounters of the Christ-kind" with Jesus. Among these were the Syrophoenician woman and the woman "taken in adultery."

The story of the Syrophoenician woman is another first for Jesus' ministry. It is His first outreach to the Gentiles, and He does it at her request (Matt. 15: 21-28, Mark 7: 24-30). The Syrophoenician woman was a Canaanite from the district of Tyre and Sidon, a pagan. Her story directly follows the two accounts by Jesus of what is clean and unclean in the sight of God (Matt. 15: 1-20, Mark 7: 1-231). It is a time of withdrawal from the hoards of people for special instruction of the disciples. (Mark 9: 29-49)

She comes and begs for a healing of her daughter who is possessed. Today we know from Scriptural research that biblical possession often referred to medical diseases such as epilepsy or mental illness.[188] Whatever the nature of the child's sickness, Matthew called it a "devil," and Mark, "an unclean spirit." At first, Jesus won't even talk to her and ignores her request. In Matthew's account, the disciples get exasperated at her persistence and ask Him to help her—just to shut her up. His reply to them is that He has come only to the lost sheep of Israel. In Mark's Gospel, there are no intermediaries mentioned; she requests the healing directly. Jesus' reply sounds so callous. He said to her it's not fair to take the children's food (the people of Israel) and give it to the dogs (the traditional term in that society used to describe non-Jews). She doesn't

---

[188] Wahlberg, 9.

take umbrage at that remark because her intent is for a healing for her child, and she refuses to leave until that is accomplished. For her to come to Jesus and make this request shows first of all, she recognized who He was—as Messiah—and accepted His authority over illness. She worships Jesus the Messiah, and answers that even the puppies under the table are fed the table scraps.

Jesus speaking to the woman of Canaan.

Jesus is won over and the child is healed of the evil spirit. It is the woman's faith and not her retort which influenced Jesus' action. He doesn't say what He did to give her a hard time, but to show the male-disciples about true faith. In fact, the whole story is a faith-test. Jesus is showing the disciples that faith is the answer. Belief in Him is what's necessary, even if you are a non-Jew.

While Jesus was sent to the lost sheep of Israel, in Romans 2: 9, Paul explained Jesus was sent to the Jews first, then the Gentiles. Hundreds of years before Jesus' birth, Isaiah 42: 1 predicted, "He shall bring forth judgement to the Gentiles." (KJV) In other places, the Scripture repeats that Christ will be the delight of the Gentiles. Subsequently, the Roman Centurion is also an example of Gentile-belief in Jesus. The gruff soldier who believed for his servant's healing is also an example to the Jewish disciples. Jesus told the Centurion, "Such faith I have not seen in Israel." (Luke 7: 1-10).

The term "dogs" is not used to imply an unclean cur of the street but is a term which applies to the non-Jews such as Gentiles and Sodomites. The actual phrase would mean a little dog, as in a pet kept in the house, maybe a lap dog. Wahlberg called that, "an interesting but not ameliorating point."[189]

Wahlberg termed the Syrophoenician woman, "Uppity," and claimed she was one of the reasons why the Bible says "Jesus grew in wisdom." The Syrophoenician woman helped Jesus realize His mission of Messiah-ship was also to the non-Jews, Wahlberg said.[190] The Syrophoenician woman addressed Jesus as "Kyrie," which means Lord. In Mark's Gospel, the Greek word "Kyrie," is used as a title, always stipulating "Son of God," [191] and is not just the respectful form of address, "Sir." The woman is a pagan who knows who He is—at the time the male-disciples need special tutoring and really don't recognize Jesus as Messiah—only as someone extraordinarily special.

When Jesus points out faith in action to the male-disciples, it is usually a woman who is the example. This is true of the woman of faith healed of the blood issue, the Syrophoenician woman, and the old widow who gives all her pennies in the Temple collection. Jesus expressly compliments each of them, the woman of the blood issue, the Syrophoenician woman for their belief. It is their faith which is causational in their respective healings. It is their faith in Jesus, the Christ, which sets them free.

In the story of the woman taken in adultery, Jesus sets another woman free. Remember the goals of Christ's mission read in the synagogue at the start of His ministry? One of those was freedom for captives, for those in bondage. Everyone always wonders what

---

[189]   Wahlberg, 13.

[190]   Ibid., 9-14.

[191]   McGrath, 27.

it was that Jesus wrote in the sand in the story of the woman taken in adultery (John 8: 1-11). Perhaps He wrote, "Doesn't it take two to tango?" or "Where is her partner? Why aren't you accusing him also?" Perhaps He just doodled or wrote out the next weeks' travel agenda. Many believe He wrote out some pertinent facts about the sexual sins of the accusers. However, Scripture scholars believe it was an indication of His boredom with their question! The King James Version says, "He wrote as though He heard them not," and a cross reference to Amos 5: 13 says, "Therefore the prudent shall keep silence in that time; for it is an evil time."

The story indicates a trap, a double trap. But Jesus gently turned the situation into his own "sting," in which the accusers become the accused by association. The Pharisees' scheme was to trap Jesus, not the woman; she is ancillary. It probably wasn't difficult to plan the operation and catch "her in the very act," since adultery was quite commonplace. After all, men's wives were unclean for at least a week or 10 days every month, so having sex with her was often unavailable. Trapping the woman was peripheral—she had no importance in their society—except to be used by men.

What a great victory it would be for Jesus' enemies to make the peaceful, love-promoting preacher look ridiculous! He would have to agree she had to be stoned to death on the spot—and take part in it as a good Jewish male—since the law commanded stoning as a punishment for those taken in adultery. The second part of the trap is to get even with Jesus. The Pharisees and other Jewish leaders obviously noticed his "unusual" treatment of women—even that women were some of His closest friends, an anomaly indeed for a Jewish rabbi. This made them dislike Him even more. What better way to show Him up than to negate once and for all His acceptance of women as human beings, which was absolutely contrary to the standards of the time. Why, He even had the audacity to suggest that adultery could be committed AGAINST the woman if she was divorced. (Mark 10: 10-12, Luke 16: 18)

The problem with the scheme was these blokes were dealing with Jesus, who knew the Father's words in Scripture far better than they. The opening verse of the chapter said He spent the night on the Mount of Olives and returned at daybreak to teach in the Temple precincts. Getting alone with the Father for prayer and Holy Spirit-infusion was Jesus' pattern. It was how He kept going through His ministry and how He knew what the Father wanted in each situation. Jesus knew what the Law said and prescribed. He knew Ezekiel 33: 11 said, "I do not wish the sinner to die but to turn to me and live." Jesus knew stoning was not the punishment solely for the woman caught in adultery but for both. The Pharisees only brought the woman.

Leviticus 20:10 says, "And the man that commits adultery with another man's wife, even he that commits adultery with his neighbor's wife, the adulterer and the adulteress shall surely be put to death."

Jesus' answer does not disregard the law. He merely tempers it with equality and justice. He says, "Don't treat women any differently than you treat men." He adds, "Who among you is capable of judging another? Judgment for guilt or innocence is God's prerogative." He neither condones the particular sin nor the sins of sexuality as being worse than any other kinds of sin. In fact, Jesus is acting as her lawyer, her advocate. I believe He actually initiates the legal practice traditionally attributed to Justinian's Law, which is the basis of our democracy's legal ethics—that a person is innocent until proven guilty.

Since women were readily associated with Eve, sin, temptation, the Fall, and believed to be tempters, men allowed themselves to be guiltless.[192] In that culture, women were assumed to be guilty of moral depravity. Women could not testify in their own behalf. So, once accused, women could not be proved innocent. To Jesus, the solution is simple. "If there is one of you who has not sinned, let him be the first to throw a stone at her." Before and after the statement, Jesus doodles in the sand. In the intervening silence, the men slouch away, from the eldest to the youngest.

Sermons or homilies on this biblical story always refer to it as the "Woman taken in Adultery." That's with a capital "A," as in the *Scarlet Letter*. Wahlberg called it, "The Woman with the Adulterous Men,"

---

[192] Wahlberg, 18.

which puts the story in a whole other perspective.[193] In older days, the sermon's topic was, invariably, on how women were inherently evil and inclined to be the temptress and cause of sexual sin but the male preachers never asked where was her male companion.

"Jesus knew that guilt could not be assigned according to one's sex," Wahlberg said, "and that private guilt could destroy a person."[194] In Jesus' day there existed a presumption of guilt and condemnation associated with women and sexual sin. A penchant so strong . . . it was an automatic bias against any woman who committed a sexual indiscretion. And in those days, just as today, men were regarded less critically for sexual sins. Wahlberg stated, "The question must be asked: where was the man caught in adultery with the woman? Did he run away? Did he hide? Did the men who caught the woman protect him? When I raised the question of the man's whereabouts to a large group of women, one woman suggested calmly, 'He probably ran outside and picked up a stone.'"[195]

When Jesus looks up from His doodling, He and the woman are alone. He asked, "Has no one condemned you?" She replied, "No one, Lord." I believe Jesus' response is a forerunner of the Sacrament of Reconciliation (with God), traditionally called the Sacrament of Penance (for an offense against God), and popularly known as Confession. His answer includes forgiveness, absolution, exhortation not to repeat the sin, and freedom from guilt. (The establishment of the Sacrament of Reconciliation is usually considered to be Jesus' comment to the disciples, "Whatever you bind on earth shall be bound in heaven.") (Matt 16: 19, 18:18)

Unlike the accusers, Jesus, of course, has the power to judge and to forgive. He says, "Neither do I condemn you" (Forgiveness). It meant, "I'm not going to stone you, don't be afraid. You can leave now." (Absolution) He added, "Go home and don't sin anymore." (Exhortation) In other words, "Ms., (her marital status is not important. Adultery implies at least one of the two parties involved is married.)

---

[193] Ibid., 15-22.
[194] Ibid., 17.
[195] Ibid., 16.

change your ways now. You have been forgiven. When you are sorry for what you've done and do change, that's repentance, being changed into a new being." Jesus freed her from her sin. Similarly, He liberated women from bondage, and from captivity to the very idea that women are sexually sinful by their very nature.

In the following verse, John's gospel related that the very next time Jesus spoke He showed this freedom from bondage. "When Jesus spoke to the people again (the next time), He said, 'I am the light of the world; anyone who follows me will not be walking in the dark.'" (John 8:12) Jesus didn't say, "The males who follow me," nor "The females who follow." He said, "Anyone." Everyone. That's freedom.

CHAPTER 13

The Eleven Female Disciples and the 'Parallel Parables'

Everyone. Jesus' ministry was for everyone. He clearly showed God neither favors nor discriminates between men and women. All are called equally to share in the kingdom. Jesus' entire ministry showed the parallels between the two sexes, not the differences—which were absolutely shocking to His society.

Jesus accepted the essential likeness or similarities between men and women when the culture could not. His followers were both male and female. He healed and forgave the illnesses and sins of both sexes. Women traveled in ministry with Jesus, as did men, and parallel the Twelve, the closest male-disciples. These are scriptural facts.

Whenever Jesus spoke in parables to instruct the people, He used analogies involving situations familiar to men and to women. For instance, He spoke of the vineyard, the man's domain, and a wedding, the woman's. In addition, He taught with parallel examples, one following the other to emphasize the point. These are scriptural facts.

When He spoke of God's concern for human beings, the parables included obvious god-figures. In one story that was a man, and in another, it was a woman. The father in the Prodigal son story and the woman in search of the lost coin are two examples. Yes, Jesus used a female to represent a god-figure symbol! It, like the others, is a Scriptural fact which we overlook because of our conditioning. Our conditioning says we can't describe God in female terms—that's akin to blasphemy, but it didn't bother Jesus to do so.

It didn't bother Jesus to use a female figure to represent God. It didn't bother Jesus that qualities we call "feminine" are attributes found in God. So why does it bother us? It is especially significant that Jesus used women as a god-figure image for two reasons. The first is because of the cultural conditioning, both in His time and ours. The second is because, according to Genesis, "male and female were created in the image of God." Created in Divine Image, that is, God-like.

If both sexes are in God's image, then God contains both elements, maleness and femaleness. The writer of Genesis obviously is not speaking about a physical image because Jesus, Incarnate God in a human, male body, was born hundreds of years after Genesis finally was written down.

God is pure spirit. Human beings are created in that image. The mystery of the Incarnation, of Christmas, is that the change-less God, changes; God assumes human nature. In Jesus, God will feel pain, heat, cold, being tired after a long journey, perspiration from work, temptation, joy, happiness, hunger and so on. The Incarnation of the God-man is one of the central doctrines of Christianity; the other is the Resurrection. Our belief in Christ is faith in the fact that God has chosen the human to reveal the divine. This is through the human Jesus and even through the human word, with all its imperfections.

The maleness of Christ, which is often used as an argument against women's participation in official religious functions, was necessary for His time and His mission. That's all. It was not derogatory toward women by choosing the "superior sex." If the roles were reversed and women ran the society of that time, Jesus could have been incarnated as a woman. The function of the Messiah is salvation, not maleness.

"It seems clear that when God made humankind in his own image, he/she was exemplifying something very fundamental about his/her own nature," said Ruth Barnhouse. "The complexity of the mystery of the Trinity is that there are three distinct persons in one God. On God's level of being, of course, it is a unity; but in bringing it into manifestation on our physical plane, God thought it desirable to differentiate it into the form we know as male and female."[196]

The Eleven Women

Eleven women in the gospels form a group comparable to the Twelve, the closest male disciples, or more exactly, to the faithful Eleven. They are among the many women who traveled with Jesus regularly and ministered to His needs. (Only angels and women are recorded in the Gospels as doing so.) These women performed in "the ministry of service."[197]

Service has long been a ministry of women to the church. As Pope John Paul II said to women in his letter in 1995 on the UN sponsored "Year of the Woman," "In this vast domain of service, the church has truly experienced the genius of women; from the heart of the Church there have emerged women of the highest caliber who have left an impressive and beneficial mark in history."[198]

In Jesus' ministry, the women provided food, shelter, and other ameliorations, assisting Jesus and the other men, "out of their own resources." (Luke 8:3). Many of them were closely associated with other aspects of Jesus' ministry as well. Some possibly had been healed or delivered of demons. These Eleven, perhaps a forerunner of the faithful male-eleven, are specifically mentioned in the four gospels. They are:

1. Mary, the mother of Jesus
2. Mary Magdalene
3. Johanna, the wife of Herod's steward, Chuza
4. Suzanna
5. Mary, the mother of James (the Less) and Joseph

---

[196] Ruth Tiffany Barnhouse, M.D., "An Examination of the Ordination of Women to the Priesthood in Terms of the Symbolism of the Eucharist." *Women and Orders*, 22.

[197] Elizabeth Carroll, R.S.M., "Women and Ministry," *Women:* New Dimensions, 89.

[198] Letter of Pope John Paul II to Women, June 29, 1995.

6. Salome
7. The mother of Zebedees' children (John and James)
8. Mary, the wife of Cleophas
9. Mary of Bethany
10. Martha of Bethany
11. The mother-in-law of Peter, who after her healing got up and ministered to Jesus. (Salome may be mother of Zebedee's children, James and John, and if so, then there are 10 faithful women. Different texts reference her individually, and at other times, as their mother.)

Each of the gospel accounts of Jesus' Crucifixion mentions these and several unnamed women (John 19:25; Luke 23: 49, 55; Matt. 27: 55-56, 61; Mark 15: 40-41, 47). The fact that they traveled with Jesus is well-documented. Luke 8: 1-3 says, "With Him went the Twelve as well as certain women." Women accompanied Jesus on the last decisive journey from Galilee to Jerusalem. (Mark 15: 40-41) The criteria for "witness," according to Acts 1: 21, "was someone who had been traveling around with us the whole time." Women had; they shared the "ministry of witness."

It was the hand-picked men who betrayed, denied and abandoned Jesus. It was the hand-picked men who hid, desperately afraid after His death. It was the hand-picked men who had to see the Risen Christ or put their hands into His wounds to believe. It was the women who stood, along with the Beloved Disciple (John, a teenager) at the foot of the Cross. It was the women who watched where Jesus was entombed. It was the women who went to the gravesite on Sunday morning to minister to their beloved Master's torn and shredded body. It was women, Mary Magdalene and others, who were the first witnesses of the Resurrection. It was Mary Magdalene who preached the "Good News" of the Resurrection to the male-disciples. None of that was accidental.

Women were "the constant" in the otherwise consistent emphasis in the gospels on failure in discipleship, according to Elizabeth

Carroll in her article, "Women in Ministry."[199] It was the women who Jesus praised for their exemplary faith when the men, particularly the Twelve, were continually upbraided for their lack of faith, their disbelief, and lack of understanding.

The Parallel Parables:

With the parables, which were stories Jesus told so the multitudes who followed Him could understand, the examples are exactly balanced. First, Jesus compares the kingdom of God to a mustard seed which a man sowed in his garden "till it flowered as the greatest tree in the garden." Then He compares the kingdom to being like the leaven a woman used in baking bread, "till the whole was leavened" (Matt. 13: 31-33, Mark 4: 30-32, Luke 13: 18-22).

Jesus compared faith to a seed which would die if the seed was thrown on rocky ground. (Mark 4: 1-20) Sowing and tilling of the soil were part of the man's domain. Jesus compared faith to a light which was easily extinguished if hidden under a bushel basket (Mark 4: 21-25). Candles were used in the home, the woman's area.

Jesus described preparation for the coming of the kingdom in two ways. He mentioned the Ten Bridesmaids, five of whom were ready and five who were foolish and unprepared (Matt 25: 1-13). He spoke of 10 talents and explained how the servant who buried the money was left penniless and unprepared. The other servant invested the money and profited from the interest. (Luke 19: 11-28)

Two other parallel parables show the conditions for entering the kingdom. Again, there is the vineyard analogy for the men and the wedding analogy for the women. The laborers in the vineyard grumble because some latecomers earn exactly the same pay as those who had toiled through the heat of the day. (Matt. 20: 1-16) The latecomers receive the same wage due to the benevolence of the master, who had set the wage with the initial workers. In the parable of the wedding garment (Matt. 22: 1-14), when the invited

---

[199]   Carroll, *Women: New Dimensions*, 88.

guests refuse to come to the wedding celebration, outsiders from the highways and byways are brought in (as are the latecomers to work in the vineyard). One of these latecomers refused to don the reception robe which was provided by the host. The stubborn one is cast out of the party "for many are called but few are chosen."

In the parable of the unjust judge (Luke 18: 2-8), Jesus uses a woman as a model for perseverance in prayer.[200] In the story of the old woman putting her last two pennies into the Temple coffer, Jesus uses a woman as a model for the spirit of giving. Her reward will be great, Jesus said, because she gave out of love and from her need and not from excess income. He compares her to the (male) Pharisees who tithed flamboyantly so everyone would notice but did so only from their abundant wealth.

Other examples of the balance and equity in Jesus' preaching are:

- "The Kingdom of Heaven is like a mustard seed which a man took and hid in his field." (Matt. 13:31). "The kingdom of Heaven is like the yeast a woman took and mixed in with the three measures of flour." (Matt. 13: 33)
- Of two men in the fields, one is taken; one left. (Matt 24:40) Of two women at the millstone grinding, one is taken, one left. (Matt 24:41)
- "There were many widows in Israel, I can assure you, in Elijah's day . . . but Elijah was not sent to any one of these: he was sent to the widow of Zarephath, a Didonian town." (Luke 4: 25-26). "And in the prophet Elisha's time there were many lepers in Israel, but none of these were cured, except the Syrian, Naaman." (Luke 4: 27).
- "On Judgment Day the men of Nineveh shall stand up with this generation and shall condemn it." (Luke 12:41). "On Judgment Day the Queen of the South will rise up with this generation and condemn it." (Luke 12:42).
- Also the relentless man, who knocks on his friends' door seeking nourishment (Luke 11: 5-8), parallels the persistent

---

[200] Ibid.

widow who demands justice from the unjust judge (Luke 16: 1-5). Neither gives up until he and she received what they came for. Similarly, the Syrophoenician woman will not give up until her daughter is healed by Jesus.

- Finally, Jesus says, "Anyone who does the will of my Father in Heaven, he is my brother and sister and mother." (Matt 12: 50, Mark 3: 35, Luke 8:21).

The God-Figures:

The God-figure searches for the lost in the three consecutive parables of the lost sheep (Luke 15: 4-7), the lost money (Luke 15: 8-10), and the prodigal son. (Luke 15: 11-32) While we readily acknowledge that the shepherd signifies Jesus the Good Shepherd (John 10), and the father of the prodigal is analogous to God the Father, we never even think of the woman as a God-figure! "Our first inclination in the coin story is to see just a woman doing something women do, sweeping," Wahlberg said.[201]

To see woman-as-God is to see the story in terms which shake up our familiar categories. To see a woman-as-God is to break out of our slots for women—our conditioned categories. Jesus did not have our hang-ups about picturing God as either sex. But because of our trained perceptions—the traditional association of God is with the male sex—we have been unable to see in this story the woman as a deity. We don't have room in our heads for that kind of woman.

Second, the God-woman is obscured because she is doing a housekeeping chore. Everyone knows that housekeeping chores "are not important," either in a Jesus story or in the current world. Such tasks which are done in the seclusion of the home are not credited as being important to society. What the God-woman is doing is regarded as non-essential labor, "women's work," both in the first century and the 21st century. The irony is obvious. Our society tells us, if one cooks for one's family, it is not work. If one cooks for others, a

---

[201] Wahlberg, 24.

paid job, it is work. If one does cleaning or child care for others it is considered work. If one does it for one's family, it is "not working." Traditionally, whatever woman does is regarded as not worth pay or status. It's thought of as nice but unimportant.[202]

We don't see her as "seeking the lost," only searching for something of economic value which she, or someone else, carelessly misplaced. From that point of view, we look at her story as significant only because of what is missing and not because of her prototype, or her search. However, we never think of the shepherd as careless for allowing one of the sheep to wander away, although a sheep had great economic value in their pastoral society. Neither do we think the prodigal's father is tyrannical and a poor parent. We don't value-judge and think he must have done a shoddy job in raising the son who, as the name prodigal indicates, was wasteful and extravagant. We also don't usually see the son as wanting his father to be dead—that's what asking for his inheritance "now" meant. It was quite an insult from his bratty boy. We don't see the father as weak and insipid by giving into the son's demand. We see the father as so loving that he can't refuse the son anything.

The God-woman is obscured, according to Wahlberg, solely because she is a woman.[203] "When we read or hear the story, our perception of it is immediately limited to the sex role implications we have all internalized," she said.[204]

It is not merely the woman as the God-figure which makes this parable so significant. The woman represents God searching for the lost but also, according to Tavard in *Women in Christian Tradition,* her coins represent *all* the wisdom of God.[205]

> The drachmas represent all that God has created: principalities, powers, virtues, thrones, denominations, angels, archangels, cherubim and seraphim and the first born, whom Life and Resurrection lost, sought and found fallen.[206]

---

202   Ibid., 24-25.
203   Wahlberg, 24.
204   Ibid.
205   Tavard, WCT, 153.
206   Ibid.

The God-qualities in each of the three stories are human qualities, not sex-linked characteristics. Each of the three demonstrates concern and anxiety. The father is compassionate and waits; he never searches for his son. He forgives and anxiously hopes for the young man's return. He patiently waits and watches and runs to his errant son when the deviant fellow returns. The woman and the shepherd are aggressive. They take action and search for the lost. Both the woman and the shepherd find the missing object. The father puts shoes on his returning prodigal, the sign of son-ship, and throws a banquet in his honor. All three God-figures rejoice at the ultimate outcomes.[207]

The father is the most passive of the three, although passivity is usually culturally assigned to females. Culture says women are less aggressive than men, but here the woman is as diligent as the shepherd in searching. We don't even know that it was she who lost the coin, though it was the shepherd's responsibility to guard all the sheep.

Men and women—as well as God—can show love and concern, or can aggressively perform an action to achieve a goal. God can passively wait for us, or He can initiate action to search for us and lead us. Luke in these three stories is showing us that God shares in many characteristics that we exhibit ourselves. As a spin-off, we are thus encouraged to be God-like.[208]

For Jesus, "God is a spiritual parent."[209] That's why He could use images of either sex to describe God.

Leonard Swidler suggested that Jesus deliberately used the analogy of God-as-woman to make a point with the scribes and Pharisees since they denigrated women and the tax-collectors.[210] Jesus was dining with the latter at the time of these parables.

L. Swidler pointed out the Trinitarian implications of these three parables. Obviously, Jesus is the shepherd and the Father is the father of the Prodigal, so the Holy Spirit logically must be the feminine image.[211] Besides, the Holy Spirit does seek the lost.

---

[207] Wahlberg, 28.
[208] Ibid., 27-29.
[209] Ibid.
[210] L. Swidler, 183.
[211] L. Swidler, 183.

Is the Holy Spirit really the feminine manifestation of God? It's not shocking at all, although it may appear so initially. Throughout Scripture, the Hebrew word used to refer to God's spirit is *ruach*, a feminine gender word.

The Holy Spirit represents God's wisdom and, in the Bible, God's wisdom is always referred to in feminine terms. The whole Book of Wisdom is a celebration of the spirit or Wisdom of God. It is about "she," even in English-language translations. Many of the identifying attributes of Wisdom are the same used by Jesus to describe the Holy Spirit, or the Advocate, the Comforter, the Paraclete (John 15, 16).

The word, Sophia, is a specific feminine word used to describe God's wisdom. In fact, a whole theology of Sophiology developed throughout the Christian churches, particularly in the Eastern and Orthodox Rites such as Russian Orthodoxy. Tavard defines Sophiology as "a systemic attempt to discover the feminine element in God and to understand it in terms that are compatible with traditional Trinitarian faith."[212]

L. Swidler quoted the *Syrian Didascalia* as an example of the instances in Christian history when the Holy Spirit has been associated with a feminine character. The example speaks of the various offices in the church and it states, "The Deaconess, however, should be honored by you as the image of the Holy Spirit."[213]

There are two reasons why the logical association of the female with the Holy Spirit was never widespread, according to L. Swidler. These are the general cultural subjugation of women and the abhorrence of pagan goddesses. But, "Christian abhorrence of pagan gods did not result in a Christian rejection of a male image of God," L. Swidler noted.[214]

As for the Resurrection itself, we know Mary Magdalene was there but we often forget that other women were at the tomb initially, also. John's gospel just refers to Mary Magdalene but each of the three synoptic refers to her *and* others. Matthew 27: 55 says women

---

[212] Tavard, WCT, 159.
[213] As quoted in L. Swidler, 183.
[214] Ibid.

were at Calvary, too: Mary Magdalene; Mary the mother of James and Joseph; and the mother of the sons of Zebedee, and in verse 61, that "Mary Magdalene and the other Mary" were sitting opposite the tomb to see where they laid Jesus, according to the *Ignatius Catholic Study Bible*. Likewise in Chapter 28, Matthew mentions that the two Mary's on Sunday morning witnessed the earthquake at the tomb, and were addressed by an angel—who told them to tell the disciples that Jesus is risen and they would see Him in Galilee. In Chapter 29, verses 9 and 10, Jesus speaks to them and they worship Him. He reiterates the same message the angel just gave, "go and tell," then "go to Galilee." (Matt. 27: 1, 5, 9).

Mark mentions in Chapter 16, verse 1, that Mary Magdalene; Mary, the mother of James; and Salome brought spices to the Tomb on Easter morning. The angel spoke to them (verses 4-8) but they were afraid and didn't tell anyone. However, in verse 9, Mark says Jesus appeared first to Mary Magdalene who went and told the disciples, who were mourning and weeping. But in verse 11, Mark said, "But when they heard that He was alive and had been seen by her, they would not believe it." In verse 12, he said Jesus appeared to two others enroute to the country (on the road to Emmaus, see Luke 24: 13-35). Whether it was because the story was so mind-boggling, as it is, or because of the culturally-imposed fact that women were not considered valid witnesses, the male disciples chose not to believe—even though they themselves had witnessed Jesus raising three people: Jarius' daughter, the son of the widow of Nain, and Lazarus. So, why couldn't it be possible for Jesus himself?

Mark also shows us another parallel with examples of both men and women. The male disciples didn't believe the women, nor did they believe the (allegedly) male disciples from the Emmaus story—and men's testimony was considered valid in their world (verses 12 and 13). In verse 14, Jesus upbraids the Eleven "for their unbelief and hardness of hearts, for not believing those who had seen Him." Luke includes men and women in the words "those who saw him."

Luke said in Chapter 23, verse 55, that the women from Galilee, who had come with Him, saw where He was buried and in verse 55, they went home and prepared spices and ointments. In Chapter 24 the women returned to the tomb, saw two young men who repeated Jesus' previous words about His own Resurrection. "And they (the women) remembered his words," Luke said, "Returning from the tomb they told all this to the Eleven and to all the rest. Now it was **Mary Magdalene** and **Johanna** and **Mary the mother of James and the other women with them** who told this to the apostles," in verses 9 and 10. Again, in verse 11, this inner, elite circle of men thought it "an idle tale," and they did not believe them." Luke said in verse 12, Peter then ran to the tomb, looked inside, saw the linen cloths, and left bewildered.

Despite the slight variations in each of the four Gospel accounts, all we really know is this truth: that the Resurrection happened, the women saw and believed, and the men were skeptical.

CHAPTER 14

In Divine Image:
It Reflects the Feminine in God

If male and female were created in the Divine Image and God is generally recognized as "Father," mustn't God also be "Mother?" Isn't mother the parent who births and nurtures the children? Doesn't God do that to us, the divine offspring?

Pope John Paul I, during his brief but significant 33-day papacy in 1978, recognized exactly this! Often called "the Smiling Pope," he shocked a conservative Italian audience one Sunday by referring to it. ***"God is a father, but even more, He is a mother," the pope said.***[215]

Jesus referred to this same motherly dimension of God's concern when He said, "Jerusalem, Jerusalem, you kill the prophets and stone those who are sent to you! How often have I longed to gather your children, as a hen gathers her chicks under her wings, and you refused!" (Matt. 23: 37, Luke 13: 34)

Using feminine analogies to describe God's love was not a problem for Jesus. God is our spiritual parent. But the inference of the feminine in God makes some of us recoil. Why? We are limited trying to give personal pronoun status to an omniscient and omnipotent God. God is without limit, without labels, without pronouns.

How do we relate to Jesus the Christ? We relate through His gentleness, empathy, compassion, understanding, forgiveness,

---

[215] As quoted in John Muthig, "Pope Asks Prayers for Mideast," N.C. News (U.S. Catholic Conference News Service, Washington, D.C.,), *The Monitor*, Vol. XXV, No 32, (Trenton, NJ), September 14, 1978, 5.

patience, serenity and softness (not hardness) and, of course, His love for us. Those words are generally considered to be "feminine" attributes. Is Christ those things? Yes. And if these feminine attributes are in Christ, they are in God. If God wasn't those things, we wouldn't come and cling; they are manifestations of divine love and relationship.

Yahweh of the Old Testament is often wrongly portrayed as harsh, angry, and vengeful. The anger is only directed at the people's unfaithfulness, disobedience and stubbornness in doing their own thing. Before the anger there was always a warning, always chances for the people to change their ways. Only when they didn't, zap. Yahweh had repeatedly told them He was a jealous god—jealous for their exclusive love and worship.

Stereotypes of gender limit people, as well as linguistically limit our perception of God. Many men contain those same characteristics found in Jesus, though of course, not tempered by Divinity. Further, women want men to be strong enough to be gentle, to be able to cry without embarrassment as a psychological release, to be understanding with children, and to be sentimental enough to remember birthdays but intuitive enough to neglect to remember ages!

Similarly, women are leaders. They have analytical minds and work with detailed precision. Did you ever notice how many intricate steps there are in today's quilt-making? It isn't yesteryear's just patching together old pieces of fabric.[216] Also, women are resourceful, strong, aggressive, wise, protective, determined, logical, objective, task-oriented—all so-called "masculine" characteristics.

And that's all they are—merely words, descriptive adjectives. People—men and women—resemble God in more fundamental

---

[216] My sister, Sheila Kramer, began quilting about eight years ago, which is a short time for quilters. She enters contests, called "Challenges," and wins frequently; takes classes in special techniques like beading; and makes marvelous quilts. It took nine months for her to make a unique quilt of Celtic scrolls, lettering, crosses, and shamrock-designed stitches for me for my birthday. It takes precision, calculation, determination, creativity, fine craftsmanship and time to a make a quilt. These are the same attributes used by Michelangelo, Monet, American Impressionist Mary Cassatt, and all great artists and musicians.

ways. First of all, we are spirit, as God is. Human beings are "finite copies of infinite God."[217] Our God-likeness is what separates us from other species:

- Self-consciousness. That is, we human beings know we are alive. Animals don't.
- Creators. We can think and imagine, take what is, and create something that never was.
- Communicators. We communicate and we speak because God eternally communicates between Father, Son and Spirit, and because God spoke to humankind. When God speaks to us, we can expect to understand. God's words, Paul said, are written in our hearts. Communication is originally found in God.
- Lovers. We love and enjoy fellowship because God does, within the God-head and without—to us.
- Self-determining. We have will and volition. Our lives are shaped by choice, not programmed by instinct as are animals.

Through choice and creativity, we have developed human wisdom. As wonderful as it is, it is nothing in comparison with God's wisdom. It is ancient conviction that wisdom and woman were related, inseparable, Bruns said.[218] Divine wisdom was not another God, separate from Yahweh but Yahweh considered from a different perspective.[219] Divine Wisdom is an integral part of God.

The perspective of the feminine in God starts in Genesis. "The spirit of Elohim hovered over the water." (Genesis 1: 2). God refers to divine nature in the plural, since Elohim in Hebrew is *a feminine noun with a masculine plural ending.*[220] Eloh is the feminine singular

---

[217] Rev. Malcolm Smith's teaching tape, "Your Thought Life I: Jesus, Lord of the Mind," IMS 217, Logos Tapes, Hazlet, NJ. I am indebted to this tape for some of the material on how humans reflect the God-in-us.

[218] Bruns, 38.

[219] Ibid., 39.

[220] Barnhouse, 22.

word for goddess with the masculine plural ending, "im."[221] Ruach, for spirit or breath, is a feminine word.[222]

> It may not be purely coincidental that the first inkling of the covenant shows the Spirit of God 'brooding' over the waste (Gen. 1: 2) Brooding evokes the very feminine image of the mother bird waiting patiently for her eggs to hatch, or also hovering over the nest while she encourages her young ones to get up and fly. It is precisely in the process of creation that God can be seen in a 'feminine' attitude, an attitude which pervades both the Old and New Testaments when writers and prophets perceive the fullness of the divine love for His people. God loves mankind with a motherly love. As 'the power of the Most High,' this primordial love, in the epiphany of Luke 1: 35, 'overshadows' the virgin. Thus God as Father, Word and Spirit manifests himself to humankind in a love which human experience associates with a mother's love.[223]

When Jesus is baptized by John, and the spirit in the form of the dove rests on Him (Mark 3: 13-17), it is a completed cycle of what begins in Genesis, I believe. In Genesis, the spirit 'hovered over the waters.' It is the beginning. In Jesus' Baptism account, it is a new beginning. It is the beginning of a new order. The feminine spirit, *Ruach,* dove-like, rests over the waters of Baptism. Using a dove as a Symbol of the Holy Spirit starts in Genesis and not just at Jesus' baptism. The Holy Spirit brooked over the waters of chaos and brought order.

By Noah's day, the world is again in turmoil. According to Marilyn Hickey in her publication, "Time with Him," she explained what she called "the three dispensations" of the Holy Spirit:

---

[221] Dobell, 41.
[222] Barnhouse, 23.
[223] Fr. George Tavard, "Sexist Language in Theology," *Women: New Dimensions,* 145.

After a terrible deluge of rain, Noah finally sends forth a Dove to seek dry land, but it returns after finding no place to rest. This represents the Holy Spirit going forth in the Old Testament and prophesying through His prophets. He finds no place to rest, and returns back to the bosom of the Father. The second dispensation of the Holy Spirit is seen when the dove is sent forth again, and returns with an olive branch—a symbol of Peace. This same Holy Spirit came upon the Prince of Peace, Jesus at his Baptism, but He also returned to his Father, just as the Dove returned to the Ark. The third dispensation of the Holy Spirit is shown when the dove is sent forth and does not return. When Jesus returned to the Father, He sent his Holy Spirit to the earth, and from that very instant we have His abiding presence upon the earth in our own hearts and lives.[224]

In both the King James and Confraternity editions of the Bible, the dove in Genesis is definitely called "she," reiterating the correlation between the Holy Spirit and the feminine characteristics of God. "So she returned to him in the ark; for the water covered the whole earth. He put forth his hand and caught her and drew her to him in the ark . . . The dove came back to him in the evening, and there in her mouth was a green olive leaf." (Gen. 8:9, 11)

There are other examples of the feminine in God throughout scripture. In the Old Testament, in Exodus, Yahweh says, "I will stretch out my hand and smite Egypt" (Exod. 3: 20). *Yad,* the Hebrew word for hand, is feminine.

Leviticus calls for the offering of the whole people to be an unblemished male, which is often analogized to Jesus' sacrifice. Leviticus also calls for the Peace offering to be either an unblemished male or female and the sin offering for the private person to be an unblemished female. (Lv. 3: 1-6, 4: 32, 5: 6). Jesus is called the Prince of Peace; He is also our peace offering. Although the peace offering

---

[224] Marilyn Hickey, *Time with Him*, Bible Study, Jan. 3, 1980, Vol. 3, No 1, (Denver, CO), 4.

can be male or female, I believe this reiterates there are both male and female elements in God. Women throughout history were active in peace movements for example, in the Vietnam War years in the U.S., many Catholic religious sisters, mothers, and other women were involved in pro-peace, anti-death penalty and pro-life activities, being against killing in all arenas.

In the Book of **Esther**, a beautiful woman is used to save the Jewish people from the anti-Jewish ravages of Haman, the evil instigator. The king is so enthralled with Esther that he promises her whatever she wants, "even half his kingdom" (Esth. 5: 2-8) Those are the same words used by Herod when he promises Salome anything for her dance in the New Testament. That resulted in the beheading of John the Baptist. Apparently, Herod didn't want to do it but he also didn't want to be embarrassed by refusing her request.

In the book of **Ruth**, she, a foreigner, a Moabite woman, marries Boaz of Bethlehem, and is an ancestress of David and Jesus. Her piety, self-sacrifice and moral integrity are admired. As an ancestress of Jesus, the universality of the messianic salvation is foreshadowed, says the introduction to the book of Ruth in the *New American Bible* (Catholic).

Numerous women are mentioned as forbearers of Jesus in 1 Chron., Chapters 1—4. The men in power come to the prophetess **Huldah** in 2 Chron., to seek God's direction. **Hannah** in the book of Samuel vowed to dedicate her child to the Lord if she could become pregnant. Her Canticle of Thanksgiving for Samuel's birth (Sam. 2: 1-10) strongly resembles **Mary**'s Magnificat in Luke. In Job 1, before his travails, Job feasted with his children—daughters and sons. After Job's 'renewal,' Job's daughters and sons are restored to their inheritances; usually daughters did not inherit if there were living male sons (Job 1, 42: 10-25, and Nm. 27, 1-11) Job's daughters did inherit—and they were wealthy. This shows that all are restored in God's kingdom.

The most notable references to the femaleness in God are in Isaiah, Chapter 66, which speaks of true and false worship and Mother Zion. Again there is use of the outstretched hand of God imagery, "My hand made all these things." (Is. 66:2). The footnote in the *New*

American Bible on verses Is. 66: 7-9 says that Mother Zion gave birth without pain, showing "the absence of labor in Zion's childbearing is a symbol of the joyful begetting of the new people of God."

Verses 10-13 talk of the new babe (Zion or Israel, the people of God) sucking at her (Mother God's) abundant breasts and says, "as nurslings, you shall be carried in her arms, and fondled in her lap; as a mother comforts her son (child), so I will comfort you." (Is. 66: 12-13).

Perhaps even more important than all the feminine references as being in God, is that God's relationship to the chosen people is nearly always described in feminine terms. This is particularly true of the many examples of marriage as an analogy between God and believers. Tavard said:

> There is an analogy, basic to the Catholic theology of the sacrament of marriage, between the gift of love in the transcendent Trinity and the gift of love between man and woman. From Origen through St. Bernard through St. John of the Cross, this analogy is constantly used to describe the development and highest degrees of the spiritual life. The mystery of the bridegroom and the bride reflects the mystery of God's inner love. We should endorse Ann Relford Ulanov's summing up of the Catholic conception of love: 'The mystery of the unconditioned Divine, the Father, seeing unconditional worth in the human, the son, and bestowing that worth in an act of self-giving love, the Spirit, is fully reflected in the mystery of unconditional love between lovers.'[225]

Another example is the use of the feminine word, *yad*, or hand, used in the context, "God stretches out his hand to his people."[226] Use of the word Elohim by the early Hebrew writers could have been used with double entendre; reflecting belief in the multiplicity and transcendence of God, and also the inherent inclusion of maleness and femaleness in the divine Nature.

---

[225] Tavard, "Sexist Language," 145.
[226] Barnhouse, 23.

Perception of Yahweh as one being with several dimensions was a major step toward monotheistic worship. Dr. Barnhouse explained it this way:

> One of the great landmarks in the development of human consciousness was precisely that in which the ancient Hebrew people were enabled to perceive God in monotheistic terms, rather than as a motley collection of gods and goddesses. But in doing so they were not abolishing the feminine aspects of deity in favor of the masculine aspects; but rather they were learning to think of God in a way which could be inclusive of both. In these terms, then, we may say that God is androgynous. It naturally follows that Christ is androgynous as well . . . . It seems obvious that given the social and cultural conditions and the general level of human development at the time, there was no choice: for the divine message to be received by imperfect humanity, Jesus in the first century had to be and therefore was male, even though the living Christ is androgynous . . . The term androgynous denotes a quality of consciousness, and does not in any way refer to the biological sex differentiation of male and female.[227]

In the book of Wisdom, which we've already shown is equated with the Holy Spirit, Divine Wisdom is equated with creation and the Word of God. This reinforces the Trinitarian interaction between the Spirit and Wisdom, between Christ the Word and the Father. For example:

o   Yes, *she (wisdom) is an initiate in the mysteries of God's knowledge,* making choice of the works He is to do (Wisdom 8:4).
o   God of our ancestors, Lord of Mercy, who by your Word have made all things, and in your wisdom have filled man to rule the creatures that have come from you, to govern the world in holiness and justice and in honesty of soul to wield authority,

---

[227]   Ibid., 23-4.

grant me Wisdom, consort of your throne, and do not reject me from the number of your children (Wisdom 9: 1-4).

o   With you is *Wisdom, she who knows your works, she who was present when you made the world* (Wisdom 9:9).

If Divine Wisdom, which is feminine, is in the Word, which is Christ (John 2: 1-3), then the feminine is also in Christ. As Christ is in God, so there is feminine in God. Fr. Tavard in *Women in Christian Tradition* explains:

> Creation takes place in Christ, the wisdom of God, who therefore encompasses in himself all creatures, the invisible world of the angelic spirits and the world of man, fallen, and restored. The English language fails to express this properly for wisdom, Sophia, is a feminine term in both Hebrew and Greek. We ought to say, were it linguistically possible: Christ, the wisdom of god, encompasses in herself.[228]

We relate to Jesus, the Christ, in every aspect of His self. We relate as creature to the Creator. We relate in brother/sisterhood through incarnation. We relate as bride to the bridegroom through redemption. We relate as children to our spiritual parents—both father and mother—through Baptism and filling with the Holy Spirit. Quoted in Tavard, the Christian writer, Gregory Palamast, said:

> Christ has become our brother by union to our flesh and our blood; and he has in this way assimilated himself to us . . . . He has bonded and adapted us to himself as the bridegroom does with the bride, by becoming one flesh with us through communion to the Blood; he has also become our father with us through the Holy Baptism which makes us like him, and he nurses us from his own breast as a mother, filled with tenderness, does with her babies.[229]

---

[228]   Tavard, WCT, 153-154.
[229]   As quoted in Tavard, 158.

131

According to modern psychology on the collective unconscious, especially the writings of Carl Jung regarding the animus and anima, each person contains within his or her self, the opposite psyche. The animus is consciousness, extraversion and rational functions of thought, which are "masculine." Anima is the unconscious, introversion, irrational functions of sensation and intuition, the "feminine."[230] One or the other is more evident at all times but *everyone contains both elements* interacting to comprise the individual. Jesus was human, He contained these also.

There is another dimension to this maleness/femaleness which is worth noting, and that pertains to Eucharist. According to Dr. Barnhouse, the gifts of bread and wine represent humanity, including women as well as men.[231] The bread represents the physical means of sustenance and wine the spiritual," she wrote.[232] In the Roman Catholic liturgy, she explained further, "*The perception is of the wine as masculine and the bread as feminine, together forming the whole community of Christian believers.*[233]

It's interesting in most Catholic churches it is the Host, or bread, which is universally distributed today, and only the priest-celebrant, deacon, and Eucharistic Ministers always partake of the wine. That is especially true in very large gatherings such as at a papal mass. Some churches, of course, have communion under both species for everyone but often people chose not to take the wine. Aside from allergic or other reactions, that probably stems from the many years the wine wasn't available to the congregation. Also, centuries ago, congregants dipped their bread into the wine, called Intinction,[234] but that was discontinued because of fear of spreading the bubonic or Black plague. Probably the use of the wine for congregants stopped totally after that. (See results of the Council of Trent.) Self-intinction

---

[230] Ibid., 167.
[231] Barnhouse, 20.
[232] Barnhouse, 20.
[233] Ibid., 21.
[234] Intinction today by the individual is prohibited in the Western Rite but a priest or deacon may do so and give it to the recipient. However, it is widely used in Eastern Rite services.

is not permitted today for Roman Catholics. Distributing wine to the whole congregation of those who receive Holy Communion has become more prevalent recently. There can often be 10 or more Eucharistic Ministers in large parishes, plus the celebrant and deacon, and each one is distributing communion.

Also, in the Eucharistic sacrament, either element—bread or wine—is considered to have both properties. Leviticus 17:11 says, "It is the blood, as the seat of life, which makes atonement." Or, in the words of the vernacular and many Pentecostals, "We are saved by the blood!"

According to Dr. Barnhouse, seeing the wine as masculine and the bread as feminine, parallels the deep symbolism rooted in human consciousness of a male pagan deity, Bacchus, as lord of the vine, while fertility, the goddess Ceres (from which we get our word, cereal) presided over the grain.[235] "In Eucharist there is also the traditional meaning of the bread and wine as the body and blood of Christ," Dr. Barnhouse said, "and the fact that the priest represents both God and humankind."[236] She added: "God is both sacrifice and victim. Humankind, included in God's human nature through the incarnation, is thus also present. We are assured through our participation in these rites we become members of the mystical body of Christ."[237]

The Greek word for spirit is pneuma, a neuter gender word. Although gender in word usage does not really connote sex, the implication is that it does. In this case, pneuma, is a sexless word, which "well-suited the thinking of the male-oriented theologians." Bruns explained:

> The father is obviously masculine, the Word (Logos in Greek is also masculine in gender) whom he begets is masculine; and the Spirit which they beget together is neuter. It is perhaps a tragedy that this concept of the Spirit as feminine was

---

[235] Barnhouse, 35-6.
[236] Ibid., 21.
[237] Ibid.

neglected. There is no more reason for Jews and Christians to think of God as masculine (independently of the purely literary and cultural influence which determined the kind of terminology used in our Scriptures), than as feminine.[238]

God is God—neither male nor female. Yet, God contains both elements. Humans were created in Divine Image, which generally means that like God, we are spirit. It also means that as the Spirit, or Wisdom of God, is defined as female, there is a feminine side to God. It's nice to realize that the feminine in God is represented by the Holy Spirit, sometimes described as the Love between the Father and the Son.

---

[238] Bruns, 40, 38.

CHAPTER 15

Women as Jesus' 'Own,' His Friends, Disciples, Anointers

In a day when a rabbi could not speak to women in the street, it is a fascinating deviation from the culturally assigned roles to know Jesus had close personal friendships with women, particularly the sisters of Bethany, Mary and Martha.

His friendship with them was because of who they were, not because He was also friends with their brother, Lazarus. In fact, Scripture says little about Lazarus' relation to Jesus and a lot about that of his sisters. Jesus could come to their home in Bethany and relax from the rigors of His ministry. He could chat amiably with friends and share in the hospitality provided by the women and eat some decent "home cooking." It was a non-threatening environment, secure from threats and conniving by the Pharisees.

Of course, Jesus would teach and the women would listen. Most of the time both would listen, but frequently Martha was more anxious about the serving than the listening (Luke 10: 38-42). In fact, she knew Jesus well enough that she could complain to Him, "Lord, do you not care that my sister is leaving me to do the serving all by myself? Please tell her to help me."

Anyone who's ever had a lot of company for dinner can relate to Martha's plight. It usually happens a lot around American Thanksgiving, when the men who might normally help out are watching football on television and the women are in the kitchen preparing the feast.

What is Jesus' answer? "Mary, you better hurry up and lend a hand?" No. Rather he gently rebukes Martha. "Martha, you worry and fret about so many things, and yet few are needed, indeed only one. It is Mary who has chosen the better part; it is not to be taken from her."

First, Mary, apparently, was sitting close to Jesus, absorbed in His lesson. Sitting at someone's feet indicated discipleship in their culture. It was a position of learning, the student imbued with knowledge from the master or teacher. Even way into the Middle Ages, when printing and written manuscripts were becoming fairly common, the usual position for instruction was at the feet of the instructor. This is Mary's position. It is the same as the male-disciples. Jesus makes it pointedly clear that is exactly where she should be.

Jesus with Mary and Martha

Second, Jesus is telling Martha that worrying "never does any good," and that the heavenly Father will take care of our physical needs as He does the flowers and birds, if first we seek His kingdom and his kingship (Matt. 6: 25-34). Martha wasn't doing that. In fact, she was ignoring her spiritual life for her housework, however necessary it was. That's exactly where women get into trouble, get locked into housekeeping as a stereotypical jail. It didn't matter how well Martha knew and loved Jesus overall; what mattered was she was ignoring her spiritual needs.

In Joyce Landorf's fictionalized account of the relationship between Martha and Jesus, *I Came to Love You Late,* this is gently elaborated. Martha is speaking to her friend, Andrew, Peter's brother, and she asks, "Is he displeased with me for doing the thing I do best— serving? It's the only thing I can give to him. Is it wrong to serve or to need help and seek Mary to share the work load?" Andrew explained Jesus was not reproaching or scolding her but pointing out priorities. "When have you ever sat at his feet?" Andrew asks. She stammers her reply, "I have never taken the time. There always seems so much to do."[239] Jesus slips into the room and the conversation. "That's exactly what I meant, Martha; I want to see a balance between doing and being in your life. You need to learn when it is time to stop your industrious serving and quiet yourself for listening and storing food for your soul. Did you know that the soul must be fed its supper too?" He asked.[240]

Martha begins to understand. She says to herself and to us: "Being still is what Mary chose. The 'being' is the better part of 'doing.'" How could I have been so caught up in the serving—the doing? . . . The truth, the whole truth of God began to illuminate her mind. "I must serve him not out of duty alone, but cheerfully, willingly, out of love."[241]

---

[239] Joyce Landorf, *I Came to Love You Late*, (Old Tappan, NJ: Revel), 113.
[240] Ibid., 114.
[241] Ibid, 114, 132.

In setting out the priorities for Martha, Jesus also may be seen as giving a sort of "Emancipation Proclamation" for Martha [242] and all the other housekeeper women throughout history. Sr. McGrath wrote:

> The lot of women in ancient civilizations was one of heavy and drudging toil. Not scorning Martha's service to him, Jesus would lighten her load and encourage her to seize the freedom to cultivate her gifts of the mind and spirit. His loving rebuke chides not Martha so much as the system which burdened her. On the other hand, Jesus praises her sister Mary for doing that which the religion of Israel did not encourage; she directly approached Christ, the source of spiritual knowledge and power, without the mediation of any man. This 'better part' of direct contact with Jesus and his truth 'is not to be taken from her.'

> "It is an ironical comment on this story, is it not,' says Dr. Maude Royden, 'that the church has sought to take it from her ever since."[243]

Perhaps if Martha was less concerned with having the party go well—so she could be praised as an efficient housekeeper—the whole company, including Mary, the men, and Jesus might have lent a hand. Most guests ask how they can help out.[244]

The story has several ramifications. First is an invitation to spirituality, then acknowledgement of the chore of housework with its secondary importance in a woman's life. L. Swidler said that in this Biblical account, Jesus is not limiting women's role to that of only housekeeper or child bearer.

> Jesus rejected the stereotype that the proper place of all women 'is in the home,' during a visit to the house of Martha and

[242] McGrath, 29.
[243] Ibid.
[244] Jesus even knew how to grill fish; after the resurrection, He did a barbeque on the beach for the fishing disciples. Although Scripture says women ministered to His needs, He probably was a good cook; He was a bachelor!

Mary . . . Martha apparently thought Mary was out of place in choosing the role of the 'intellectual,' for she complained to Jesus. But Jesus' response was a refusal to force all women into the stereotype; he treated Mary first of all as a person (whose highest faculty is the intellect, the spirit) who was allowed to set her own priorities . . . Again, when one recalls the Palestinian restriction on women studying the Scriptures or studying with rabbis, that is, engaging in the intellectual life or acquiring any 'religious authority,' it is difficult to imagine how Jesus could possibly have been clearer in his insistence that women were called to the intellectual, the spiritual life just as were men.[245]

Wahlberg takes the exact opposite perspective of the above interpretations of the story. It is quite a change from her usual point of view, which strongly supports Jesus' emancipating attitude toward women. The difference is due to the entrapment of the culturally defined "women's role." Wahlberg doesn't see apparently that Jesus is eliminating that very limited aspect of a woman's life—both for the individual and for society. No longer must women solely be looked upon as a housekeeper, according to Jesus.

Martha and Mary symbolize the polarization of women's roles. Martha is presented as a busybody, a complaining housewife, and Mary has been elevated to the ideal spiritual woman, somehow liberated from the domestic role . . . . Many women greatly identify with Martha. In the kitchen is exactly where society and the church have put women.[246]

Wahlberg is exactly right so far, but she blames Jesus for making Martha feel even worse.

---

[245] L. Swidler, "Jesus Was a Feminist," 182-3.
[246] Wahlberg, 81.

To her, she is serving and her sister is goofing off. She resents Jesus' elevating what Mary is doing and putting down what she is doing. Her duty in the kitchen comes before her desire to be with Jesus . . . . Martha embodies the dilemma of all women . . . Women are burdened unfairly with serving in the home, the church, and society's institutions—and then blamed with being too concerned with that function. It is a no-win position . . . . If they prefer being Marys, they nevertheless have to perform Martha jobs . . .

More and more women today are declaring a self-identity that could be compared to Mary's—independent, seeking, earning, self-affirming, interested in theology. Throughout Christian history, women who have been Marys have had to achieve under great handicaps. Many potential Marys have been lost to Christianity because of lack of encouragement or opportunity. In the Catholic tradition, in order to be a 'Mary,' a woman had to give up family life and become a mystic or a sister in an order. There were no female Augustines. In the Protestant tradition there have been few women spiritual/ intellectual leaders—no women Luthers, no female Barths or Bonhoeffer's.[247]

Today, many women prefer to be Marthas—and—that's okay. It is okay even though the society says, "do your own thing." It is okay if that's what a woman is happy doing, if that's what she wants. It is *not okay* if society conversely says to women, "that is all you may do."

On the other hand, it is also okay to be a Mary; something that Marthas of the world still question. Women have got to get over the idea that being a Mary-person is selfish; it's not. Women's responsibility, then and now, is first to fellowship with God, to nourish her own spirit. Loving and serving one's family is fundamental; it's vitally important but follows her first responsibility. The latter statement doesn't mean neglecting a husband or family for churchy activities

---

[247] Ibid., 82-84.

or prayer meetings, and so on. It means putting things in proper perspective. It means being free from sexual stereotypes—and that's what Jesus promulgated.

Jesus rejected the concept of women as "mother-only" when a woman in the crowd yelled the compliment to Him, "Happy the womb that bore you and the breasts that nursed you." He doesn't interpret it as a compliment to himself or to His mother; His answer is that His true relatives are those who believe the word of God and follow it, and not just His physical mother. Jesus respects women as the bearer and nurturers of life, but, repeatedly, says a woman's worth is more than that. L. Swidler said Jesus' answer "rejects the baby-machine image of woman."[248] McGrath explained the comment shows, "A woman is more than a womb. She is a fully human person with intelligence to understand and fulfill the word of God.[249]

What else is unique about the friendship Jesus had with Martha and Mary? John 11:5 says, "Jesus loved Martha and her sister and Lazarus." We don't know from the Gospel accounts the marital status of either sister, or their brother. We do know from Scripture that married and single women, were disciples of Jesus. Perhaps Mary and Martha were single. Perhaps, again, Jesus was starting a trend the church is only now resuming: outreach to single adults.

All Christian churches over the last number of years languidly have realized that singles, both men and women, are one of the "new frontiers" for evangelization efforts, along with the unchurched (or lapsed churchgoers), minorities, and so on. It is a major reversal for most churches since their orientation, particularly in the Catholic Church in the 20th and 21st centuries, has been that singleness is a non-permanent state, a passage enroute to the more 'acceptable' lifestyle of marriage. Churches notoriously excluded the non-marrieds or never marrieds from parish and congregational life because they "didn't fit." The orientation centered on the family and the children, usually

---

[248]   L. Swidler, 183.
[249]   McGrath, 37.

attending the parish parochial school,[250] or nowadays, mostly attending religious education classes since there are fewer parochial schools. There are fewer because the parish school is the most expensive part of a parish budget and with changing demographics, many city schools have been closed in favor of suburban or regional schools.

If Mary, Martha and Lazarus (disciples John and Paul, too) are the singles of the Biblical disciples, they are a good example for singles today. Then, as now, "singles were desperate to come into contact with the single person, Jesus Christ. When the single finds the relevance of Jesus in his or her life, emphasis on all other activities is put into proper perspective."[251]

Whether they were single or not, Jesus was close personal friends with Mary and Martha. We know from the Scripture that He constantly referred to them by name, as He later did to Mary Magdalene at the tome-site after His Resurrection. That's significant because Jesus called himself "the Good Shepherd." (John 10: 1-18) He referred to His followers allegorically as sheep, those who knew the shepherd's voice and answered when he "called them by name."[252] Similarly, Yahweh called the Israelites by name, showing personal relationship. "Do not be afraid for I have redeemed you; I have called you by your name, you are mine." (Isaiah 43:1, 49:1)

Jesus called the sheep "His own." The fact that women can belong among the sheep is especially important because they are Jesus' own.[253] "His own" is also used to introduce those present during the account of the Last Supper (John 13: 1). "It is clear that John has no hesitation," Fr. Raymond Brown said, "in placing a woman in the same category of relation to Jesus as the Twelve would be placed if they are meant by 'His own.'"[254]

John repeatedly used the word disciples to indicate persons of both sexes. In the account of the Last Supper, John only says, "his

---

[250]   Barbara O'Reilly, "Churches Are Mounting Special Ministries to Cope With the Needs of Single Persons," Religious News Service, Nov. 2, 1979, 1-2.
[251]   Ibid., 6.
[252]   Brown, 118.
[253]   Ibid.
[254]   Ibid.

disciples" were present without delineating any further. John doesn't say it was only men, although they were there. Neither do any of the other gospel accounts about the supper or its preparation mention who fixed it.

It was the disciples who came and asked where they would eat the Passover; the disciples who prepared it. The disciples included women and were not limited to the Twelve, although we've come to interpret it as such. The gospels relate, Jesus sat down (at the table) with the Twelve, or He came in the evening with the Twelve (Matt. 26: 19, Mark 14: 12, Luke 22:8). The Scripture relates that Jesus sent the disciples to prepare the room and the supper. Only in Luke, it is mentioned that Peter and John were sent to make the arrangements for the room.

I believe Leonardo Da Vinci did a great disservice to women with his wonderful painting of his conception of the Last Supper. That has become our standard for viewing the situation, and I believe it was just part of the total picture. Many times at a group party, photographs only show some of the guests. What Leonardo did was a forerunner of television, to use the close-up effect to tell the focused story.

There is no Scriptural proof that women and other male disciples were not present at the supper, generally accepted as the scene for the institution of the Eucharist. In fact, it would be quite culturally contradictory if they were not.

Passover was a time of deep religious observance and significance. It was a time of family gatherings and celebrations and religious commemorations of the Egyptian deliverance. It can hardly be expected that two migrant ex-fishermen, Peter and John, would know how to prepare a roast lamb dinner, the most special dinner of the year. Peter was married after all, and in their culturally separated roles, women did the cooking. A man, properly, would not even be in the kitchen—the woman's domain—although he might cook outdoors over a fire as Jesus did on the shore of the Sea of Galilee.

It doesn't seem reasonable that Jesus went out of his way to make sure women were treated equally and without inferiority—knowing they would be at the foot of the cross and in the garden on Sunday morning and the men would not—and to exclude them deliberately from this most precious celebration. Besides, they were "His own," and close friends. He would have wanted to say farewell to them as well as the male disciples. Jesus knew this was His last dinner before the Crucifixion; it was the earthly supper on which the most sacred mystery of the church-to-come would be eternally based.

When Pope John Paul II visited the United States for his first papal visit in October 1979, it was in the midst of the tumult over Women's Ordination in the Episcopal Church, and the growing movement for women's ordination in the Catholic Church. The Pope was very politically savvy as well as a great humanitarian. He spoke to a gathering of women-religious at the National Shrine of the Immaculate Conception. In his remarks, the Pope deliberately mentioned the Last Supper and he said, very carefully, "The gospel does not mention that women were present at the Last Supper." He neglected to say that neither does the gospel say women were *not* present. The only ones, the gospel says, who were there were "Jesus' disciples," "His own."[255]

There is an additional reason to doubt that women were not present. Women were present at the foreshadowing of the institution of the Eucharist, which is the multiplication of the loaves and the fishes.[256] Like the story of the Samaritan woman at the well, we miss a lot of the underlying meaning of these passages of Scripture because our culture is not Jewish and we are so far removed from that tradition. As much as Americans are aware of what George Washington and Abraham Lincoln did for the United States, the ancient Hebrews or Israelites knew the history of the grumbling and hunger of their ancestors in the desert, as relayed in Exodus 16: 2-4, 12-15. They knew Moses' statement, "This is the bread which the Lord has given you to eat," referred to the manna, God's heavenly bread, as easily as they knew their own first names.

---

[255] Brown, 119.

[256] I am indebted to a homily by Fr. Bob McCarthy for the following account of the loaves and fishes.

Jesus mentions this Moses-reference in the multiplication story. There is a direct correlation with the miracle of the manna in the desert, and the "Give us our daily bread" line in the Lord's Prayer. It is interconnected.

Jesus is speaking to the multitude, which included men, women and children, as did the wandering Israelite tribes on their 40-year desert journey. Although only men are 'counted' in the multiplication story (Matt. 15:30) basically, what Jesus is doing and saying through His action of feeding the masses is, "In the desert the Israelites could not manage to live forever even with that heavenly-sent bread, given day by day to sustain their lives. But there is another bread which gives Eternal Life, which I am giving to you." Then He continues, "If you eat my flesh you shall live forever."

Jesus' use of the word bread in the Lord's Prayer is not haphazard. The word "bread" had such sacred religious significance it couldn't be mentioned in prayer. Jesus even said in teaching the disciples how to pray, "Give us this day your daily bread," breaking another taboo.

What Jesus is doing, and the listeners are aware of the full implications of the story, is appropriating the power of Moses. Moses calmed the disgruntled Israelites by getting bread from Yahweh for them to satisfy their hunger. "Who can do what God's chosen one, Moses, could do?" they asked themselves. This crowd is also disgruntled with hunger, as were their ancestors, another similarity. Jesus physically feeds them with bread and fish and tells them He is the Bread of Life, that He alone can satisfy their spiritual hunger. They eat—and are filled.

By Jesus' words and actions, He shows them that Moses' power was not as great as His. He is greater than Moses, the revered emissary of God. Moses lead the people from the tyranny of Egypt into the freedom of the Promised Land, and Jesus, the new Moses, will provide freedom from the tyranny of sin and the promise of eternal life.

Jesus clearly is reminding them that Moses didn't give the bread, that it came from "My Father." Again, Jesus alludes to the God of their ancestors, causing them to remember their spiritual roots. There is even reference to the Passover lamb, the Pascal sacrifice, with His words, "My flesh will be given for you."

The Last Supper's institution of the Sacrament of Eucharist is another repetition of this whole situation. Even the word, Eucharist, means "to give thanks." That is what Jesus did with the multiplication (John 6: 11) and at the Last Supper (Luke 22: 14-20). He gave thanks that "I am" is good and sent salvation to the people.

Mary anointing the feet of Jesus

In preparation for His imminent suffering and burial, a woman pre-anoints Jesus' body with precious ointments. It is one of the few Bible stories repeated in all four Gospel accounts. Although they all mention such an incident, it may or may not have been the same woman. In the gospel of John, the woman is the beloved Mary, sister of Martha and Lazarus. (John 12: 3-8)

Specifics of the account differ in each Gospel, but the principle is intact. A woman pours costly oil on Jesus and He passively accepts this ministering. He praises her actions to the skeptical men. We are taken off guard by His reaction. Whomever she was, she anointed Jesus' feet with precious, expensive ointment, showing compassion. We can assume that she felt a special spiritual kinship to Jesus. She alone apparently can "feel" His agony and anticipation at the approaching Crucifixion.

He praises her action emphatically and rebukes those who criticize the extravagance. He says it is preparation for His day of burial—which will come sooner than any of them realize, except Jesus.

In the next section of the same chapter, John 12: 23-36, Jesus foretells His death and Resurrection, so we can assume it weighs very heavily on His heart; after all, He asked the Father to remove the burden if possible. (Matt. 26: 39, Mark 14:36, and Luke 22: 42)

The anointing of Jesus is done either the day before the palm-strewn hosanna parade when Jesus triumphantly enters Jerusalem, or within a week of it. (John 12: 12-19)

"We don't expect Jesus to receive from others. We expect Him to give, to preach, to teach, to suffer. This is a religious stereotype which parallels the social sex stereotype. That is, we are socially conditioned not to expect men to be passive and for women to be active in a self-assertive sense," Wahlberg said.[257]

John's gospel says the woman is Mary of Bethany. In Matthew's account (Matt. 26: 6-13), as in John's, the site is in a house in Bethany. Matthew says it is the home of Simon the leper and the woman's identity is anonymous. John relates they gave a dinner for Jesus; Lazarus, newly raised, was at the table and Martha waited on them. In Matthew's account, none of the diners or participants is named except Jesus. The woman, still nameless, comes in and pours the oil on His head. The men at the table complain of the "waste," saying the money could be used for alms. Jesus retorts that her good work, her charitable deed, is superior to almsgiving.

Mark also places the scene at the home of Simon the leper in Bethany. Again, the anointing is on Jesus' head. In the symbolism of the Old Testament, oil represented the Holy Spirit. To anoint was

---

[257] Wahlberg, 52.

to pour oil with the idea of consecrating the person or thing to God, or to set them apart for an office (Gen. 31:13, Ex. 28:41). Since kings and priests were the persons most frequently anointed on taking office, they were frequently spoken of as God's anointed (2 Sam. 23:1, Isa. 45:1). Similarly, Jesus Christ, as king and Priest, was called the 'anointed one of God.' (Acts 10:38)[258]

This woman—especially in the accounts of Matthew and Mark—is actually anointing, or ordaining, Jesus to His messiah mission, I believe. She is anointing Him to His ministry of priest-sacrifice, priest-redeemer. She is His bishop. Jesus will tap that special infusion of Holy Spirit power and strength during the upcoming Passion and Crucifixion. It was fitting and proper that she do so, just as Jesus had to be baptized by John the Baptist "to fulfill all righteousness." (Matt. 3:15)

The Jewish kings, including David, had to be anointed before assuming office. The Old Testament prophets, too, were specially called and anointed to properly proclaim God's message. Jesus is the last of the Prophets since he is the Perfect Prophet. All His divine statements were fulfilled.

Luke's interpretation is different and is the most frequently related, possibly because the woman is portrayed as a dreadful sinner (Luke 7: 36-50), something many men believed anyway about women in general. But the role of sinner is not usually the one we associate with Mary of Bethany. However, in Luke, the Pharisees take Jesus to dinner at the home of another Pharisee. A woman, allegedly of ill repute, enters. She cries her heart out, cleansing her soul as she weeps on His feet. I believe this is a forerunner of Jesus' action shortly after in which He, wearing a slave's apron, will wash the disciples' feet at the Last Supper. There is no doubt her action preceded His. Perhaps, like the Syrophoenician woman, this woman helped Jesus to grow in wisdom. Jesus says to the disciples at the Last Supper, "I have given you an example, follow it," but He is imitating the woman's action.

---

[258] Alexander Crudens, M.A., A.D. Adams, M.S., Editors, *Cruden's Complete Concordance to the Old and New Testament,* Zondervan Publishing House, (Grand Rapids, MI), 1975, 18.

He seems to be so moved by her humility, devotion and service, that He used her as a role-model. However, when she washes his feet, she has no apron, no towel. She dries her tears and His feet with her hair, a sign of humility. Then she kisses His feet. A kiss, in Biblical times and countries, according to *Crudens' Concordance,* "was given as a sign of reverence and subjection to a superior of love and affection, and of adoration."[259]

First she poured oil on Jesus' head. Then, while kissing His feet she anoints them with the oil or ointment. In modern day ordination to the priesthood, the candidate is anointed with oil by the bishop, on his head, his hands and his feet. Even her kissing and tear-drying are precursors of modern ordination in that it is physical touching, more often called Laying on of Hands, which the bishop does to the candidates, passing on spiritual power and grace.

There is also a parallel with Jesus' crucifixion itself—the body parts she kisses, and on which she pours the ointment, are the head and feet. During the scourging and after on the trek to Calvary, Jesus' head wears the crown of thorns, which sources say, was pushed down on his head like a cap with its long, sharp brambles, pounded on, digging into His brain. Similarly, His hands and feet are pierced by the vile horrific nails, like big spikes. They were not the nails you'd use at home to hang a picture on the wall but heavy and strong enough to hold a grown man to a plank, at least several inches in length and width.

The Pharisee homeowner, or Simon, is incredulous at the woman's actions. Jesus rebukes him reminding him that he didn't even do the common courtesy to his guest. The custom of the society was for a host to greet his guests with a kiss on the cheek and to provide water to wash away the dust from their feet. The woman is criticized by all but Jesus for doing the male host's failed responsibility. You have to know the other guests at the table noticed this lack of hospitality to Him because it was a serious violation of their custom, an affront really.

Because of the woman's great love and sorrow over her past life, her many sins are forgiven. Because of her faith, Jesus tells her to go

---

[259] Crudens, 357.

in peace. The men, once again, wonder who He is that He forgives sin. She knows.

Mark and Matthew both relate the man, Simon, was a leper. If so, assumedly, he had been healed by Jesus, otherwise he couldn't associate with non-lepers and had to live, ostracized, outside of the town. Where was his thanks?

If the Pharisees hadn't been so hung up on the purification laws—and the revulsion of the thought of being touched by a woman in public, disreputable or not—maybe they should have realized their responsibility to treat Jesus as the honored guest. And how humiliating and embarrassing for the men to be shown up by a woman! You have to know the other guests realized that also.

Again, why is it in countless homilies that preachers have been more concerned with her alleged reputation than with her action? Why do they choose the one account out of four which mentions this anointing in which she is labeled sinner? Why don't they say the men apparently knew exactly who she was and why that was what was embarrassing for them?

There was only one other time when Jesus is the recipient of such a costly present. It was a gift from and for kings, given for what the infant Jesus would become. It was a gift of gold, frankincense and myrrh, and presented to a poor woman in a house for the newborn baby king (Matt. 2:10-11). That present is never considered wasteful or extravagant. Why not? Is it because the givers were wise learned men and not female?

Magi (Wise Men) at Bethlehem presenting gifts for baby Jesus

Frankincense and myrrh were burial spices. Myrrh, which is generally considered to be the same as the English laudanum, was also used in the oil of holy anointment, the purification of women, and was the "gall mixed with wine" given to Jesus on the cross to dull his pain, which He refused to taste.[260]

So why was the woman's gift considered extravagant? The difference is in our conception of the giver. We perceive the Biblical narrative through sexually-stereotyped colored glasses. The acts of wise kings were not to be discounted, but the acts of a foolish woman

---

[260]   *Smith's Bible Dictionary*, 433.

are easily discredited,[261] especially if she as a former harlot. The acts of service, actually the ministry of service, performed by the woman are easily discredited by the patriarchal world. To the guests at the dinner, what she did was not as important as what she as—a sinner. Jesus said "No way" to that. He showed ministry by women is important because they are.

It is often said that Jesus sent the Holy Spirit to bring *agape*, a Greek word used to show mutuality of love, or Gods' way of loving us, to believers. It is also true that one of the gifts or charisms of the Holy Spirit is that of service. Sister Margaret A. Farley in her article, "New Patterns of Relationship: Beginnings of a Moral Revolution," said service is a position of privilege, not inferiority.[262]

The ministry of service, translated "provided for" or "ministered to," is from the Greek word, *diekanoun,* the same basic root for deacon. In the early church, the deacons and deaconesses did the same thing: they instructed catechumens and they distributed food to the poor. Deacons to men and deaconesses to women.

We never look at the woman with the precious ointment as providing a service for Jesus, of ministering to His needs, as did the Ten or Eleven women who traveled with Him. Isn't it time that at the next ecumenical or Holy Thursday Foot Washing service, the group which has endured more discrimination than any other—women—have their feet washed (whether they actually were present at the Last Supper or not). Foot washing services are usually held for reconciliation and forgiveness between families, Protestants and Catholics, Blacks and Whites, and so on. It's time the men, including clergy, wash the feet of women, in repentance for the sin of sexism.

---

[261] Wahlberg, 55-6.
[262] Margaret A. Farley, RS.M, "New Patterns of Relationship: Beginning of a Moral Revolution," *Woman: New Dimensions,* 56-58.

CHAPTER 16

The Most Maligned Woman in the Bible: AKA "Apostle to the Apostles"

Which woman has the unfortunate distinction of being the most maligned woman from the Bible? No, it's not Jezebel; Delilah; nor Hosea's wife, the prostitute Gomer, who is a symbol of Israel's unfaithfulness to Yahweh. Try the New Testament. Nope, it's not Herod's step-daughter, Salome. All of these women deserved their notoriety. No, it's not Mary of Nazareth. The answer is Mary Magdalene.

She did nothing to warrant such a misfortune. Yet, it lingers.

Mary was the first to see the risen Christ—and what an honor that was! She told the male disciples and the other believers that Jesus is alive. "I have seen the Lord," she said. Despite her alleged naughty reputation, Mary is and was known as "the Apostle to the Apostles," throughout the history of the church, a big contradiction in its own treatment of her. Additionally, her feast day is major, which is a significant privilege in the church.

With these historical facts, who would have thought Mary Magdalene would need champions in papal armor to restore her true identity as apostle and disciple—and to overcome the incorrect notion that she was a sinner and harlot? How did she get this terrible reputation, to be the most maligned woman from the Bible?

Her name is Mary of Magdala; that refers to the town she was from, Magdala, a port city.[263] People in Jesus' time didn't use last names, so calling her "Mary Magdalene" is almost a misnomer. Mary's name is unique among Biblical women, since most New Testament women are identified by their relationship to men: "Mary, the wife of Clopas" is a different person than "Mary, the mother of James," or "Joanna, the wife of Cuza." Even Jesus' own mother was known as "Mary, the mother of Jesus." Magdalene is identified by her hometown.[264]

Throughout most of church history, she was referred to as a harlot—despite no scriptural passage saying that. Two Scriptural references say she was among women cured of evil spirits and infirmities, and that seven demons had gone out of her (Luke 8: 1-3). It is well-known today that the words "possession and evil spirits" in the Gospel refer to physical, emotional and psychological ailments. So she was cured—of seven ailments—perhaps diseases, maybe sinful behavior. We just don't know.

She is mentioned in Scripture a total of 11 times and is never heard of again after the Resurrection. You have to believe as a faithful disciple of Jesus, she was with the group praying on Pentecost morning, and was instrumental in the early church and its ministries, especially witnessing to female converts. But everything else is conjecture— what she looked like, whether she was married, widowed or not.

In the Gnostic Gospels—which were radical in their time for their ideas about gender—including the so-called "Gospel of Mary," shows women as strong and willful, according to Darman in *Newsweek*.[265] He quoted Harvard Divinity professor, Karen King, "The texts argue that the distinction between male and female is one of the body, which will dissolve. The basis for leadership lies in spiritual development."[266]

---

[263] Jonathan Darman, "An Inconvenient Woman: In Search of the Real Mary Magdalene," *Newsweek*, May 29, 2006, Vol. CXXVII, No 22, 47-51.
[264] Ibid., 46-48.
[265] Ibid.
[266] Ibid.

The Gnostic Gospels were widely criticized as being profane and non-authentic—perhaps because they often showed women in a better light. "As church teachings evolved, women took on a more sinister role: carriers of earthly sin," Darman said.[267] Bishops barred women from the ordained ministry and accused them of spreading sin,[268] Darman wrote. "It was only a matter of time before the Magdalene came under attack."[269]

It was an autumn Sunday in 591, the 6th century, when Pope Gregory I preached at the Basilica of San Clemente in Rome to a church full of monks. He believed the faithful—most of whom could not read or write—needed a story of penance and repentance, which was both alluring and inspiring, and from Jesus' immediate inner circle.

Perhaps he never thought of the term "sex sells" but he knew the principle. Peter's repentance, after he denied knowing Jesus three times, was to go out and cry—not a symbol of masculine bravado. In patriarchal times, Gregory certainly wouldn't pick that illustration of grief and repentance, besides, what's more interesting or alluring than sex? Gregory needed a model from Jesus' inner circle and something vague enough that it could not be questioned. So, Gregory alleged that Mary had been a whore, or prostitute, before she came to be healed by Jesus, in other words, she was now reformed. Big time.

Essentially, in modern day language, Gregory "marketed" her, so her image would conform to his purposes, a forerunner of some present day advertising and publicity campaigns. "She had coveted with earthly eyes, but now through penitence these are consumed with tears," Gregory said,[270] creating his "papal debauchery" about Magdalene. He continued in the same mode, "She had coveted with earthly eyes, displayed her hair to set off her face, and perfumed her flesh in forbidden acts."[271] Obviously, from that description—Mary was a dangerous sinner, a total deviant. But today we wonder about

---

[267] Ibid., 48.
[268] Ibid.
[269] Ibid.
[270] Ibid.
[271] Ibid.

how it could be "read" as so disreputable. Almost everyone nowadays fixes his or her hair to show off the face and uses perfume, after shave, and scented body wash in the shower or bathtub. The pope's new identity for Mary would shape her image for more than 1400 years, Darman said.[272]

Gregory's remarkable assertion was supposedly based on the sinful, unnamed woman who washed Jesus' feet in Luke 7, a contention which is disputed by contemporary scholars, Darman said.[273]

As mentioned above, there is no Scriptural reference that Mary of Magdala's evil spirits were sinful, let alone those of the flesh. Darman says Gregory's creation of Mary as prostitute, "proved that the path of Christ was an escape for the pressures of the sinful world."[274] In the first century, Darman explained, a woman could be considered "sinful" for talking to men other than her husband, or for going to the marketplace alone.[275]

Mary Magdalene's story was marginal enough, but still close enough to Jesus, to be reinvented. Most of Gregory's listeners probably didn't know the difference, anyway, especially if they couldn't read the Scriptures! She became "hot"—with legends and cults formed around her fabricated background, even that she traveled to France after the Resurrection and lived there. In the Renaissance, Darman noted, painters reveled in her story—she's Mary the sorrowful, "beautiful and buxom or drawn and austere"[276]—while the Virgin Mary presented a more difficult subject to depict: how to be controversial, yet modest, graceful and chaste?[277]

I remember hearing homilies which continued to denigrate Mary in the 20th century, as if her memory was the "Cult of the Wicked Woman." Whenever the story of the woman who washed Jesus' feet was the gospel at church, the homily was about the sinful Mary Magdalene, not about the anointed service which a woman gave to

---

[272] Ibid.
[273] Ibid.
[274] Ibid, 49.
[275] Ibid.
[276] Ibid., 50.
[277] Ibid., 49-50.

Jesus. She was apparently so degenerate, according to those homilists, that only the love of Jesus could save her, offered through the church, of course.

Even the hit musical, "Jesus Christ Superstar" in 1971, presented Mary as a prostitute, using her body to lord over men. Her character's main song is, "I don't know how to love him." The lyrics: "He's just a man and I've had so many men before, in very many ways, he's just one more." Mary Magdalene is just never thought of as an intelligent, confident woman, let alone a believer and evangelist. She was defamed and slandered in the 2003 hit novel and movie, *The Da Vinci Code*, as being the paramour of Jesus and the mother of His alleged child, all of which is fiction.

For the first time since Gregory's day (591) the church declared in *1969* that she should not be thought of as the sinful woman of Luke, Darman said. That's 1,378 years of misinformation. Even further, Pope John Paul II called Mary by her old title, "Apostle to the Apostles" in an official church document in *1988*. He noted in Christianity's most arduous test of faith, that is, the Crucifixion itself, "the women proved stronger than the Apostles."[278]

In *The Da Vinci Code,* Mary is still more important for her body than her mind, and as a single Mom, too. "Why do we feel the need to re-sexualize Mary?" asked Karen King, who wrote "The Gospel of Mary Magdalene." She says, "We've gotten rid of the myth of the prostitute. Now there's this move to see her as wife and mother. Why isn't it adequate to see her as disciple and perhaps apostle?"[279]

Two pertinent Scriptural facts are unmistakable. Women stood at the foot of the cross in position of discipleship and a woman was the first to see and speak with the Risen Christ. A woman, who was not a valid witness in their time, was the first to preach the central message of Christianity—Jesus is risen from the dead.

Perhaps it was because women never deserted Jesus as the men had. Perhaps it was the greater spirituality in all women since Eve's desire to be wise and god-like. Perhaps it was just the completion of

---

[278] Ibid., 50.
[279] As quoted in Ibid., 51.

orderliness, the alpha and omega-ness, which began with women. That is, beginning with Anna's prophetic forecast of the Messiah-ship of Jesus in the Temple; the message of Messiah-ship was told first to a woman, the Samaritan woman at the well; and the message of Resurrection was told to a woman, Martha at Lazarus' tomb. After Jesus' actual resurrection, the first to see Him were women, including the woman, Mary Magdalene.

Perhaps, basically, women were the first in all these areas because they believed and the male-disciples did not. Peter and "the beloved disciple" (meaning John) did not believe until they saw the angel in the empty tomb. (John 20:9) Thomas, another of the Twelve, and a skeptic, did not believe even on the basis of Peter and John's testimony. He had to put his fingers into Jesus' wounds before he believed. Only then did Jesus become for him, "My Lord and My God." (John 20: 17-18)

Perhaps women were granted these great privileges because the Resurrection meant a whole new world, a new order, a new way of doing things and looking at people. Who would be able to appreciate this more than women?

There is no doubt that Jesus specifically told a woman, Mary Magdalene, to tell the disciples, particularly the male Eleven, that He was alive. Her message included His words to her—that He would meet them in Galilee (Matt. 28:10, John 20: 17-18). He commissioned her to preach the "Good News."[280] His first action after Resurrection was an abrogation of the Law, McGrath noted. It's in agreement with the principle that "death frees from the law," that was—to use the reliable testimony of a woman as witness:

> The unbelief of the apostles, the contempt for women implicit in their attitude, has had thousands of repetitions' in the history of the Churches. One of the most ridiculous comes from the mid 1930's in a report from a commission appointed by the Archbishop of Canterbury, which is entitled, 'the Ministry of Women' using the Mary Magdalene incident as

---

[280] McGrath, 32.

one basis for the church rule denying to women the right of proclaiming the Gospel to women. The commission argued that, "The appearance to St. Mary Magdalene after the Resurrection was not reckoned among the appearances which 'may be termed official, on which the belief of Christendom was to rest' (London, 1935, p. 33). Apparently, Christ did not understand the difference between his official and his unofficial appearances, nor appreciate that both the ecclesial college of his apostles, and late assemblies of ecclesiastics, could override his express command to a woman to preach his truth.[281]

Perhaps the reason why the appearance to a woman was often not given much credence, although undebatable in the Gospels, is that "women are culturally seen as gossips, they go and tell their neighbors." [282] Even in proclaiming such an event as the good news of Resurrection, they were seen first by the men of their day, and later by men in the ecclesia, as cultural stereotypes. "In this way our customary social formulations about women have blinded us to the perception of them as preachers, witnesses and doers of the Word,"[283] Wahlberg said.

The women's movements, even with some of their accompanying negative ramifications, must be credited with awakening our awareness that most people categorize others solely on the basis of their jobs, or work roles. For instance—and thankfully this is changing—a woman was deemed important if her husband had a good job, was a professional, owned his own business or was vice president of a company, and so on. She was important because her children won scholarships or participated in athletics. She was considered important because of who they were and what they did and not because of whom she was and what she did. The woman even lost her identity when she married, going from say Penelope J. Pena

---

[281] Ibid., 33.
[282] Wahlberg, 100.
[283] Ibid., 101.

to Mrs. Reginald Livingston.[284] Forever afterward, she is identified only by her title, Mrs. Livingston.

This role-limiting has certainly been true within the church structure, especially regarding priestly ministries, said Wahlberg. "Most people have minister/priest categories which permit only males. Even if women are performing the acts of a minister or proclaimer of the gospel, they are not so recognized or labeled. If women are denied by culture and religion a certain label or acceptance in a role or job, the tendency of people in that culture and religion is to ignore them in that capacity or to call it something else."[285]

Two women wrote a book from their perspective as seminary students prior to the Episcopal ordination of women to the priesthood in the 1970's. In their book, *Women Priests, Yes or No,* the authors said many of the actions of priests are actions which culture generally today assigns to women. Whether readers support the idea of women's ordination in *any* church, or not, to most people, these words ring true. Many of the duties of a priest are duties, which in this society happen to be considered as belonging in woman's realm. "When a woman dons vestments we suddenly recognize that in this society they resemble more what women wear than they do the garb of men. When a woman breaks bread and serves wine, then cleans the vessels when all have been fed, we suddenly recognize that she has served a meal and done the dishes, just as women do at home. When a woman hears confession or gives absolution, we recognize that women are the listeners and comforters at home, too."[286]

Mary Magdalene had the great honor of first seeing Jesus and speaking with Him in the garden on Easter Sunday morning. She is the primary witness to all the fundamentals of the Christian faith—the life and ministry of Jesus, His death, burial and Resurrection. She proclaimed to the male disciples, "I have seen the Lord!" For that statement she is known as the "Apostle to the Apostles," and not

---

[284] These names are made up and do not reflect individuals.
[285] Wahlberg, 100.
[286] Emily Hewitt and Suzanne Hiatt. *Women Priests, Yes or No.* (New York: The Seabury Press, 1973).

just recently. It dates from as early as the year 1148 in the writings of Bernard of Clairvaux, and even earlier, in her 9th Century biography written by Rabanus Maurus.[287] That biography states Mary "was elevated to the honor of the apostolate and instituted evangelist (evangelista) of the Resurrection."[288]

"In the Western church she received the honor of being the only woman (besides the Mother of God) on whose feast the Creed was recited precisely because she was considered to be an apostle—'the apostle to the apostle' (*apostola apostolorum*)," Fr. Raymond Brown explained.[289]

Our perception of Mary Magdalene is hardly that of an apostle and evangelist. Rather, we see Mary as sinner and penitent woman, said theologian Elisabeth Schussler Fiorenza.[290]

> Modern novelists and theological interpreters picture her as having abandoned sexual pleasure and whoring for the pure and romantic love of Jesus, the man. This distortion of her image signals deep distortion in the self-understanding of Christian women. If as women we should not have to reject the Christian faith and tradition, we have to reclaim women's contribution and role in it. We must free the image of Mary Magdalene from all distortions and recover her role as apostle.[291]

The fact that Mary Magdalene is mentioned by some of the earliest Christian scholars to be an apostle, and the fact that she fit the criteria for apostleship set by Paul—seeing the risen Lord Jesus and preaching the "good news"—should put the damper on all the negative comments which say, "If Jesus wanted women to be important in the church, He would have made them apostles."

---

[287] McGrath.

[288] Ibid.

[289] Brown, Footnote No. 14, 117.

[290] Elisabeth Schussler Fiorenza, "Feminist Theology as a Critical Theology of Liberation," *Women: New Dimensions,* 49.

[291] Ibid.

He did. I'm sure the other unnamed women at the tomb that Easter morning are apostles, too. The Church and it members overlook these Scriptural facts.

Mary Magdalene as faithful disciple? Well, that's just so boring. A faithful, female disciple. Not again. What is this church coming to?

CHAPTER 17

Women in the Early Church and as Medieval Abbesses

The preaching of the Samaritan woman at the well was responsible for the first converts to Jesus, the messiah, in the New Testament. Mary Magdalene and the other women at the tomb on Easter morning were the first members of the new church, or body of believers, in the risen Lord Jesus Christ. Peter, John and the other disciples, male and female, came later.

We have seen that in John's gospel the word "disciple" indicates both men and women; the Bible doesn't say one way or the other if women were present at Jesus' post Resurrection appearances, except in Acts 1:14. But *it would be unlikely if they were not*. As at the Last Supper, it would make no sense if female disciples—among Jesus' closest associates—weren't present at these important appearances. Assuming that women were also among the disciples when Jesus made His glorified appearances, (John 20: 19-31) they also received the graces when the disciples were commissioned to spread the Good News of Resurrection, of healing, of Divine Love.

It was hardly coincidental that the Holy Spirit was given to the believers on the occasion of Pentecost. To Christians, Pentecost is the seventh Sunday after Easter and seven is always considered in the Bible to be the Lord's number. To the Jews, Pentecost occurs 50 days after the first day of Passover. Jesus told the disciples to go and wait for the outpouring of the Holy Spirit. Prior to Pentecost, the male disciples were gathered in the upper room in Jerusalem to pray and wait for the Holy Spirit's outpouring "together with some women, and Mary, the Mother of Jesus." (Acts 1:14)

The very fact that most of the women who were at Pentecost are not identified is very representative of their culture—women were too unimportant in their minds to make a big to-do over; however, 1) it must have been a significant number for them to be mentioned at all and 2) the fact they were mentioned shows how important it was for them to be there!

To Christians, Pentecost is the "birthday of the church." To Jews, Pentecost was and is also called Shabuoth, or the Festival of Weeks. It signified the harvesting of the spring wheat crop and commemorates the day the Law was given to Moses on Mount Sinai. The original promises of a covenanted relationship with God were made to Abraham; Mary's yes started the fulfillment of the Old Covenant and the initiation of the New. The old law was given to Moses; Jesus' coming started the new law. Just as the appearance of God on Sinai was the birthday of the Jewish nation, the outpouring of the Holy Spirit on Pentecost was the birthday of a redeemed nation, the Christian church.

Of course, Mother Mary and the other women, perhaps Mary Magdalene, were present. God does not do incomplete things. It is especially significant that the author of Acts names Mother Mary. Her presence on Pentecost is also parallel to the Sinai-Pentecost correlation.

"Israel is personified in Mary," McGrath said. Mary is "the woman, who on the invitation of God, takes possession of the promise. The dwelling of Yahweh in the midst of His people is first realized in Mary."[292]

Mary was Spirit-filled at the Annunciation. Pentecost is her rebirth.

On Pentecost, the women, as well as the men, were filled with the Holy Spirit. A woman's legal status at that time was that of a minor-child, who could not give testimony in court. Their society frowned on a woman even speaking in public—can you imagine that

---

[292]   McGrath, 35.

these women didn't share what they knew about Jesus? If course they did! I believe they shared the Good News as forcefully as the male-disciples, as dynamically as anyone!

Who converted the females anyway if men were not allowed to speak to women? Wouldn't you share such blessings with your friends? The women not only preached the Good News, they converted others to it. Maybe they didn't preach at a podium to a huge, mixed crowd in a large open square, but they preached to one another, quietly, genuinely. The women certainly shared with their female colleagues and friends. A husband instructing his household about his own conversion is one thing but making many female converts is another. "The numbers of men and women who came to believe in the Lord increased steadily." (Acts 5:14) Of course, women were at the Pentecostal infilling . . . .

Prior to Paul's conversion, he persecuted both men and women who were believers in Jesus, because they were active in propagating it and thus dangerous. (Acts 8:3) He understood in the Christian faith women had a participatory role. In fact, Paul's first convert was Lydia, a professional businesswoman from the town of Thyatira. She was in the purple-dye trade and apparently was much respected in her community. (Acts 16:14) Somehow Paul got to talk with her, or she was so impressed with his living out his new Christian walk, that she made sure to find out what he was talking about. Lydia is followed by other women. Paul described them as "rich," "Greek" (which is how all non-Jews were called) and "from the upper classes," (Acts 17:4, 12, 34), indicating converts whose opinions were influential.

Women received and practiced the gifts of the Holy Spirit. Philip's four daughters are listed as having the gift of prophecy, "one of the higher gifts for which all should strive." (Acts 21:9; 1 Cor. 14:1-2) Other Scriptural references indicate they were not alone in the manifestation of this gift. (Acts 2: 17-21) Prophets are second only to apostles in the "ranking" of pre-eminence in early church life. (1 Cor. 12: 28)

Teaching and preaching are other gifts of the Spirit. (1 Cor. 12: 8-9, 28-29) Priscilla, of the husband and wife ministering team of Priscilla and Aquila, is the prime example. Both, like Paul, were tentmakers and Paul lived with them in Corinth (Greece). Greek women had fewer restrictions than did Jewish women. The couple traveled with Paul to Ephesus (Turkey) where they met Apollos. It was Priscilla (also called Prisca) who was Apollos' primary instructor. He was, literally, her convert, so obviously she was able to speak to him.

The couple is mentioned six times in Scripture. (Acts 18: 2, 18, 26; Rom. 16:3, Tim. 4: 19; 1 Cor. 16:19) Five of those times, Priscilla is mentioned first, indicating she was the more important of the two. That was "contrary to ordinary Jewish usage," according to McGrath.[293]

"There is no hint that she has no right, as a woman, to teach a man. Priscilla taught and told Apollos what to do and gained nothing but praise from Paul," McGrath noted.[294] Priscilla, according to some scholars, wrote the Letter to the Hebrews, the only unsigned Pauline Epistle.[295]

Even Euodia and Syntyche, who had the coworkers quarrel (Phil. 4:2), have their names written in the Book of Life (Phil 4:3) for helping Paul spread the gospel. Apparently, they had the same level of responsibility for teaching the gospel as did Paul's male associates, Silas, Clement, and others.[296]

Phoebe of Cenchreae was one of the first deaconesses. (Romans 16: 1-2) Paul specifically mentions that she was the bearer of the letter to the community in Rome, a service often performed by male deacons.

> Phoebe has been the victim of translation errors for centuries. Twenty-two times Paul used the word "diakonos" to apply to himself, Timothy, Apollos, Epaphras, Tychicus, and Phoebe. In many translations that was rendered as "deacon" when it applied to males, but when the same word applied to Phoebe it was translated as "servant,"[297] as in the *King James Version*. In the *Jerusalem and Revised Standard versions*, Phoebe gets the

---

[293] Ibid, 40-1.
[294] Ibid.
[295] Morris, 121.
[296] McGrath, 42.
[297] McGrath.

correct and equal translation; deaconess. In *the Confraternity Edition,* she is described as 'our sister who serves in the Church.' It should be remembered that all ministry was known as *diakonia* and was viewed as loving service to the community. People were specifically consecrated, or ordained, to a particular service for the community.[298]

Origen, one of the early Christian writers, who lived from 185 to 254 and wrote in the early 3rd century, said that the passage on Phoebe in Romans 16: 1-2 gives, "Apostolic authority for the construction of women ministers in the Church," Morris commented.[299] Similarly, John Chrysostom wrote in his "Commentary on the Epistle to the Romans" that "Paul accepted Phoebe as an ordained deaconess," Morris noted.[300]

Women clearly assumed positions of administrative responsibility in the formative days of the early church. Perhaps that was due to the Scriptural fact that all assemblies of Christian communities, mentioned in Acts and the Pauline Epistles, were held in the houses of women: examples Chloe; Lydia, the mother of Mark; Nympha, Priscilla and many more.

Perhaps even more noteworthy is the fact that John's second Epistle is addressed to the "elect Lady," whom Morris described as "a woman, obviously an overseer of the church community." [301] The third epistle is addressed to "Elect Gaius," assumedly the male overseer of another Christian community. There is no difference, but interpreters usually consider "the elect lady" *as merely one of the churches, and not as an overseer or a real person.* Morris explained *"eklekta"* or elect, was used to denote a clerically ordained person. The "elect lady" would have been a person elected and ordained for special service of the Christian community, that is, an "overseer."[302]

---

[298] Ibid., 59.
[299] Morris, 119.
[300] Ibid., 120.
[301] Ibid., 1.
[302] Ibid. 2.

This does not mean that as an ordained overseer she also was ordained to consecrate the Holy Eucharist. We know that for reasons of the taboo of women during menstruation, they were considered unclean and liable to contaminate others and even to be under the domination of the devil. Therefore, they were withheld from the service of the altar although able to undertake many other services such as overseers of communities that in apostolic times started in their homes.[303]

Morris also noted the word *"episcopus,"* meaning bishop in current vocabulary, is derived from the Greek feminine word meaning overseer, *"episcopae."*[304] Even the male *"episcopus"* was sometimes translated "overseer," as in Acts 20:28. (*Jerusalem Bible*)

History may be hidden from evasion of facts through prejudice. Worse it may be due to a purposeful and malicious hiding of events. Pliny the Elder tells us in his book, *Natural History*, that information was intentionally hidden regarding the work of women. The women overseers', *episcopae*, of early Christian communities and the abbesses with quasi-episcopal jurisdiction, show a tradition that lasted for centuries and yet is little known. It is a tradition in which women had a prominent role.[305]

Additionally, the title *episcopa*, as applied to women, is found on the stone and Mosaic inscriptions from antiquity. "The very stones cry out truths that have been hidden away. These inscriptions prove that women once held a place in the hierarchical service of the church that is now denied to them," Morris said.[306] Morris cites the Church of St. Praxedis in Rome, Italy, adjacent to St. Mary Major Basilica, as

---

[303] Ibid.
[304] Ibid., xi.
[305] Morris., xi-xii.
[306] Ibid, 4.

one example of these inscriptions. The church contains a mosaic with the word 'episcopa' over the head of a veiled woman and the person's name runs lengthways down the side. It is inscribed "Theodo(ra)." The name was tampered with and appears as "Theodo," although the figure and head represented are that of a veiled woman.[307]

The church of St. Praxedis, a female martyr, was one of the oldest titular churches—where bishops presided and baptisms were performed. Wherever women catechumens were baptized, there was an established order of deaconesses, Morris said.[308] A titular church would be comparable to a modern day cathedral. St. Praxedis herself is believed to have been an "elect lady," either from the fifth or ninth century.[309] There is a Praxedis mentioned in the Bible. She, along with Prudentiana, were daughters of Pudens, and mentioned in 2 Timothy 4:21, but, if it was the same woman, that would have made her alive in the first or second century.

The real question is not about Praxedis—but exactly *which* Theodora Episcopa is remembered by the mosaic statue. First of all, about her chiseled-away name. In an attempt to validate the age of the mosaic in the church, Morris explained, an independent scholar who specialized in ancient tile, was allowed to test the mosaic pieces. The scientific determination said the word 'episcopa' over the woman's head was very old, as was the name inscribed down the side of the mosaic portrait. However, the scientists determined the "ra" had been eliminated from her name at some later time and "more modern" mosaic cubes had been replaced to make the name appear as if it had always been Theodo.[310] But who did that, and whomever approved it, forgot it described a veiled woman!

On one of the church columns outside the chapel with Theodora's mosaic, there is a list of important people from the early church. One of those listed is Theodora Episcopa (July 20, 818). Also, the mother of Pope Paschal is buried in the church.[311] Either she or another

---

[307] Ibid.
[308] Ibid.
[309] Ibid, 4.
[310] Ibid., 5.
[311] Ibid.

woman, Theodora of Alexandria, both widows, headed a community of widows and virgins. Theodora of Alexandria is also buried in the church.[312] The statue and mosaic may commemorate either of them, or another woman.

Whomever she was, her name, Theodora, means "gift of God," an interesting side note to the history of female *episcopa*.

> To have women overseers (*episcopae*) of churches and Christian communities of both men and women was a common practice from apostolic times that continued throughout many centuries and was only very slowly suppressed.[313]

Morris noted that one of the earliest of the church councils, The Council of Tours, mentions "Episcopa Terni" in its Canon 20 and deaconesses and sub-deaconesses in canons 13 and 14.[314]

It is well-recognized that deaconesses not only existed within the structure of the Catholic Church, but extended directly from apostolic times, into at least the 6th, 10th or 13th century. We hear very little about it today, but even as late as in the 19th century, it was rather well-known, Morris said. In *A General History of the Catholic Church* by M. L'Abbe J.E. Darras, published in 1866, a half-page is devoted to deaconesses, although he assumes the practice was short-lived ("only during the first ages"), Morris related.

Deaconesses originated at the time of the Apostles. According to Morris, the most sensible and experienced widows were selected for this honor. The age for admission was first fixed at 60 years, but afterwards at 40. The deaconesses did for women what the male deacons did for men. These tasks included visiting all who needed care from the Church: those who were poor, sick, or had other misfortunes. They instructed the catechumens, presented them for Baptism, and molded the newly-Baptized in the Christian life. Both deaconesses and deacons reported to the bishop. The role of deaconesses went out

---

[312] Ibid.

[313] Morris, 3.

[314] Ibid., 6.

of use by degree, Morris said.[315] The deaconesses, who later became known as canonesses, had the right along with the clergy, to say the Divine Office.[316]

In France in one of its Cathedrals, fairly close to Paris, there is a glass enclosed display of the gloves, ring, crosier (or staff), pectoral cross and miter of a medieval abbess. They were gold and ornate—all symbols of her episcopal office and pastoral authority—and exactly what a bishop wears and uses. Modern day visitors from the U.S., who never heard of the abbesses, assume her function must have been that of a 1960's mother-superior in a Catholic high school. No way. She had power and jurisdiction—and they were the same as the bishop, except she did not hold priestly ordination. Most Christians today have no idea of this role which women held in the church; the male hierarchy today certainly doesn't talk about it. Do they even know about it? I'm sure it's not a favorite topic at the seminary, if it's even mentioned. Yes, women did hold ecclesial office in the church.[317]

Monastic leaders often were ordained for the function of leadership although the men and women whom they supervised were usually not ordained for their services. The *Wisigothic Sacramentary* from the 5ᵗʰ Century *gives instructions for the ordination of abbesses, Morris said.*[318]

Abbesses were ordained to their ministry as head of the community. It was the same way the early Christians were ordained to the ministries of the deaconate and the same way priests were

[315] M. L'Abbe, J.H. Darras, *A General History of the Catholic Church: From the Commencement of the Christian Era Until the Present Time.* (First American Edition from the Last French Edition, New York: P.O.'d. Shea Publisher, 1866), Vol. 1, 74-75.
[316] Morris, 12.
[317] I attended 17 years of Catholic schools—from kindergarten through college graduation—and I never heard a word about medieval abbesses or their clout. I saw these robes and symbols of the abbesses' authority during a trip to Europe in 1967, years before I started this research. These women existed. I found some of their names by searching on-line, including St. Hildegarde, several de Bourbons, and so on.
[318] Morris, 13.

ordained to their ministry. "It was a form of ordination though not priestly ordination," Morris explained.[319]

The abbesses had independent jurisdiction with spiritual and temporal control. They supervised churches and parishes; received tithes; maintained buildings and land; and provided for the salaries of priests. The right of the abbess to raise money was never questioned until the Council of Trent.[320] The council's 25 sessions were held from 1545 to 1564, primarily in response to the Protestant Reformation and also due to abuses in the Catholic tradition, such as selling indulgences.

Morris detailed the histories of all the women's abbeys in Western Europe—and there were many from Ireland and England to Germany, Austria and Spain—in *The Lady Was a Bishop,* but here we will just consider some of those aspects just because of the lack of familiarity about the Abbesses today.

Women's abbeys prospered as well-established religious centers with thousands of people under the jurisdiction of the abbess—priests, nuns, monks, lay employees and parishioners. Two of the abbeys, as recorded in church documents, were the sites of church councils, and probably chosen for those councils because of the influence of the abbess. St. Hilda's community in Whitby, England, was the site of a Council in the 7th Century and the famous Abbey of Notre Dame de Jouarre (approximately one hour by train from Paris) was the site of a major Council in 1133.[321] Although there is no longer an abbey, the rest of its cloister and buildings are there today and Jouarre still functions as an active Benedictine monastery. In France the abbeys were called "royal abbeys" because so many of the abbesses or other community members were daughters of royal families.

The abbesses had exactly the same powers and authority as did the bishops, except one—they did not have priestly ordination. But they did have complete authority over priests and clerics residing within their territory. In fact, the abbeys and their lands and property were equivalent as a distinct and separate diocese within a diocese.

---

[319]   Ibid., 23.
[320]   Morris., 23, 30, 17.
[321]   Ibid., 34.

Most of the women's abbey's had a special protection from the Holy See called the "Right of Exemption," which ultimately led to their undoing. The Right of Exemption was guaranteed by the Vatican and it included immunity from paying taxes and tithes to local bishops for the abbey, its churches, property, land, residents, and clergy. The exempt abbeys were directly answerable to the Holy See. Naturally, the bishops did not like the "Right of Exemption," since the abbeys and their territories were huge and very rich. Bishops conspired in every un-Christian way to void the "Right of Exemption," including falsification of documents, forgery, military threats, political conspiracy, supply boycotts, and even coercion—all attempts to get money from the abbeys.

One of the most important abbeys was the Abbey of Fontevrault in Chignon, Anjou, in northwestern France. Today the abbey and its remains are a popular tourist attraction because of its involvement with French history and its royal monarchs. The Order of Fontevrault and the abbey were started in 1099. Not only did it have its quasi-episcopal abbesses, one of its one-time residents, Eleanor of Aquitaine, was queen of both England and France. She and several royal family members from both countries are buried there.

A Benedictine monastery, Fontevrault established three houses in England, which also were exempt from the jurisdiction and taxes of local bishops, Morris said.[322] "The priests and monks, together with the nuns, took vows of obedience to the abbess in imitation of the obedience of Jesus to His mother, while the abbess in imitation of Mary, served the community devotedly in an administrative capacity," Morris said.[323]

The first abbess of Fontevrault was elected and installed on October 28, 1115, before five thousand nuns and five thousand monks, all of whom took vows of obedience to her. This continued until elections of abbesses were discontinued and suppressed by the French

---

[322] One of the abbesses was Charlotte de Bourbon, who shocked her family and the Abbey when she converted to Protestantism and married William of Orange in 1575.

[323] Morris, 35.

Revolution at the end of the 1700s.[324] In 1636, the monks rebelled saying obedience to the abbess, that is, of a man to a woman, was "against nature and God." The abbess rebutted the monks' contention with the fact that this act of obedience was fundamental in the rule of the Order of Fontevrault, founded by Robert d'Abrissel. The rule was based on the disciple John becoming the adopted son of Mary at Calvary.[325]

That abbess also used the example of Deborah, the prophetess and judge in the Old Testament, to buttress her arguments against the monks and noted the same argument was mentioned by John Calvin in his criticism of the right of queens to rule in secular society.[326]

> The idea that nuns, like married women, must be subject to men arose at the time of the Renaissance when the Greco-Roman culture adverse to women was revived. The obedience of clergy and monks to the abbess was considered a worthy ideal in the 12th and 13th centuries, one based on the imitation of Jesus Christ and not degrading to man but by the 16th and 17th centuries, it was looked upon as being contrary to the nature of man and to the will of God.[327]

Regarding the monks' rebellion, the Council confirmed the authority of the abbess and the force of age-long tradition prevailed, Morris noted.[328] The abbess had both spiritual and temporal responsibilities. At the Order of Sainte-Croix at Poitiers, more recently a flourishing Benedictine community, Papal Bulls said the abbess alone could confer the investiture on the abbot.[329]

Along with the "Right of Exemption," the abbeys were also directly dependent on the Holy See and reported only to the Vatican.[330]

---

[324] Ibid., 45.
[325] Morris.
[326] Ibid., 51.
[327] Ibid.
[328] Ibid.
[329] Ibid, 52.
[330] Ibid., 54.

Exempt orders from the Holy See was the usual practice and not extraordinary. Morris said:

> What is astounding is the terrible change of attitude that took place after so many centuries of a Christian tradition, a tradition in which women's administration has been accepted and enjoyed. Only after the 12th Century during the Renaissance was there a slow return to Greco-Roman culture that the service rendered by abbesses was looked upon as wrong. Enforced domination by later bishops over exempt abbeys like Jouarre was a flagrant contradiction of the earlier Christian ideal of monastic freedom. The dislike of women having any right to rule shows the whole idea of what it means to rule has become re-paganized. [331]

Administration was no longer considered a service, but a right of dominion, a right to laud it over another, which was a pagan idea of government and not the Christian one of humble service. From a lovely and commendable act in imitation of Jesus' obedience to His mother, and of John the Evangelist in service of his adopted mother, the mores changed to it being 'wrong' for a man to make a vow of obedience to a woman. Morris explained:

> *All these things have become hidden history. Nobody hears anything about it. It is hushed up, and the Christian tradition is presented as an all-male right of authority as though it had been so always.* In fact, the quasi-episcopal status of abbesses did not come to an end until the time of the French Revolution and in the case of Las Heulgas de Burgos (Spain) the same status continued until 1874.[332]

Morris related there was a "slow whittling away of the abbesses jurisdiction." By 1705, the clergy of Castellana appealed to the Sacred

---

[331]   Ibid., 55, 56.
[332]   Morris, 56-7.

Congregation in Rome. They wanted to merely bow before the newly elected abbess rather than genuflect; and have the confessor for the abbey appointed by her vicar, and not chosen by the abbess, the traditional practice.[333] It was granted, again diminishing the abbess' authority.

The rise of democracy and the Industrial Revolution in Western Europe resulted in an inconsistent situation for women. While the world became "freer" through democracy, women abbesses lost their authority. While the Industrial Revolution put men to work in factories, and romanticized the labor of men to varnish its oppressive aspects, it became the fashionable ideal for women to be idle. Kolbenschlag said:

> One of the great paradoxes about the progress of developing societies is that it is often achieved at the expense of a progression in women's function and status. While it is true that in most societies—primitive, ancient and modern—some division between male and female roles have prevailed, industrialization has exaggerated and radicalized these divisions. Primitive and even colonial women played a much more integral role in the business of survival. Their identity as workers and managers was taken for granted. The 'valiant woman' described in Proverbs 31 is high in self-esteem and in the eyes of the community because her role is integral to the private and public life of the community.

> In our own culture women of the colonial and frontier eras were closely tied to the economic enterprises of the emerging society . . . . In effect, women of the colonial era were not forced to choose between work and domesticity as alternative vocations. Domestic work was, in fact, often performed by unmarried young women in order to free the married woman for work in the family industry. Ironically, the work roles of married and unmarried women have been reversed in modern times.[334]

---

[333] Ibid., 74.
[334] Kolbenschlag, 78-9.

By the mid-18th century, the disassociation of home and work, according to Kolbenschlag, "Isolated the woman in a privatized sphere of domestic responsibility."[335] In Victorian thinking, the rugged virtues were replaced by piety, delicacy and gentility as the index for social mobility. Its cult of "true womanhood" denigrated work to the point where it was seen as an unfortunate social condition, "a fall from grace."[336]

> The myth of the leisured lady endowed the middle class woman with more protection, more pedestal worship, and more restriction. The more idealized her role, the narrower it became . . . The practice of female idleness spread through the middle class until work for women became a 'misfortune' and 'disgrace.' In time the prospect of women leaving home for work inevitably came to be regarded as a kind of 'mortal sin' against the family.[337]

Two examples of how women lost authority through democratization and industrialization are the traditional female-only job as a brewer and the other is the medieval abbess. A brewer was a skilled craftsperson, making a marketable commodity which was financially lucrative. Eventually this trade was deemed "unfit" for women: today, it's a shock to learn that brewing was once a female-dominated and "stereotyped" role. Men didn't do it. With the abbesses, the church had been consistently the most powerful spot for women—especially with the ecclesial hierarchical rank of Abbess—and not the accidental power of royal birth. Europe's democratic revolutions squashed this opportunity for women. The French Revolution closed most of the abbeys in France. The invasion of Italy by the Napoleonic forces brought an end to the whole system of Exemption in Italy. By 1809, Pope Pius VII, was a prisoner, and

---

[335] Ibid., 80.
[336] Ibid.,81.
[337] Ibid.

the King of Naples was Napoleon's brother, Joseph. He was followed as King by Joachim Murat.[338]

One abbey Prioress wrote to King Murat saying, "It was only prejudice and ignorance that considered it abusive for women to hold a place in the church hierarchy and to have quasi-episcopal jurisdiction." [339] It was not a question of priestly ordination, she wrote but that deaconesses from apostolic times had formed an administrative order in the church "into which women were formally initiated by the laying on of hands."[340] She mentioned that abbesses and congregations of the monastic system in both the Latin Rite and the Greek or Eastern Rite received Exemption and had jurisdiction over their own "separated territories."[341] That was usual for royally instituted foundations, such as the Benedictines and other 'derived orders,' she noted. Adding, it was a commonly accepted arrangement that abbots and abbesses acquired a rank of honor in church hierarchy.[342] The abbess wrote—but to no avail.

The abbesses with these quasi-episcopal powers were not just in France and Italy. They ruled abbeys in almost every country in Europe including Germany, Spain, Belgium, Austria, England and Ireland. In Ireland, the most noted of the abbesses was St. Brigid of Kildare, who may have been ordained as a bishop, serving not in a quasi-episcopal capacity but as co-episcopa.[343] Morris said Brigid's story is considered a 'legend' by prejudicial writers who do not know about the quasi-episcopal status of abbesses."[344] Morris adds that legends often turn out to be based on historical facts. In Brigid's case it seems possible.

According to her biographer, Cogitoser, Brigid was ordained a bishop by Bishop Mel. Nevertheless, she called a hermit from his solitary life to govern the church with her. Like her abbess-colleagues

---

[338] Morris, 75.
[339] Ibid., 76.
[340] Ibid.
[341] Ibid., 77.
[342] Ibid.
[343] Ibid.,14, 137.
[344] Ibid., 137.

on the Continent, Brigid had the jurisdiction of a bishop but possibly not sacerdotal, or priestly, ordination. Morris explained that is why she had a shared ministry—because a woman could not consecrate the Eucharist—"at least not until the age of 60."[345] We do know Brigid did preach to the people and had jurisdiction over large territories and held churches and believers together.[346]

What we forget, being so far removed from those times, is that women from earliest days were ordained to administrative positions within the church. These women received titles: Episcopa, Sacerdota Maxima, Praeposita and Custos of Churches.[347] They had all the powers of a bishop with regard to the jurisdiction of churches and peoples within their territories, Morris said. "It cannot be concluded they were called *sacerdos,* that is consecrated for celebration of the Eucharist, at least not until past 50 or 60 years of age."[348]

While the mistaken idea of genetics prevented women from consecrating Eucharist—to avoid the possibility of contaminating the Blessed Sacrament—(until perhaps after they were menopausal) there is documented evidence women as abbesses and deacons had "the duty of hearing confession." [349] Morris said there were four rules of religious orders that allowed the abbess to hear confession: the Rule of St. Columban, Rule of St. Donatus, Regula Cujusdam ad Virginis, and the Rule of St. Basil.[350] The abbesses apparently gave absolution to men who confessed to them until this was changed later when considered an abuse. They may have continued to confess and absolve women, which was not abusive, Morris noted.[351]

"In 1210, Innocent III withdrew the right of abbesses of Las Heulgas de Burgos (Spain) from hearing confession. By that time, it was considered an abuse and must have entailed absolution," Morris

---

[345] Ibid.
[346] Ibid, 138.
[347] Ibid.
[348] Morris.
[349] Ibid, 140.
[350] Ibid.
[351] Ibid., 142.

said.[352] She notes that the Church's General Law on Confession was only set after that—during the 4th Lateran Council in 1215.

> In 1255, at Poitiers, deacons were forbidden to hear confession. No doubt abbesses had the ordination of deaconess or arch deaconess. The ordination of deacon at one time was sufficient for hearing confession and that may be why the abbesses of Las Heulgas felt they had a right to do so.[353]

The Abbess of Fontevrault in France had the Right of Absolution in cases of ex-communication. They also were granted the right to nominate confessors and preachers. The abbess of Fontevrault received these privileges from Pope Honorius III in 1224, who charged the abbess "with the maternal care of the flock of our Lord," Morris said.[354]

At the time of the Reformation, the abbeys and the abbesses were no less immune to the changes than anyone or anything else. Several entire monasteries converted to Lutheranism or other denominations. In other abbeys, individual members converted and this caused serious discord.

One abbess whose story is poignant is that of Charlotte de Bourbon (born in 1546 or 1547, death May 5, 1582). Her mother left her when she was two weeks old at the Abbey of Jouarre to be raised as a nun![355] Although Charlotte protested she was too young, at the age of 15, she was elected as abbess of the Abbey of Jouarre. She served from 1561 to 1572. Under the influence of her sister, Francoise de Bourbon, she converted. (One source says to Lutheranism and another source says to Calvinism.)[356] After unsuccessfully attempting to convert the whole abbey, she escaped from the abbey and France in 1572, and

---

[352] Ibid.

[353] Ibid.

[354] Ibid.,76.

[355] "Charlotte de Bourbon" from Wikipedia on-line. See also sites on Fontevrand Abbey, Abbey de Jouarre, Medieval Abbesses and related sites. Accessed in 2010.

[356] Morris says Lutheranism and Wikipedia says Calvinism.

fled to Germany. There she married Protestant William (The Silent), Prince of Orange-Nassau in 1575; they had six daughters, one of whom was Louisa Juliana, Electress Palatine. William was the main leader of the Dutch revolt against the Spanish.[357]

I find Charlotte de Bourbon's story quite sad for several reasons. As a baby, she had no say in what her parents chose for her life's profession—entering the convent. Her personal religious convictions were such that she had to flee for her life in a so-called "Christian society." Also, her daughter was Louise Juliana of Nassau, whose descendants started the House of Hanover, ancestors of the present-day British royal family.[358]

In hierarchical processions, the abbess walked behind the bishops but in front of the clergy and carried her pectoral cross, Morris related.[359]

> From apostolic times women ranked in the hierarchal order and have been considered worthy of an ecclesiastical ministry, all

---

[357] Morris, 77, and "Charlotte de Bourbon" from Wikipedia on-line.

[358] My parents were born in Ireland and I am quite familiar with Irish history. It occurs to me, as a purely personal insight, which I have never seen written elsewhere, one of Charlotte de Bourbon's descendants, perhaps her great grandson, or great nephew, was King William of Orange, or King "Billy," who fought at the Battle of the Boyne in Ireland in 1690. It was his success at the Battle of the Boyne which imposed "the Supremacy of Protestantism" in Northeast Ireland, today known as Northern Ireland. That started the para-military group, "the Orange Order." Catholics and Protestants for hundreds of years have been "refighting" that Battle—politically-motivated "religious wars" until the Belfast Peace Agreement ("The Good Friday Agreement") in 1998, lead by former U.S. Senator George Mitchell. It is totally incongruous since, as an abbess, Charlotte de Bourbon, was one of the most influential women in the Catholic Church. Yet, 118 years after she left France, her kinsman would fight to squelch Catholicism in Ireland. The situation worsens when you realize, the little known fact, and this is found in some books on Ireland, that William of Orange, a Protestant, was an ally of the pope in the battle. In effect, "King Billy," carried the Catholic standard in the battle. He defeated the Catholic King of England, James II, who was carrying the Protestant banner. In those political days of the Papal States, the Vatican celebrated William's victory for having subdued the French king, Louis XIV, James' ally.

[359] Morris, 76.

the more so, when an abbess. Abbesses have had high place in councils ranking above the clergy; at one time they held the right to confess and to preach; they have had the right to suspend clergy subject to them when necessary and to confer offices and benefices. In short, they have been considered of first rank.[360]

The last of the great abbeys was Las Heulgas de Burgos in Spain, which was Exempt from its founding in 1188 until 1874. It was founded in exact diligence to the traditions and ideals of the Cistercian Order; eventually the custom of the abbess hearing confession, which was practiced at Burgos, was withdrawn as being an abuse.[361] At one time, there were 60 villages and churches under the jurisdiction of the abbess.

The duties of the abbesses at Burgos were far-reaching. The abbess had the right to establish new parishes in her territories and to bestow the duty of "cure of souls" on her clergy. Neither the bishop nor the Apostolic Delegate had the right to visit the churches, the parishes, the clergy or the beneficiaries in her district without her permission. In the same way as bishop, the abbess had the right to punish and to summon any priest preaching heresy in her diocese.

Both the abbess and, the bishop, had the right to punish lay people who committed a criminal offense within their district—whether they were from the district or outside of it. The same as a bishop, the abbess had the right to promulgate dispensations and graces received from Rome for her district and diocese. She had the right to examine the veracity of public criminal cases who claimed a pardon. She could establish works of charity such as a hospital within her district. She could examine the ability of the apostolic notaries and also the Imperial or Royal notaries and had the duty of punishing any offense done in executing those offices.[362]

The abbess could also hear matrimonial cases and criminal cases, as could a bishop, and she acted through ecclesiastical judges nominated

---

[360] Ibid., 77.
[361] Ibid., 84.
[362] Ibid., 85.

by her. She could examine clergy members for their suitability. She had the right to appoint a confessor for the nuns and lay sisters; they could not go to another confessor without the approval of the abbess.[363] The list of her responsibilities and duties goes on and on but one of the most interesting was her right to issue licenses to priests, giving them the right to say Mass in her churches.[364]

Priests are ordained for a particular diocese and are assigned to obey that local bishop. To minister as a priest in another diocese, he needs permission, called Faculties, from that second bishop—and from his own bishop to practice outside his assigned territory. Canon 274 was established at the Council of Nicea, which is in present day Turkey, in 325, at the time of Constantine. The abbesses granted Faculties also to the priests serving in her territory.

Regarding hearing confessions, the abbesses of the order had apparently practiced it since the abbey was founded in 1188. Morris said she believed it must have been a Cistercian custom, practiced in France. Las Heulgas of Burgos and two other monasteries at Leon and Calhorra, followed the established Cistercian practices in extreme conformity.[365]

But in 1200, it was considered an abuse and Innocent III, having been informed about this, sent a Bull, *Nova Quaedum*, prohibiting the continuation of this practice. It in no way deterred the abbesses from any of the forms of jurisdiction just described, which were then considered quite normal and in no way an abuse. Had it been otherwise, the Bull would have been directed against the abbess with regard to her powers of jurisdiction too.[366]

Military orders of men were formed to nurse the wounded from the Crusades. The abbess usually had power over the men's orders and hospitals as well, if they were within her territory. The Women's Orders nursed also. Morris said this was particularly appropriate for the women's orders which were descendants of the communities of deaconesses, who had the duty of caring for the sick in the early church. The hospitals were

---

[363] Morris, 86.
[364] Ibid.
[365] Ibid., 87.
[366] Ibid., 86-7.

often founded by the side of the monastic institutions. This was also to follow Christ's command that for cure of the sick, there was need for penance and prayer.[367]

Papal Bulls repeatedly confirmed the rights of the abbesses to Immunity and Exemption. For example, a Bull by Pope Urban VIII in 1629 to Abbess Anna of Austria confirmed Exemption. By 1873, a Bull was issued by Pius IX which ended all quasi-episcopal jurisdiction in Spain. It was the Bull *Pontificis Maximi Acta,* and it affected both men's and women's orders.[368]

Morris attributes much of the changing thought on women to John Knox. Knox revived the idea that women had no right to rule over men in his vitriolic accusations against Mary, Queen of Scots, and Elizabeth I of England, called "Against the Monstrous Regiment of Women." He coined the phrase, "It is against nature and against God for a man to be in obedience to a women.[369]

The document, Morris said, corresponds to the main points of the Concordat between Pius VII and Napoleon, which was still in force. The Bull said, due to a change in civil society, the custom of Exemption for Episcopal jurisdiction, was now inopportune and possibly harmful. The abbeys were put under the jurisdiction of the local diocesan bishop.[370]

In defense against the Bull, a document prepared by the abbey, cited two papal Bulls from Pope Clement III in 1188 and 1197, formulating the separated abbey. The defense referred to seven confirmations of the exempt status by six different popes: Honorius III, Sept. 11, 1219; Gregory IX, July 20, 1234; Innocent IV, April 29, 1246; two by Innocent VIII, July 30, 1487, and August 13, 1489; Leo X June 1, 1521; and Urban VIII who confirmed all the previous Bulls in his of Oct. 2, 1632.[371]

"By the 16th Century, the opinion of Aristotle (on women) vied with that of Christ," Morris said.[372] She explained a return to the Greco-Roman cultural influence brought about the return to the low evaluation

---

[367] Ibid., 90.
[368] Ibid., 94, 96.
[369] Ibid.
[370] Ibid., 97.
[371] Morris, 97-8.
[372] Ibid., 100.

of women. Leadership in the church took on patriarchal domination instead of the Christian ideal of humble service, she said.

> As a result of the suppression of religious orders through the French Revolution, women lost their chief centers of education. The Napoleonic Code's civil law placed wives in complete subordination to husbands in a way worse than in Roman and pagan paternalistic times. The Concordat with Rome allowed religious property to remain in the hands of the government. Some redress was made by means of government salaries for the (male) clergy. No provision was made for nuns who likewise lost their property.[373]

Pius IX took away the right of Spanish abbesses to Exemption on the grounds it no longer was in keeping with new 'democratic' ideas. At that time democracy did not include women.[374]

On Jan. 20, 1874 the Abbey of Las Heulgas de Burgos and its quasi-episcopal jurisdiction was suppressed by the local cardinal. It ended almost 1900 years of female authority in the ecclesiastical and hierarchal structure of the Catholic Church. Those years, and that amount of women's power within the church, are now mostly forgotten. Today, it is almost as if it never happened.

And, as broadcaster Paul Harvey, used to say, "Now you know the rest of the story"—it is no longer hidden history.

In the latest chapter on medieval Abbesses, 11th Century German Benedictine abbess, Hildegard of Bingen, will be named Doctor of the Church in Oct. 2012. She will be the fourth woman Doctor. She was a mystic, composer, illustrator, prophet, ecologist and strong promoter of women's leadership in the church. Although often referred to as Saint, she will be officially canonized, as will Kateri Tekawitha, the first native American, in Oct. 2012.

---

[373] Ibid., 101.
[374] Ibid, 104.

CHAPTER 18

The Myth of the "Mary-Myth"

The abbesses are not the only women in the church history whose contributions were ignored, glossed over or deliberately hidden. They are only the most dramatic example of erosion of women's authority within the church; their power eroded by degree as shown previously. But there is, of course, one woman whose impact on the church blossomed. She is Mary, Jesus' mother.

I think if we could meet her that we might leave the interview and call her "a gutsy lady." She certainly was that. Despite what the Palestinian gossips must have said, she believed God would make her apparent 'unmarried pregnancy' into a glorious victory. That certainly happened.

But there are things we overlook about her relationship to Jesus, His fledgling church, and through history. She has been the object of veneration beyond compare by church members. Some Mary-critics say that veneration moved into adoration, superseding God, boarding on idolatry. This was a prevalent belief about Catholics during the Protestant Reformation and after. In history, this preoccupation, seeming or otherwise, with Mary is sometimes called "the Mary-Myth." Of course, many Protestants, including Martin Luther himself, and especially the Anglican Church, have strong devotion to Mary.

Catholics today are finding that Mary is perhaps the Catholic Church's greatest asset in ecumenical areas. Yes, that's true, as surprising as it may sound!

"The Mary of faith, of discipleship, is very appealing to Protestants who are seeking to relate to Christ in a human way," said the late

Bishop Joseph McKinney of Grand Rapids. "That is her true role," the bishop said, and "not as the fourth person of the Blessed Trinity, where some Catholics have mistakenly placed her."[375]

Nowhere else is there a person who so unflinchingly believed in Jesus as Savior and as God. Nowhere else is there a person in Scripture of such faith. The prime example of Mary and Jesus' relationship and her faith is the story of the Wedding Feast at Cana. (John 2: 1-12) She tells Jesus that the couple, their friends, relatives or neighbors, have run out of wine and Mary infers they will be embarrassed to continue the party 'empty-handed.' He replies in effect, "So what? That's not my problem." ("Woman, what do I have to do with you? My hour has not yet come." (Verses 4-5). "Woman, why turn to me?" (*Jerusalem Bible*). What would you have me do, woman?" (*Confraternity*).

The Confraternity Edition has an interesting footnote on that statement. Literally, it means, "What's that to you and me?" and was an expression which could vary in meaning with its context and with the speaker's tone of voice.[376]

It occurs several times in the Old and New Testaments, practically always implying dissent. Though there may be some disagreement in it even here, the circumstances show that it was not a rebuke. 'Woman' was an honorable address in the language spoken by Jesus and Mary. "My hour' could be said of any critical period of one's life. Here it is used of the opening of Christ's public ministry, or that of the ministry as a whole.

"The hour" pertained to the Father's domain, according to Fr. Brown's commentary on the passage.[377]

Mary knows that Jesus' time of miracles hasn't begun yet. She's not pressuring Him to do something against His will. But she also knows that He has the power to correct any situation, to do something about anything and everything. Scripture scholars believe Jesus'

---

[375] McKinney spoke at the Ecumenism Workshop of the Eastern Regional Conference on the Catholic Charismatic Renewal, held in New York City, 1979, which I covered as a reporter. He was an auxiliary bishop of Grand Rapids for many years. McKinney died in 2010.

[376] *Confraternity,* (NT), 130, Footnote #24.

[377] Brown, *"Women in the Fourth Gospel,"* 121, Footnote #25.

retort to Mary agrees with the Synoptic tradition that "Mary had no role in the ministry as Jesus' physical mother." The Jesus who asked His disciples not to give any priority to family, (Mark 10: 29-30; Matt. 10:37; Luke 14:26) was not Himself going to give priority to family.[378]

Brown explained Jesus' response makes the story very hard to understand. Apparently, it is a refusal, and yet, Mary goes ahead as though it was not a refusal, and Jesus does what she requested.[379] Perhaps Jesus answered her request for one simple reason: Mary's faith. Whatever the reason, she turns to the waiters and says, "Do whatever He tells you." There is no doubt. She does not say "Well, He may help, but maybe you'd better go to the store just in case."

Do many of us have faith like Mary's? Do we do "whatever He tells us?" Do we believe Jesus will act in our behalf even when it appears the answer to our prayer-request is no?

Obviously, Mary is one of Jesus' disciples. She is mentioned among the women who traveled with Him, the women kneeling at the foot of the cross, and among those who received the Holy Spirit on Pentecost. Brown comments that being a disciple, that is hearers of the Word of God, do not replace Jesus' mother and brothers as His true family—but because Mary and other relatives hear the Word of God and do it, they are part of the true family of disciples.[380]

This is also John's understanding of the role of Jesus' mother in relation to discipleship. At the Foot of the Cross (John 10:25-27), there are brought together the two great symbolic figures of the Fourth Gospel whose personal names are never used by the Evangelist: the mother of Jesus and the disciple whom Jesus loved. Both were historic personages, but they are not named by John, since their primary (not sole) importance is in their symbolism for discipleship rather than in their historical careers. Fr. Brown explains:

---

[378] Ibid., 121.
[379] Ibid., 120.
[380] Ibid., 121.

As in the Cana story, (especially 2:4), the mother of Jesus was denied involvement as his physical mother in favor of the timetable of the 'hour,' dictated by Jesus' Father, but now that the hour has come for Jesus to pass from this world to the Father (13:1), Jesus will grant her a role that will involve her, not as His mother, but as the mother of the Beloved Disciple. By stressing not only that His mother has become the mother of the Beloved Disciple, but also that this Disciple has become her son, the Johannine Jesus is logically claiming the Disciple as His true brother . . . . A woman and a man stood at the foot of the cross as models for Jesus' 'own' his true family of disciples.[381]

Mary has not become "simply a disciple among many," Brown noted. "She has eminence as the mother of the ideal Disciple. John treats the physical brothers (7:5) as nonbelievers and so he chooses to deal with the brotherhood of the Beloved Disciple, who is not a physical relative of Jesus."[382] Mary participated fully in the life of the new church. According to the thinking of that time, she was actually one of the "priesthood of all believers," or those who offered their lives to make God known to others.

The use of the word priesthood in the early centuries of Christianity referred to the "priesthood of all believers," and that included women, and, as such, Mary was the "greatest of priests," Brown said.[383] Brown is a Sulpician priest and renowned Scripture scholar and spoke as the guest homilist at the 50th anniversary Mass in late 1979, commemorating the founding of St. Mary's Seminary, Roland Park, Maryland. He told the hundreds of priests and bishops, his fellow alumni of the seminary and their clerical colleagues, there are actually three types of priesthood: the priesthood of Christ, the priesthood of all believers, and the priesthood of offering sacrifice.

---

[381] Ibid., 122-123.
[382] Ibid., 122, Footnote #28.
[383] Barbara O'Reilly, "Mary: 'Greatest of Priests,' Scripture Scholar Declares." Religious News Service, Section II, Oct. 8, 1979, 9.

"The notion of Mary as priest has a strong Biblical foundation because every Christian is a priest and she is the first among Christians," he said.[384] "In terms of the priesthood of all believers, Mary, the mother of Christ, is the greatest of priests. She stands above the disciples, the saints, the theologians, and the popes because she heard the word of God and kept it. 'Be it done unto me according to Thy Will,'" Brown explained.[385]

The priesthood, as it is known today, had its basis in the Old Testament, he said, and not the New Testament. It is modeled on those set aside to sacrifice in the name of the people. It was several hundred years after the death of Christ that the term 'priest' was applied to the ordained priesthood of the Eucharist. [386] Today, when we mention priesthood, Brown noted, no one thinks of the priesthood of Christ—which is unique and sovereign and cannot be shared by anyone—or of the priesthood of all believers. Vatican II revived the priesthood of all believers concept when it reaffirmed that every Christian living a life dedicated to Christ is a minister in priestly service, Brown said.[387]

"It would be a struggle for ordained priests to come to grips with the priesthood of the laity in coming years." He stressed that everyone baptized in Christ "is a member of the royal priesthood of God," but urged the clergy not to be fearful of losing the distinct nature of the ordained priesthood.[388]

The priesthood of Christ was one of sacrifice and the priesthood of all believers is one based on service, grounded in obedience, and exemplified by Mary. Brown suggested the ordained priests draw upon these the *charisms* of the other two priesthoods: sacrifice and service, and prioritize them to face the challenges of the years ahead. "The struggle over who should be ordained will not matter," Brown said, "until we understand this sense of service."[389]

---

[384]   Ibid.
[385]   Ibid.
[386]   Ibid.
[387]   Ibid.
[388]   As quoted in Ibid.
[389]   Ibid.

Mary's priesthood started at the foot of the cross. Her ministry of love and care goes beyond the Beloved Disciple and extends to all the followers of Christ. McGrath said, "The virtual exclusion of the Jewish woman from the covenanted and cultic life of the *q'ahal* (the ecclesia, the church) seems here to be formally brought to an end. Mary is given an official place in ministering to all mankind of the redemption accomplished on the cross. Is it too much to see here the full integration of all women into the Church of the New Covenant?"[390]

Catholic Madonna was rejected through, "The Mary Myth."

---

[390]   McGrath, 36.

It is interesting that Protestantism readily accepted the principle of the priesthood of all believers,[391] but virtually rejected Mary. "Hating what they called Mariolatry, the Reformers substituted for it an intense Bibliolatry which, instead of elevating, depressed the status of women, McGrath stated."[392]

"Not only did the Reformation end the honoring of Mary (although Luther himself kept a real devotion to Our Lady) . . . it also tended to cut women off from financial independence," she added.[393] "The reformers narrowed the sphere of woman exclusively to the home. It was the Reformed Churches which introduced the vow of obedience of wife to husband into the marriage service."[394]

Luther, a former Catholic priest, was strongly influenced by Paul and Aquinas in his view of sex. "He called women 'priests of the Evil One,' who could have nothing to do with 'Divine Service, the priestly office, or God's Word.' Instead they were to remain at home, sit still, keep house, and bear and bring up children,'" McGrath said.[395]

McGrath also wrote, "The Puritan groups within the Anglican Church opposed the Prayer Book because it said, with Luther, that women might baptize in case of necessity." "This, they declared in the tradition of female uncleanness, was a 'prophanation of His Holy Sacrament not to be endured.'"[396]

We hear a lot in America about the "Protestant Work Ethic," and how it is the resounding base on which our economy functions. The work ethic, or effort, demands that we must see and measure success. It's hard to get contemplative, that is, non-productive work-wise, in this society. Dr. Anthony Padovano, during a lecture on prayer, explained that is one of the reasons Americans have difficulty, and edginess, with silence. "Our lives are determined by our social

---

[391]   McGrath., 93

[392]   Ibid.

[393]   Ibid., 93.

[394]   Ibid., 93-4.

[395]   Ibid., 94.

[396]   The teaching today is that any baptized Christian may baptize another in an emergency. Catholics do it; nurses in premature babies units at hospitals do it at the request of parents when the infant is dying, and so on.

usefulness; if we are unemployed, we feel we are no one, with no worth," Padavano said.

In my opinion, 'The Work Ethic' as far as women are concerned, meant staying at home, "not working" as most adults do. It is that concept that women need to change. Of course, raising a family and caring for a home is work but if it's not paid employment the world tells us, "It doesn't count unless you're paid." In other words, women seek a cyclic reversion to the yes, more 'traditional' method, where the women worked equally with men, contributed to their society in a significant manner, and still parented children.

Perhaps one of the reasons Protestantism rejected Mary so dogmatically was the fear of the Pagan myths of female goddesses reappearing. In some ways these pagan myths of the mother goddess was partially absorbed by the Christian Mary, the mother of God. Catholic Mariology, according to Fr. Tavard, is based on the fact that our traditional presentation of God failed to reveal the feminine dimension of the divinity. Instead, this was communicated to us through the embodiment of it in Mary the Virgin.[397] "The Central problem of recent Catholic tradition in this area," Tavard said, "is namely its schizophrenia: contradictory streams of thought to see woman as weak and as a symbol of temptation and to idealize her as a symbol of transient goodness."[398]

Tavard explained, "Encomiums of the feminine ideal and praises of the Virgin Mary notwithstanding, the position of woman in the Catholic Church reflects the idea of her debility rather than any other of the elements of the total Catholic tradition."[399]

Mary is both counterpart and daughter to Eve, Tavard noted. Eve is the initiator of the Fall and Mary, who believes first, is the instrument of the Incarnation.[400] Similarly, Tavard believes, it is no accident that Mary Magdalene is the first witness of the Resurrection. He said it was "providential" since a woman was the one "having fallen first,"

---

[397] Tavard, *Women in Christian Tradition*, 146.
[398] Tavard, *WCT.*, 149.
[399] Ibid.
[400] Ibid., 53.

at least according to "Romano's First Hymn on the Resurrection."[401] Tavard said, "Within the renewed order of the universe, according to the economy of salvation, woman is first in faith and highest in the hierarchy of the restored image of God."[402]

In Catholic thinking, "Mary is confirmed as the model of women—both in terms of servanthood and in terms of the ideal. She is both the handmaid of the Lord and the feminine sign in Heaven. The two aspects of womanhood—service and bringing to perfection—are now joined inseparably," Tavard said.[403]

In the early Protestant writings, Tavard said, Luther treats woman as a sex object. To Luther, woman has been provided as a legal outlet of sexual desire in the male, to provide him with a remedy against sexual sins.[404] Similarly, marriage was not originally listed among the Reformation sacraments, because according to Luther, only those which directly express justification are sacramental.[405] "This effectively removed marriage from the realm of the sacred and placed it among secular realities," Tavard said.[406]

Calvin disagrees with Luther's interpretation and says the woman was not created just to sleep with the man but was given as his companion. "Mankind, which was like a partly built edifice, has been perfected and finished in the person of the woman. Adam saw himself complete in his wife (from Commentary on Genesis, pp 55, 60) . . . Then mankind could not subsist without woman," Calvin said, as quoted by Tavard.[407]

Since "sex object" was the label for any woman, it's no wonder Mother Mary was denigrated—she who had been made the paradigm for womanhood. Theologian Elizabeth Schussler Fiorenza explained this dichotomy:

---

[401] As quoted in Ibid.

[402] Ibid., 153.

[403] Ibid., 170.

[404] Ibid., 172.

[405] Ibid., 175.

[406] Ibid.

[407] Ibid., 176.

From the outset it can be questioned whether the myth (of Mary) can give to women a new vision of equality and wholeness, since the myth almost never functioned as symbol or justification of women's equality and leadership in the church and society, even though the myth contains elements which could have done so. As the 'queen of heaven' and the 'mother of God,' Mary clearly resembles and integrates aspects of the ancient goddess mythologies, e.g. Isis or the Magna Mater. Therefore, the myth has the tendency to portray Mary as divine and to place her on the equal level with God and Christ . . . Epiphasius, Bishop of Salamis (in the early church) makes a very clear distinction between worship of God and Christ and veneration of Mary. Through the centuries, church teachers maintained this distinction, but popular piety did not quite understand it. The countless legends and devotions to Mary prove that people preferred to go to her instead of going to a majestic-authoritarian God.[408]

The Mary-Myth is still with us. It affected the lives of many people, but it never had an impact upon Church structures and power relationships, Theologian Fiorenza said.[409] On the whole, "The Mary-Myth had its roots and development in a male, clerical and ascetic culture and theology. It has very little to do with the historical woman, Mary of Nazareth," Fiorenza noted.[410] She explained further:

While other parts of the Mary-myth, such as her bodily assumption into Heaven, or the doctrine of her Immaculate Conception, were integrated and accepted very slowly into the Christian church. Throughout it all, Mary was considered the Virgin-Mother. In contrast to Eve, she was and remained, the 'pure virgin' who was conceived free from original sin and

---

[408] Elizabeth Schussler Fiorenza, "Feminist Theology," *Women: New Dimensions*, 44-45

[409] Ibid., 45.

[410] Ibid.

remained free from sin for all her life. She remained virgin, before, during and after the birth of Jesus. This myth of Mary sanctions a double dichotomy in the self-understanding of Catholic women.

First, the myth of the virginal mother justifies the body-soul dualism of the Christian tradition. Whereas man, in this tradition, is defined by his mind and reason, woman is defined by her 'nature,' i.e. by her physical capacity to bear children. Motherhood, therefore, is the vocation of every woman regardless of whether or not she is a natural mother. However, since in the ascetic Christian tradition, nature and body have to be subordinated to the mind and spirit, woman because of her nature has to be subordinated to man.

Second, the myth of the virginal mother functions to separate the women within the Roman Catholic community from one another. Since historically women cannot be both virgin and mother, she has either to fulfill her nature in motherhood or to transcend her nature in virginity. Consequently, Roman Catholic traditional theology has a place for women only as mother or nun. The Mary-Myth thus sanctions a deep psychological and institutional split between Catholic women. Since the genuine Christian and human vocation is to transcend one's nature and biology, the true Christian ideal is represented by the actual biological virgin who lives in concrete ecclesial obedience. Only among those who represent the humble hand-maiden and ever-virgin Mary is true Christian sisterhood possible. Distinct from women who are still bound to earthly desires and earthly dependencies, the biological virgins in the church, bound to ecclesial authority, are the true 'religious women.'[411]

---

[411]   Ibid., 47-49.

Fiorenza further explains that traditional Mariology demonstrates, "The myth of a woman, preached to women by men, can serve to deter women from becoming fully independent and whole human persons."[412]

> As long as we do not know the relationship between the myth and its societal functions, we cannot expect, for example, that the myth of the mother goddess in itself will be liberating for women. The myth of the 'mother god' would define, as the myth of the 'mother of God' did, woman primarily in her capacity for motherhood and thus reduce women's possibilities to her biological capacity for motherhood . . . . The absolute precondition of new liberating Christian myths and images is not only the change of individual consciousness but that of societal, ecclesial and theological structures as well.[413]

Some Catholics may have distorted Mary's place by seemingly ignoring God, especially when they petitioned heaven with prayer requests. But the majority of Catholics, I believe, realized that Mary was an intercessor with us to Jesus. In the Catholic tradition, the body of believers includes the Communion of Saints, those already with Christ in their Heavenly reward. If they are alive in Christ, what is the difference between praying with them, or praying with your next door neighbor? Some Fundamentalists scoff at "the Catholic saints" but fervently practice the Scriptural command, "Where two agree on any one thing, it shall be done for them" (Matt. 18:19). So, they ardently pray and agree with their neighbor for God's intervention. I see it as the same thing as praying to Mary or a saint for his or her intercession with Jesus. He is the one who answers prayer.

There is an old legend that praying to Mary for her intercession was important because Jesus could not deny her anything, after all, look at Cana. Is that one of those legends based on fact? Is it

---

[412] Ibid.
[413] Fiorenza., 40.

true? Maybe, maybe not. Perhaps, between the lines is the unspoken truth: that if He cannot deny her, it's because she was the "greatest priest," the greatest of all believers, and a member of His family of disciples.

CHAPTER 19

Medieval Mystics—Bridging the Gap

Medieval mystics were the spiritual bridge between the Dark Ages, through medieval and industrial Europe, ultimately to modernity. They included both men and women, Christian leaders of their eras, some now recognized as canonized saints. The mystics kept the concept of a "living God' alive amid rampant church scandals, widespread illiteracy, entrenched misogamy, and all sorts of inroads of ancient paganism and heresies contemporary to those times.

This is particularly true of the many women mystics, whose writings have grown in popularity in the late 20th and early 21st centuries. This current popularity is two-fold. 1) The mystics often referred to God, Jesus and the Holy Spirit, in consoling, feminine language and images; and 2) the mystics recognized the feminine aspect of the godhead as something normative.

God is also mother, the mystics said. They saw God as nurturer and lover, as parent, as non-frightening, not as mean, stern disciplinarian, not the shrill scold voice of the church, as many people perceive today. The most popular of these mystics nowadays is Julian of Norwich, England.

In his regular column run by Catholic News Service in many diocesan newspapers, Fr. John Catoir wrote, "Blessed Julian of Norwich compared the love of Jesus to a mother's love. A mother's love, in ordinary circumstances, is completely dependable because it is the truest form of self-giving on earth."[414] Catoir continued, "Jesus gives us his love in a similar way. Blessed Julian refers to the divine presence as 'Mother God': 'The Lord carried us lovingly within himself (a reference to the womb) when he suffered the sharpest thorns and the most daunting agony.'"[415]

Referring in that particular column to the pain of the recent sex scandals in the church, Catoir called for people to put their faith in God, not humans. Fr. Catoir used Julian's analogy in his own way. "Our Mother God is unifying the Church at this very moment in a way long overdue."[416]

Then and now, spiritual insights had to be inspiration from the Holy Spirit—because it certainly didn't stem from medieval culture nor from church tradition.

The mystics, with their intense personalized spirituality, were the unsung heroes and heroines of those largely undereducated periods. They bridged the gap between the darkness of the Dark Ages, to and through the gradual enlightenment of the Renaissance—even with its Protestant Reformations—and onward.

The mystics have been studied extensively by scholars but much of their work—and even their names with a few major exceptions—are not well known to everyday Catholics or other Christians. Those better known include three men—Meister Eckhart, St. John of the Cross, Thomas a Kempis—and, two women, modern day Doctors of the Church, Saints Teresa of Avila and Catherine of Siena.[417]

Called Dame or Blessed, Julian of Norwich, lived from Nov. 8, 1342 to approximately 1416, around the time of Chaucer. Her real name is uncertain—she is called Julian because she was an

---

[414] Fr. John Catoir, Catholic News Service, "Coping with the Church's Human Element," *The Monitor,* Trenton, NJ, July 4, 2002, 7.

[415] Ibid.

[416] Ibid.

[417] There were no women doctors of the church until Pope Paul VI named Catherine and Teresa as doctors in 1970. Therese of Liseux was added as the third female Doctor in 1977. Hildegard of Bingen will be No. 4. Much literature about each remarkable woman is available, including on-line, so this work is not the arena to detail their individual achievements.

'anchoress" in the church of St. Julian in Norwich, England.[418] She was probably a Benedictine nun from the house of Carrow near Norwich.[419]

Her major work, *Sixteen Revelations of Divine Love*, written around 1393, is based on her own visions of Jesus during a serious illness 20 years earlier in 1373. Significantly, it is believed to be the first book written by a woman in the English language.[420]

From that standpoint alone, you'd think she would be included, or at least mentioned, in some collegiate English literature courses; however, she probably never has been. She certainly wasn't mentioned when I was in school. Like the female mystics themselves, their works are often overlooked.[421]

The purpose of the anchorite (male) or anchoress (female) was to withdraw from secular society to lead an intensely prayer-oriented, ascetic, and Eucharistic-centered life.[422] And anchoritic life was one of the earliest forms of Christian monastic living; however, it is distinct from that of a religious hermit.

Widespread in the early and high Middle Ages, the practice was especially popular in England.[423] Many of these ancient anchorite spots can be still seen in Western European churches.

An anchorite or anchoress literally lived in a side room, virtually a cell, as part of or built adjoining the church. The 'anchorhold,' or cell, was deliberately walled in. Once the inhabitant was inside, the bishop would brick up the entrance in a special ceremony.[424] For this kind of isolation and piety, it seems to be unambiguous, that being an anchorite or anchoress had to be a divine calling. Claustrophobics need not apply! The anchorite or anchoress frequently served as a

---

[418] Wikipedia, "Julian of Norwich," accessed on-line 2010.

[419] Catholic Encyclopedia, on-line, "Julian of Norwich."

[420] Wikipedia, a quoted in: "Julian of Norwich," *Showings on-line*. Paulist Press. 1978.

[421] I attended a Catholic college and never heard Julian mentioned in History, Theology or English literature courses.

[422] Wikipedia, "Anchorite."

[423] Ibid.

[424] Ibid.

spiritual advisor or spiritual director to both clergy and everyday folk.

Food and water was brought from the outside and waste handled through a chamber pot. Hearing Mass and receiving Holy Communion was possible through a small, shuttered window, called the "squint" in the common wall facing the sanctuary. There was also a window on the opposite wall—the only outlet to the world—through which the "anchor" could see the daylight and talk with people[425] (or hear village gossip!).

Today, the Catholic Church continues the anchorite tradition, though infrequently, as one of its "Other Forms of Consecrated Life," (Code of Canon Law 1983, Canon 603, as revised by Pope John Paul II in 1983). One of these was a woman I met and interviewed in the 1990's, Florence Patricia Hughes. She gave me permission to write about her unique role.

Florence was from St. Elizabeth Anne Seton parish, Whiting, NJ, and was an anchoress in the Diocese of Trenton, NJ. An older woman at the time, she was a widow, mother and grandmother. Always an active Catholic, she had been a Third Order Carmelite most of her adult life. She lived at home, supported by her and her late husband's pensions, and her Social Security. She was not supported by the diocese, or by her parish, and did not live in community.

She had a strict study, prayer and intercessory prayer schedule, including reciting the Clerical Office. Florence attended Mass daily, driven by friends, usually Bob and Blanche Weber, also of Whiting. She had a priest spiritual director with whom she spoke regularly. Often she taught religious programs or Bible studies in the parish or to Catholic women's groups, such as the NJ based Catholic Women of Zion, which celebrated its 20th anniversary in 2009. CWOZ is similar to the non-denominational and international Women's Aglow Fellowship in that there is prayer and praise, a talk by a featured speaker, healing prayer and it's usually held during a meal at a local restaurant. However, CWOZ centers its ministry around the Eucharist,

---

[425] Ibid.

and Mass is celebrated by a visiting priest. It's an outreach to women for whatever she needs spiritually.[426] Similar groups for women exist in other states, one for instance is in the Maryland/ Washington, D.C., area, since women leaders recognized how important it is for spiritual nurturing for today's women, and apart from the children or spouse.

Florence had a special ministry to pray for priests and for women, which she did. She was a happy person, wore regular clothes outside, although at home she wore a sort of uniform, loved reading and enjoyed visiting with friends, family and grandchildren. She died in Sept. 2003.

Florence was unique in her calling in the diocese. She had to receive special permission from the bishop to embark on such a life, which was solitary, prayerful and basically impoverished. She said everything she had done in her working years and raising a family had prepared her for her ministry, which was primarily one of prayer and teaching.

Back to the mystics. Julian of Norwich's name increasingly is well-known among women today because she called God (1) mother; and said (2) *she* is loving, wise, merciful and benevolent. The period in which Julian lived was one of turmoil and constant wars and revolts. People lived hand to mouth—of course, there was no inside plumbing nor electricity—and there were only primitive methods of cooking and transportation. Everything was difficult. Most people could not read or write; to tell Biblical stories, stained glass windows were used to depict aspects of Christianity.

Julian's spirituality was optimistic. She spoke of God in a personal way. Julian said that God was full of joy and compassion; she said, "*She* is a God of love, who wants to save everyone." Both of those concepts were largely unknown in her time, especially since the people's daily lives were so harsh.

In one of her writings Julian said Jesus was truly Mother, who feeds us with the Eucharist: "*As truly as God is our Father, so truly is*

---

[426] For information about CWOZ, call founder Mary Ann Collett at 732-295-5913, ext. 334.

God our Mother . . . . But our true Mother Jesus, He alone bears us for joy and for endless life . . . . The mother can give her child to suck of her milk but our precious Mother Jesus can feed us with himself and does, most courteously and tenderly with the Blessed Sacrament, which is the precious food of true life."[427]

She apparently asked God why suffering was necessary. God's answered in her 13th vision (out of 20)[428] "that it was necessary"—but that "all would be well, all manner of things shall be well." That became her "signature statement" and her most famous quoted remark.[429] For Julian, suffering was not a punishment which God inflicted, the common understanding of the time, but was a part of life. No wonder she's a favorite today—her message is needed now more than ever!

Julian is not a canonized saint in the Roman Catholic Church but is classified as Blessed—that is, on the road to sainthood. She is venerated as a spiritual authority in the Roman Catholic Church, as well as in the Anglican Communion and the Evangelical Lutheran Church in America. Her feast is celebrated on May 13 in the Catholic Church and May 8 in Anglican and Lutheran churches.[430] There is even a church hymn, *Julian of Norwich,* incorporating her theology. It was written by an English man, Sydney Carter, and is sung in worship services today.

Loud are the bells of Norwich and the people come and go. Here by the tower of Julian, I tell them what I know. (The chorus)

Ring out, bells of Norwich, and let winter come and go All shall be well again, I know. (Chorus)

---

[427] As quoted in, Joan Ohanneson, *Women Survivors in the Church* (Minneapolis, MN: Winston Press, 1980), 12 (see Chapter 1, Footnote 21), from *Showings*, trans. Edmund Colledge and James Walsh (New York: Paulist Press, 1978), 296-99.
[428] *The Life of the Soul, the Wisdom of Julian of Norwich,* Edmund Colledge, OS.A., and James Walsh, S.J., translators, (Mahwah, NJ: Paulist Press, 1966), 8, 22.
[429] Wikipedia. "Julian of Norwich."
[430] Ibid.

Love, like the yellow daffodil, is coming through the snow.
Ring for the yellow daffodil and tell them what I know.
(Chorus)

Ring for the yellow daffodil, the flower in the snow. Ring for
the yellow daffodil and tell them what I know. (Chorus)

All shall be well, I'm telling you, let the winter come and go;
all shall be well again, I know. (Chorus)[431]

Some of the other well known women mystics of the Middle Ages are Birgitta of Sweden; Hildegard of Bingen; Mechthild of Magdeburg; Margery Kemp, and Catherine of Genoa.[432] There are numerous others. These were wise women, way ahead of their time in spiritual revelations and a personal relationship with the God-head. This is especially relevant in a time when most people, particularly women, were uneducated and ostracized, and when men dominated the world and the church. Women then—in the deep mid ages—that is 1500 or more years after Jesus' life on earth—still were believed to be uneducable. The only exception might be daughters of royalty or the very rich and that was only because they were privileged, not because the tutors thought them smart enough.

Like the Mystics' forerunners—the women of Scripture in Jesus' ministry—the Holy Spirit finds individuals, some of whom happen to be women, even in the darkest times, who can relay the divine message even when no one else even gets it!

Current singer/songwriter Kathryn Christian of Williamsburg, MI., used many of these women's works and prayers, as well as Scriptural references, in her music. In a phone interview, Ms. Christian said she was influenced by her friend, Christian writer Edwina Gately, and reading the works of the Mystics themselves.

---

[431] Sydney Carter: "Julian of Norwich," accessed on-line, 2009.
[432] Sydney Carter: "Meister Eckhart and Medieval Mysticism: Other Medieval Mystics Texts." Accessed on-line 2009.

For instance in her CD *Ascension,* released in 1998, in the song/ hymn *Antiphon of Divine Wisdom,* Ms. Christian uses the poetry of Hildegard of Bingen and King Solomon's words from the Bible's Book of Wisdom. The CD's cover notes say the Greek translation for the wisdom of God in scripture is *Sophia,* a feminine word; thus the use of the word Sophia "describes an attribute of God rather than a separate identity." Her song includes the visual images of the Holy Spirit as a dove (from Genesis, the *ruach* (breath, spirit) of God hovering over the water), and from Jesus' Baptism when the Holy Spirit descended as a dove over Jesus. The following words were copied from her songs.[433]

> Sophia—you of the whirling wings, Sophia—circling, encompassing, radiance of God. (The Chorus)

> You quicken the world in your clasp, one waits in heaven, the other sweeps the earth and your love flies all around us.

> All wise, good and clear, steadfast, pure and holy, overseeing love, more lovely than the sun.

> Sophia—let all the world give praise to you, Sophia, circling, encompassing, radiance of God.

In her song "Mechthild's Prayer," Ms. Christian uses the poetry of Mechthild of Magdeburg, sung as a duet between the person and God, with a male friend singing God's part.

> (Person): *Lord, you are my lover, and my longing, my flowing steam, my sun.*

> (God): *It is my nature that makes me love you intensely, for I am Love itself.*

---

[433] Kathryn Christian, *Ascension,* words used with permission.

(Person): *It is my longing that makes me love you intensely, for I yearn to be loved from the heart.*

(God): *It is my eternity,that makes me love you long, for I have no end.*

Another selection on her CD is a famous prayer by Teresa of Avila, *"Let Nothing Disturb You."* In other songs, Kathryn Christian uses many Scriptural verses, which are outright descriptions of God as female. These include her song "Mechthild's Prayer" using the poetry of Mechthild of Magdeburg, who calls God lover. In another she uses the analogy of Mother Zion comparing God's love to a nursling's love for her charges, and so on. Her subsequent CDs carry on the same theme.[434]

We admit today that the Catholic Church in the Middle Ages was very bureaucratic, as well as dogmatic, being the only vehicle for the transmittal of Christian belief. The Protestant Reformation officially started in 1517 when Martin Luther hung his "95 Treatise" on the doors of the Wittenberg Cathedral. It was a list of things to change and correct within the church. The Reformation started as a protest, a methodology, to reform the church from abuses, not to break away from it. We know today, that as the Reformation unfolded, it was painful to the Church itself and to believers on both sides—how God must cringe when His people kill and torment one another in His name.

Historically, we also recognize today that some restructuring done in the name of alleged reform of the church was in fact political upheaval and was politically, not religiously, motivated. Not all, of course. Today's important continuing movement for ecumenism works in mainstream Christian churches to rectify and consolidate wherever the differing belief systems permit. As the roles of women in all Christian churches change (or don't), it

---

[434] I first heard cuts from "Ascension" as a reporter covering a conference in which the speaker, Ms. Gately, used the cuts to reinforce her message. Everyone attending was moved by them.

naturally has an effect on other congregations. The impact of the Medieval Mystics on current church ways of relating to God is profound; it augments current spirituality. The Mystics' words are wisdom for the ages.

CHAPTER 20

The Real Truth Beyond
The Da Vinci Code

The novel by Dan Brown, *The Da Vinci Code,* published in 2003, was an international bestseller. It was a phenomenon in the book publishing industry, selling more than 40 million copies. An exciting mystery, it was a "good read," as they say in publishing circles. As a mystery, it was challenging and compelling. It never claimed to be authentic historically, although it contained some accurate facts. It also contained many fabrications, untruths and things which are factually in dispute. It was a novel, fiction.

Many books and articles were written subsequently to refute the anti-Catholic allegations and some deliberate biases in *The Da Vinci Code.* These gave the Catholic version of the facts—that Jesus was celibate as His role as Savior mandated; that Mary of Magdala was his follower, a female disciple; that there is no historical evidence to document Brown's assertions that they married or were paramours. Numerous talks, seminars and workshops were held in the Catholic and other Christian churches throughout the world to inform the public that the book was fiction, its allegations false.

The book caused a furor with its main premises: 1) that Jesus and Mary Magdalene had a child; 2) that this fact was deliberately hidden by the Catholic Church to foster its own power base. A current very conservative group within the Catholic Church, *Opus Dei,* 3) was cited as the *raison d'être* to keep the above alleged "facts" under wraps and from becoming known.

In the book, *Opus Dei* was averred as the modern age descendant of the Priority of Sion and the Knights Templar. Both organizations, in fact in church history, were secretive, militaristic, misogamist, and in search of the always elusive—and disputably existing—Holy Grail.[435]

Mary Magdalene, the book stated, as the alleged recipient of Jesus' male human sperm, was the Holy Grail herself. Magdalene was thus a chalice-like receptacle, a take-off on one of Mother Mary's titles, Ark of the Covenant, for she who carried the Lord in pregnancy.

Neither does the book talk about marriage. It just infers there was a child. Marriage is something fervent Jews such as Jesus, would certainly have adhered to, if He had a personal intimate relationship. And He undisputedly was a practicing Jew—He went to Synagogue, to Temple in Jerusalem, followed the Jewish law, prayed several times a day, and wore the traditional prayer shawl. The only marriage ceremony recorded in the four Gospels is the one at Cana at the beginning of Jesus' ministry. He was an invited guest, not the groom. If He had married, can you imagine the gospel writers *never* mentioning it? They mention Peter's mother-in-law and Jesus' mother and cousins. They do mention Jesus had no home to call His own.

The gospels' first audiences were Jews. It seems inconceivable that Jesus' earliest disciples would not have known about it if such a marriage existed. And, besides, as stated before, Jesus was believed to have been an Essene, whose followers took a vow of celibacy.

To infer there was a child outside of marriage may be very celebrity avante-garde by Hollywood standards today, a la Brad Pitt and Angelina Jolie, and many other "stars," but it doesn't fit with Jesus' oft repeated admonition, "Go and sin no more." It just doesn't make sense.

---

[435] Opus Dei exists but it was not around for 2,000 years! It was founded in 1928, less than 100 years ago. It is known as very conservative, secretive, and apparently wealthy; its website denies all the allegations and negative characterizations in Brown's book. It says its members live and work in the secular world and are not self-flagellating monks, or ruthless priests, as depicted. Accessed on-line, 2010.

To intimate Jesus and Mary Magdalene had a sexual relationship, let alone a child, does not question Jesus' humanity, nor deny His Divinity, but, I believe, it denies His purpose as savior/redeemer. The 20th century healing minister, or "faith healer" as she was called in the media, Kathryn Kuhlman, used to say, "That Jesus was as human as if he had never been divine." He had a beard, male hormones, testosterone, a sex drive—and a unique ministry. He was warm and wonderful, perhaps right-brained, but I can't imagine that He would devote Himself to His purpose and, at the same time, to a private individual family. Who could say he or she wouldn't want to be Jesus' physical offspring?

His purpose, His "job" was Savior, to bring people back to God and save them from their sins. Along the way He established a community of believers, or church, to help individuals get to the goal of salvation. The term Christian was initially demeaning—to distinguish His followers from other Jews. Christianity, sometimes called "the New Judaism," was not well received by Jews: they thought it was heresy and cannibalistic! "Eat my flesh," and so forth. Jesus never ordained anyone, male nor female, and He surely didn't live in a Catholic parish. There was nothing like that in His time.

Yes, Jesus descended from the royal line of David; however, His parents were poor not aristocrats. Jesus was not the proclaimed, anointed High Priest of Israel, an inherited position; nor a high priest in any new religion—He was a practicing Jew. He said do the good things in life differently, with a different mental attitude from how you do it now. Do it not from fear of God's anger and retribution but because of His love. His teaching was rejected by many as being too radical.

However, *The Da Vinci Code* did introduce the historical figure of Mary Magdalene to the world and her prominence in Jesus' ministry, although for its own unsubstantiated reasons. Mary, foremost, was a disciple of Jesus, His follower, a believer in His salvific message. She was from a town called Magdala. Brown is correct in depicting the saga of Mary Magdalene—as a harlot and lost soul—as a propaganda device, initiated by a pope to discredit her reputation and foster his own agenda, that of getting sinners to repent, as we saw above. Brown is wrong about almost everything else about her. She is *documented* in Scripture as the first person Jesus spoke to after His resurrection—something *not even mentioned* in Brown's fantasy book.

She saw Jesus, spoke to him and told the male disciples that He indeed was raised—just as He said. It is for her witness, her evangelization, for which she was known throughout church history. In the Proper of the Mass she was called "the apostle to the apostles," and had a special celebratory feast day because of it. None of that is hinted at in the novel, either. After Easter, she is never mentioned again in the New Testament.

Was she at the Last Supper, their Passover Seder? That's what Brown alleges is what Leonardo Da Vinci recaptured in his masterful famous painting called *"The Last Supper."* It seems to depict Jesus and supposedly his 12 male closest cronies. Is the painted figure at Jesus' right really Mary Magdalene and not the Beloved disciple, John, as most people expect? The figure depicted may have feminine characteristics, as Brown avers, but so do many of Da Vinci's painted figures. They could be androgynous. Leonardo, according to Brown, was a known homosexual and it might have been his choice to paint people so as not to identify their sex. It's very possible and likely that women disciples, and other males disciples, plus the elite Twelve males, attended the dinner. Jesus had numerous disciples beyond the Twelve, and that included males and females, so it seems completely plausible. The possibility that there might have been others at the Last Supper beyond Jesus and the Twelve is another part of hidden history.

We just don't know one way or the other. We do know only three things about the actual dinner: Jesus washed the disciples' feet, they all ate the meal, and it's where Jesus instituted the Eucharist.

In my wildest dreams I can't imagine that this loving man would not include His mother and some of His most faithful followers and friends, who happened to be women, at this most important, profound moment in His public ministry before Calvary. I personally think many others were there, too. Probably what's depicted in Leonardo's painting was just his idea of the head table among several. There's no cell phone photo or CNN 24-hour news coverage, of course. The events which followed the dinner were very tumultuous, so people may not have been thinking at all about who were the dinner guests. Besides, John didn't write his gospel until approximately 85—90 A.D., a long time after the actual events at that Passover Seder.

Brown conjectured that Da Vinci depicted Mary Magdalene as sitting beside Jesus at the table, and not the disciple John, to foster the romantic plot in the novel. We don't know the table seating arrangement. If Mary replaced John, where is John in the painting? Nowhere. If both were there, that makes 14, which also isn't depicted in the painting! I believe Brown improvised the "whole megillah" (a fine Jewish word) of Magdalene at the table next to Jesus.[436] And some people actually thought the novel was true! Besides, these arguments are specious—neither Brown nor Leonardo were there, either. I'm sure God sat chuckling over this latest foible of the human family. Imagination is one of God's great gifts to humans.

---

[436] Megillah is a Hebrew word which means scroll. The entire book of Esther is read at Purim services and the word took on a new, slang meaning in the 1950's when Jewish comedians on TV started using it—to mean an overly extended explanation. As an Irish-American child growing up in New York City, when I heard it as a child, I thought it was really a Gaelic word, "Mc-gilla!" Definition accessed on-line, 2010.

CHAPTER 21

Veil or no Veil!—The Truth Behind Headship and Submission

Through the ages the Catholic Church has taught that taking one sentence from Scripture and interpreting it literally is erroneous. Yet, for hundreds of years, the Catholic Church literally enforced one Scriptural directive—women should have their heads covered in church—and Catholic women wore hats into church buildings and for services. Episcopal women did also. And other Christians, too.

The whole thing never made much sense to women of recent times. It certainly didn't to me. As much as many people dislike wearing a hat (at any time, not just in church, except maybe in frigid weather) or a chapel veil or mantilla, dutifully before Vatican II, we wore them. Some women still choose to do so in the 21ˢᵗ Century.[437]

Growing up, I don't even remember being told why this was required. It just was. Having your head 'covered' was what it was all about. It was interpreted literally. The 'covering" figuratively is the

---

[437] One woman, aged in her 70's, always wore a hat even when she was a Eucharistic Minister because, when she was growing up, her dad was so strict that it became a habit. Besides she liked hats and had a large collection of them. A lot of people from the parish complained and eventually she was asked by the clergy not to wear a hat! That's in the 21ˢᵗ century. In the 50's and 60's, I could never understand the significance of wearing a folded tissue, secured with a bobby pin—as many women did—to accommodate (not adhere) to the rule. I thought it was ridiculous looking and believed it was actually an aberration of the rule. These "skull tissues" certainly didn't cover anyone's head but did help the tissue manufacturer's bottom line!

integral concept in the theories of headship and submission, popular in Pentecostal churches and the Charismatic Renewals in mainline Christian churches, including the Catholic Church.

In post Vatican II days, the Catholic Church finally eliminated the hat-mandate, after recognizing it was just a residual from cultural traditions dating back to Biblical times. Church leaders realized any spiritual implications of the earlier tradition had dissipated.

Unlike the church's former hat mandate, headship and submission do not require a physical covering: that was the way it came to be interpreted. However, it does require a spiritual covering—literally by a man, your husband, father, or even a spiritual director for an unmarried woman. Headship refers to the person to whom the woman submits: "the head of the household;" submission refers to the deference she shows him and his opinions.

It stems from a time when men were educated and women were not, when women were believed to be inferior anyway. It ignores that some fathers are not college educated and their daughters may be; it ignores that some husbands and fathers are abusive. It ignores the well established fact that in many ethnic cultures, such as Italian, Jewish, Irish, Hispanic, and Black, the husband may be the head of the house, and is expected under our cultural conditioning, to support the family but *the mother* runs the household and the family. In many minority families today, it is well-known that there is no husband or father in the family at all.

It stems from the Jewish culture of the early Christian church that humans are under the authority of God and the female is under the authority of the male. Orthodox and traditional Jewish men, even today, wear head coverings all the time, to show they are under God's authority.

Proponents of headship and submission claim it is not a question of female inferiority or male superiority; they insist it is an issue of orderliness, particularly in the home. "There can't be two mayors in a town," one woman explained. "Someone has to take the final responsibility for decisions. And for our family, it works."

Submission is an attitude and not an action, explained Elizabeth Rice Handford, Iverna Tompkins and Gladys Hunt in their respective books about the topic.[438]

"When it's done out of love and not for lording it over another," a male coworker told me, "it can be very beautiful and positive in the relationship." He said he considers his spouse's opinion before making a decision and they discuss the issue. The whole thing is done out of love and not that he decided things arbitrarily, he explained.

Unfortunately, that hasn't been the experience of many women who have tried to practice headship and submission, when "lording it over them" was all they got. Additionally, in our society, the word submission has an "antagonistic" connotation. People have difficulty divorcing what is the usual definition and association of the word, when it is heard in a spiritual context. Our usual word association does not trigger the response: this has a different meaning here.

According to Father Joseph Lange, O.S.F.S., and Anthony Cushing in their book, *Called to Service,* in other cultures in the past, people did have a concrete loving experience through authority and submission but that is very rare in our democratic society. "When people hear the word 'submission' they immediately have a feeling of inferiority and subservience. The result is that the people who teach about female submission have to spend a lot of time trying to contradict the normal meaning of submissiveness as inferiority," they said.[439]

The principles of headship and submission are fervently practiced by some Christians. In varying degrees the practices are often found in fundamental-oriented Pentecostal churches. It is practiced in the Charismatic Renewal in major Christian denominations, including the Catholic Church, sometimes frequently, sometimes randomly.

---

[438] Iverna Tompkins *How to Be Happy in No Man's Land* (Plainfield, NJ: Logos International Fellowship, 1974); Elizabeth Rice Handford, *Me? Obey Him?* (Murfrusboro, TN: Sword of the Lord Publisher, 1972); and Gladys Hunt, *Ms. Means Myself* (Grand Rapids, MI: Zondervan Publishing House, 1972), 53.
[439] Joseph Lange, O.S.F.S., and Anthony Cushing, *Called to Service* (New York: Paulist Press, 1976), 164.

**Blissful weddings and romances may or
may not turn into blissful marriages.**

The basis of the practice of headship and submission are several
verses in Paul's Pastoral Epistles and their literal interpretation for
women. The whole topic, pro and con, about the practicality of
headship and submission for women today rests on the interpretation
of Paul's motives for these directives: whether they were practical
guidelines to accommodate the existing societal structure or are they
universal Christian principles?

Does wearing something on a woman's head really have anything
to do with spiritual principles? How did it evolve? How did a physical
covering become a symbol for spiritual covering on the Christian

woman? It is necessary today? Also, we must ask, does headship and submission affect how we view women's role in the church? Does it follow the example of Jesus' revolutionary encounters with women as related above? Or is it, as some contend, a denial of Christian Baptism?

The evolvement of headship and submission into the religious life of the church was part cultural, part symbolic, part accommodation and part protective for the married woman believer. It is the symbolic influence that is most responsible for the spiritual implication of the head covering; however, its wearing was due almost solely to the cultural imperative.

In Paul's writing of the apostolic days of early church, we are given a mixed picture of women's role. The tension between the practical guidelines and the universal principle is very evident in Paul's teachings. There is contradiction. For instance, in one place he says women should not speak in church and in another he cites the masterful prophecy of Phillip's four daughters and suggests everyone should follow their example. He says women should not teach, and then compliments Priscilla's teaching and preaching. According to Lange,

> Paul's directives regarding women break down into three basic areas. The woman must be veiled (in church). She may not speak or teach (in Church). She must obey the man (always). The application of the Pauline directives in the parenthesis shows the inconsistent way in which they were interpreted. Paul's directives on "order in marriage" appear in parts of his letters known as "household codes." (Except in 1 Corinthians where Paul is responding to specific questions.)[440]

These verses are:
- Ask yourself if it is fitting for a woman to pray to God without a veil. (1 Cor. 11-13)

- Also, as in all the churches of the saints, women are to remain quiet at meetings since they have no permission to speak; they

---

[440] Lange, 161.

must keep in the background as the Law itself lays down. If they have any questions to ask, they should ask their husbands at home: it does not seem right for a woman to raise her voice at meetings. (1 Cor. 14: 34-35)

- During instruction, a woman should be quiet and respectful. I am not giving permission to a woman to teach or to tell a man what to do. A woman ought not to speak, because Adam was formed first and Eve afterward, and it was not Adam who was led astray, but the woman who was led astray and fell into sin. Nevertheless, she will be saved by childbearing, provided she lives a modest life and is constant in faith and love and holiness. (1 Tim. 2: 11-15)
- Give way to one another in obedience to Christ. Wives should regard their husbands as they regard the Lord, since as Christ is head of the Church and saves the whole body, so is a husband the head of his wife; and as the church submits to Christ, so should wives to their husbands, in everything. Husbands should love their wives just as Christ loved the Church and sacrificed himself for her to make her holy. (Eph. 5: 21-26)
- Wives give way (submit, KJV; be subject, NAS and Confraternity) to your husbands, as you should in the Lord. Husbands, love your wives and treat them with gentleness. (1 Cor. 3: 18-19)

And from Peter:

- In the same way, wives should be obedient to their husbands. (1 Pet. 3:1)
- In the same way, husbands must always treat their wives with consideration in their life together, respecting a woman as one who, though she may be the weaker partner, is equally an heir to the life of grace. (1 Pet. 3:7)

The *Jerusalem Bible* footnotes on 1 Cor. 11 are interesting. In verse 4, "If a man prays with his head covered it is a sign of disrespect to his head," the notation says that head refers to "his leader," a Greek pun.[441] "Disrespect to her head" in verse 5, refers to "her husband, who is her head; she is claiming equality."[442]

Regarding the woman claiming equality, in that society equality was an impossibility. The woman was considered as her husband's property. No way is property, a possession, equal or equivalent to its owner. The woman was not considered as a person but an object, a thing.

When Paul wrote the letter to the Corinthians in approximately 57 A.D., Christianity was just in its fledgling state. Its premises of equality in God's sight were not yet well-known, or perhaps not well-understood, since that premise was so contradictory to the societal acculturation. Besides, there were few Christian couples. So, in the thinking of that culture and society, a woman claiming equality with her husband was presumptuous.

Jesus' message—His life, words, miracles, and experiences with women—were in exact opposition to that cultural stigma. He came "to set the captives free." Unfortunately, the stigma against women was so deeply ingrained that even the minds of the Christian disciples were ruled by its prerogative of male superiority/female inferiority, and male authority/female submission.

These passages are interpreted literally only for women. References to the male obligation in the same verses generally are not even quoted, let alone taken literally. Companion verses giving directives for all society and particularly the Christian community, were usually overlooked, or completely ignored. Suggestions for service and community life are not followed explicitly. There are warnings against wearing expensive clothes; dressing up to go out; and the use of gold, jewelry and braiding of hair. Such ornamentation was considered offensive. "Do not dress up for show" says 1 Pet. 3:3.

One very obvious exception to these directives for Christians is the wearing of jewelry, now worn extensively by both men and women. Pectoral crosses, chains and rings are worn by prelates, too. The wearing of gold and jewelry was a pagan custom and one which

---

[441]   *Jerusalem Bible*, New Testament, 223, footnote #11a.
[442]   Ibid., footnote #11b.

the Israelites readily adopted while sojourning in Egypt for 400 years. If these directives, particularly for women, against wearing gold in 1Peter 3: 3-4 and 1 Timothy 2: 9-11, had been interpreted literally, no Christians would wear earrings, neck chains, watches—or the elite gold badge, a wedding ring.[443]

Fr. Joseph Lange said:

> Why don't we follow the dietary laws in the Acts of the Apostles? Why is the Eucharist a sacrament and not the Washing of the Feet? Jesus tells us to do both. Why don't we all sell our possessions like the early Jerusalem community? Why don't we accept slavery as a normal aspect of society? . . . It wasn't until the 19th century that slavery was widely recognized as something contrary to the Gospel. The Spirit guiding the church has given us a different understanding of what kind of social structures are Christian. I doubt if any would promote the restoration of slavery in order to be literally faithful to the Bible . . . The point is that the Church has understood these household codes to be subject to change as the Spirit gives us an understanding of the social structures which are more human and Christian.[444]

---

[443] Legend has it that the initial wedding band was made of iron. Gradually, it changed so the woman's was made from gold. The man's ring, unchanged, was still made of iron. Allegedly, hers was switched to gold because, though a softer metal, it was purer . . . There is no mention when or why his changed to gold also . . . (or if it was a result of male purifications or envy because of the greater monetary value for gold than a base metal).

[444] Lange, 161-2.

Accommodation

But why must the woman be veiled? Why may she not speak out? To understand these things we have to remember that the early Christian church was rocked, shaken, almost self-destructed over the circumcision question. Circumcision was the sign of the Jewish covenant. The Jewish believers were strict Jews and followed the law. They didn't realize that belief in Jesus, what came to be called the New Judaism, would evolve into a new religion, a new way of relating to God. That is to the God of their covenant, Yahweh, later also called Jehovah, since Jews could not say God's name.

The Jewish converts insisted that circumcision was necessary to enter the covenant. It was followed by Baptism into Christ and salvation. Gentile converts argued they had received Baptism and the Gifts of the Holy Spirit without circumcision, so God was doing a whole new thing. Circumcision was no longer necessary to prove "chosenness" in God's covenant. It was *a new covenant*. "No mention is made in the New Testament of any dispute over the baptism of women. But if the narrower view had prevailed and circumcision of the foreskin of the males had been made a prerequisite for Baptism, women would have been denied Christian baptism," explained Elizabeth Carroll.[445] Eventually, the leaders agreed that Christian Baptism was the standard for believers and for conversion. Women were no longer physiologically excluded; they truly experienced the freedom of life in the Risen Christ.

For the first time, women could participate actively, they could pray openly. Women received the gifts of the Spirit and were using them in ministries and in service in the early church communities. But the Christians were still bound by their Jewish, Greek and Roman cultures, and these societies were patriarchal and misogynous. The milieu surrounding the Christians was shocked, flabbergasted, dumbfounded and dismayed by the openness allowed the women. We cannot forget that.

---

[445] Elizabeth Carroll, R.S.M., "Women and Ministry." *Women: New Dimensions*, 95.

To insure that the church was not split again as it had been with the circumcision question, the leaders decided there would be *accommodation,* as much as possible, with the existing social structure. This accommodation had three primary components.

First, nothing would be done by Christians which might "turn off" potential converts. They would rock the societal boat as little as possible.

Second, the new Christians had no political clout and were considered a threat to the status quo. They now said, "I do not think or do as Caesar directs, but according to what Jesus directs." So conformity to the cultural mores took the onus and label off them as "disruptors of the empire."

And third, the good order of the Roman Empire helped spread Christianity.

This is why the veil came to be so important in the female spirituality of those days. It was compliance with the accommodation principle, which Paul adapted from the rabbinic tradition of convert-making, and which is still used by modern-day evangelists to foster conversion. *The method of accommodation is to adopt the customs and mood of the person you wish to win over.* It is a companion to "the method of self-abasement where the successful proselytizer becomes the servant of all and humbles himself."[446] It was truly a compromise, and in more ways than one, for the women of Corinth.

Paul's letter to the church at Corinth is an answer to specific questions regarding problem situations which happened there. He is seeking a compromise to find an acceptable position between libertines in the pagan city and puritanical zealots. He is setting guidelines for that church community. In Corinth he is addressing a particular situation in a particular church.[447] He is disciplinary and not dogmatic. He is speaking to them from his own roots—Jewish background and religion plus a Greek education. Paul's background was formed in a rigorous patriarchal system. For that reason Fr. George Tavard called 1 Cor. 11: 5 "a very rabbinic passage."

---

[446] McGrath, 47.
[447] *Jerusalem Bible,* New Testament, "Introduction to the Letters of St. Paul," 195.

"Paul had not yet emancipated himself (and how could he have done so?) from the thought patterns of his Jewish-pharisaic training. In a strongly patriarchal family structure, women are given status in society by the man who acts as the head of the family, whatever moral and effective authority they may actually enjoy within the family circle. Such was the Jewish way of life. Yet Corinth was in a pagan land and the Corinthian Christians normally followed Greek customs." [448]

Paul's audience was very significant. He was writing in his second native language, Greek, to a Greek-oriented audience.[449] He was writing to residents of a sophisticated port and trade center, which was also a center of vice. Corinth was known as the "sin city" of the Peloponnesus.[450] Pagan deity worship was rampant. Among the pagan gods and goddesses worshipped there, the most popular was Aphrodite. Part of the cult of Aphrodite, goddess of erotic love and marriage, was its ancillary but thriving business of temple prostitution. In Paul's day, there may have been more than a thousand of these sacred prostitutes.[451]

McGrath explained: There were five classes of Greek women. The first three classes were slaves: hetairai, auletrides and concubines. The other two classes were public prostitutes, and, finally, the Greek wife. "This made it imperative that the respectable woman should emit a single signal, should make clear beyond any possibility of misunderstanding that she was respectable."[452]

The hetairai were a small group of intelligent and educated courtesans, "who enjoyed some degree of freedom and movement," McGrath said.[453] The auletrides were the dancing flute girls, who, after showing their talents during a performance, were auctioned off. Concubines were members of the household and bearers of legitimate children.[454]

---

448 Tavard, *Women in Christian Tradition*, 29.
449 *Jerusalem Bible*, 194.
450 McGrath, 43.
451 Ibid.
452 Ibid.
453 Ibid.
454 Ibid., 43, 44.

<u>Cultural</u>

As with the Jewish woman, the veil for the Greek women was the sign of her married state. It was not permitted to the harlot or slave. Also, like the Jewish woman, she had to completely cover herself with the veil when she left the house. However, Jewish women who wore the veil in the street removed it in private homes.[455] Significantly, the Christian churches and their services were held in private homes.

The respectable Greek woman was not permitted to ask questions or to express herself in public, since that privilege was reserved only for the hetairai. In public the Jewish woman could only say "Amen" during synagogue services—when allowed to be present, and then only in the outer temple precincts.[456]

Thus, wearing the veil was the cultural mandate; it was part of the dress code. It was the wedding ring for those times.

Men also wore head coverings. Mideastern men and women mostly still do; desert people always have to protect their eyes and heads from wind, blowing sand and extremes of temperature.[457] The religious use of head coverings for both men and women was rather complicated. In apostolic times, Greeks of both sexes sacrificed bareheaded. "Romans of both sexes sacrificed with the head covered and some scholars believe that Jewish men wore the *Tallith*, or veil, during prayer," McGrath said.[458] While performing sacrificial duties, Jewish priests, even the high priest, wore a cap or bonnet of fine

---

[455] McGrath, 50.

[456] Ibid., 47.

[457] Orthodox and Conservative Jewish men wear the skull cap or *yamaka (yarmulke, or kippah or kippot)*. It represents the hurried departure from Egypt and an ever-ready preparedness to follow Yahweh. Orthodox women today usually wear wigs, snoods or a regular hat to hide their hair when they go out in public. Their head covering is *tzniut*. Orthodoxy believes it is improper and lustful for any man other than the woman's husband to see her hair. Unmarried Orthodox Jewish women do not wear head coverings. Muslim women wear head scarves or the *abaya*, the full-length robe which covers them from the eyes, or the foreheads, to their feet, or the *hijab*. Muslim men wear a skull cap called a *kufi*.

[458] McGrath, 146, footnote #14.

linen in the form of a cup-shaped flower,[459] the direct forerunner of the bishops' mitre. But they were barefoot to indicate the holiness of God's presence in the temple.

In the Catholic tradition, women wore something on their heads until the rule was dispensed after Vatican II. In Paul's day, the veil was the sign of the woman's married state, which has been replaced by the wedding ring. Still, it seems incongruous that the only veiled women in our Western society today are the 'virgins'—with veils reserved for brides, First Communicants, and some nuns in conservative orders. (Also, exotic Belly Dancers use veils in their performances but their heads are not covered throughout. Anyway, their scarves are not a sign of modesty and decorum!) In Mid-Eastern cultures, the veil is definitely a sign of male dominance.

Lay Catholic men and most clerics do not wear anything on their heads. Ranking ecclesiastics still wear the zucchetto, a small round skull cap, except during consecration of the Eucharist. The color of the zucchetto indicates rank. The Pope always wears one and it is white. Cardinals wear red, bishops wear purple, abbots wear black, and members of the Capuchin Order wear brown. [460] Some religious order priests, brothers and religious sisters, also wear a habit with a hood, usually to follow the garb started by St. Francis of Assisi and other monastics. This is usually a full-length robe topped with the hood and tied with a rope around the waist. It is not the sweatshirt-type "hoodie" of modern day fashion—but may have been the "hoodie" forerunner!

When Paul asked the women of Corinth to wear a veil when they prayed or prophesied, he, literally, was asking them **to compromise**—for the benefit of the whole church. Apparently, the women of Corinth had offended some more conservative members by their exuberance during prayer and prophecy, particularly if they

---

[459] *Smith's Bible Dictionary*, "Priest," 542.

[460] *Maryknoll Catholic Dictionary*, 612. Since that item does not give the origin of the pope's zucchetto, I asked one usually knowledgeable Catholic man and deacon, then editor of a diocesan newspaper, about it. He replied, "Those Vatican corridors are very drafty!" It is a direct descendant of the Jewish yarmulke.

followed the Greek custom and did so without veils.[461] The women apparently were intoxicated by their new found liberty in Christ, just as were the Jewish (presumably male) disciples on Pentecost. Perhaps that freedom turned away the uninitiated convert, whether male or female. Anyway, Paul's compromise is an intermediary position between total freedom in Christ and societal subservience. Tavard explains:

> Paul feels caught between the claims of Christian freedom and the Jewish conventions which cannot be discarded without polarizing the Christian communities to the breaking point. He appeals to compromise which must have been formerly agreed upon: when women 'pray or prophecy' they should at least wear a veil. If they wish to enjoy the spiritual freedom of public prayer and prophecy let them renounce the material freedom of the Greeks not to wear a veil on their heads.[462]

Precedent for such conciliation had been established during the so-called Council of Jerusalem, which considered practices forbidden to Jews. Tavard calls it "a gentlemen's agreement" between Jewish-Christians and Gentile-Christians.[463] According to the disciple Paul, the standard was to emulate that of the Palestinian churches, which he called the "Churches of God" (1 Cor. 11:16) or the "churches of the Saints (1 Cor. 14:33). It didn't matter to Paul that other churches were in Greek or Roman cultures with different traditions. After all, the church at Corinth had sought his opinion. The Jewish standard was to wear the veil and Tavard said that meant, "No speaking in public and ask questions at home."[464]

---

[461]   Tavard, *WCT*, 29.
[462]   Tavard.
[463]   Ibid.
[464]   Ibid.

Protective

Paul's concern was not only to foster decorum in church services; his directives are also specifically geared toward preserving marriages. For instance, the command that a woman should prophesy while veiled had even further social ramifications. If a Jewish wife was accused of adultery, her head was uncovered by the priest (Numbers 5:18). If she was innocent, her head veiling was restored to her. If the wife removed the veil of her own volition, the husband was expected—even required—to divorce her without her marriage portion. McGrath said most scholars interpret Paul's prohibitions as referring only to married women, which further showed his interest in preserving marriages.[465] Although it may seem shocking to us who consider Christianity as a bulwark of society and the family, it was not considered so in those times. Enemies of the early church were convinced the new religion was destroying marriage and the home.[466] The early, strong emphasis on virginity and celibacy supported that contention, particularly in the apostolic church, when the believers expected Jesus' promised return to come momentarily and lived accordingly with marriage on the decline.

Paul's directives may be seen as a counter-attack to the critics of the church, who saw a serious threat to marriage and the home in the cultural taboos the Christians violated—even on the limited fashion. Women praying or teaching in public fell into this category. So did vows of virginity. McGrath explains:

> At that time, if a wife spoke in a mixed gathering or joined in a discussion in an open meeting, she forfeited her right to remain married and could be divorced without her marriage portion. For the married woman's own protection and for the prevention of scandal, Paul legislated for the Church of Corinth.[467]

---

[465] McGrath, 50, 146. Footnote #12.
[466] Ibid., 48.
[467] Ibid

In the early days of the church, prophesy was considered to be among the highest ministries, second only to apostleship. Paul comments on women doing so and recommends that all should strive to manifest, at the direction of the Holy Spirit, these higher gifts. It has been said by some scholars that prophesy in the early church was a woman's ministry. So, why then, were there prohibitions against speaking out?

Paul's cautious instructions to the Corinthians might have had other culturally-motivated basis as well, McGrath mentioned. First, impetuous fervor caused individuals to convert with little instruction. Second, the enthusiasm of the women and their exceptional gifts could constitute a danger once the fervor of the community began to wane. Third, there was continued opposition by orthodox Jews to the new religion. Spies were easily planted and they could try and destroy the credibility of the real believers.

Women were removed into separate churches and had their own cathedrals. At first, this separation started for the catechumens, those believers who were not yet baptized and who could not stay at Mass for the consecration of the Eucharist. (For more information, see Morris' *The Lady Was a Bishop.*) But practically from the earliest times women were separated, if not in different buildings, then by screens and partitions.

The practice of a "closed" confessional with a screen separating the penitent and the confessor was first mandated for women. Originally, confession of sins was done publicly following the practice of Yom Kippur, the annual Jewish Day of Atonement. It was once a year and for grave matters only, such as murder, adultery or blasphemy. Public penance was required—usually wearing of sackcloth and ashes (for weeks or months), extended fasting, or giving of alms and community service.[468]

---

[468] By the time of the cloistered monasteries, public confession was changed to confession before the abbot or abbess, since everyone was supposed to be practicing the principles of a Christian life, piety, service, and so on. Then individual confession evolved. When Irish monks were sent to the continent to reconvert the Christians after the barbaric invasions of Europe,

As a point of information, in some European countries, the men and women are still separated at services such as Mass. Men sit on one side of the aisle, the women of the other.

In 1 Cor. 14: 35, Paul warns women against raising their voices at meetings. Another possible explanation for this caution was the fact that men and women were separated in the Temple and this probably carried over into the new churches.[469] Since women could not be educated, if she did not understand a particular point, she would call out to her husband across the room or the aisle and ask him to explain it. You can imagine how noisy and confusing that might have been with questions and answers booming back and forth.

What people often forget is that the Pauline directives on silence were not for women only. Paul gave rules to the whole assembly. On the use of the Gift of Tongues, he said only two or three individuals could speak out with the Ministry gift (that's for the edification of the whole assembly) during a meeting. And then, only one at a time and only if an interpreter (another gift, the Interpretation of Tongues) was present. Prophets, Paul counseled, must also use their gift in turn and in order (1 Cor. 14: 29-33).

Symbolic

---

they took the practice of individualized confession with them. It caught on. Since Vatican II there are now three ways for Catholics to participate in the Sacrament of Reconciliation (with God, for our sins). The primary manner is individualized confession and absolution. This is especially needed for serious sin. Second is general confession (in a group, say at a church penitential service) which requires individual absolution. Last there is general repentance and absolution. This was used frequently by priests ministering to Catholic soldiers in Vietnam, Iraq and Afghanistan since it would have been impossible to hear private confessions for everyone prior to an offensive. Today, people tend to receive the Sacrament of Reconciliation less frequently than "in the old days," however, there is a greater understanding of its purpose: reconciliation for serious sin.

[469]   McGrath, 45.

The spiritual symbolism for headship and submission of being under the authority of another comes from two facts. The first is irrefutable—that human beings are under the authority of God. Even Jesus, the creator of the world (John 1:3), came under the Father's authority. When Jesus assumed the role of a human person to compete God's plan for salvation, He had to relate to the Father and to the promptings of the Holy Spirit. In the same way we must: by obedience and faith. This fact is pointed out in Hebrews 5:8. "And he, son though he was, learned obedience from the things that he suffered." (*Confraternity*)

We frequently forget that Jesus had to learn things, had to obey, and even had to suffer during the daily goings and comings of His ministry—and not just during His passion and crucifixion. We forget that "Jesus was as human as if He had never been divine," as the late evangelist Kathryn Kuhlman used to say.

Another "proof" that Jesus was under the Father's authority came from His own statements. As early as His childhood interaction with the leaders in the Temple, Jesus said, he was doing his Father's business. (Luke 2:49) When Jesus said his actions were the Father's, and that he and the Father were one, the male-disciples didn't understand and the scribes and Pharisees didn't like the analogy. The latter groups of religious leaders thought it was blasphemy even for a man to describe himself with godly attributes, let alone to suggest he and Yahweh were one.

The second reason was more directly related to the headship/submission question. It closely follows Paul's thinking on hierarchal structure. Paul saw hierarchy as a literal chain of command of God-Christ-Man-Woman. Hierarchy is defined as any group of persons or things arranged in successive orders or classes, each of which is subject to or dependent upon the one above it. Originally, the word referred to a governing body of ecclesiastics, organized according to successive ranks or orders and rules by a chief hierarch, or high priest.

"Before Vatican II, Catholics who thought 'church' thought hierarchy," said Carroll.[470]

---

[470] Carroll, 84.

The power in the hierarchy pyramid flows from the top down. The bottom, according to Betty Lehan Harragan, "is the only level which is purely subordinate because there is no one lower."[471] Except for the capstone all other levels have dual positioning: they report to the level above and have subordinates below. In Paul's order, which was the thinking of the day, no one was lower than the woman.

Paul's pyramidal evaluation of creation—from God the most powerful to woman, the least powerful—is the same organizational structure on which the Catholic Church, armies, and most major business corporations are based. It isn't coincidental that these three hierarchal 'conglomerates' are the areas where women, until recently, have had the lowest visibility and least input in the power structure.[472]

In 1 Cor. 11: 3-12, quoted above, Paul specifies, God is the head of Christ, Christ is the head of man and man is the head of woman. The basis of this hierarchal structure is Paul's interpretation of Genesis 2 as historical truth. Genesis 2 has the male naming all the animals before the female was created. He, then, even named her, a sign of his dominion (Gen. 2: 18-23). Genesis is also the basis for the statement in 1 Tim 2: 13-15: "A woman ought not to speak, because Adam was formed first and Eve afterward, and it was not Adam who was lead astray but the woman who was led astray and fell into sin."

For Paul it is a literal evaluation formulated as the patriarchal world taught him to do: the man was created first, therefore he was superior to the woman. For no other reason. She was created out of man's body, after him in time, and for his use (meaning sexually). The very expression "for his use" is a turn-off in our society, but it was the accepted milieu for patriarchal thinkers.

These things ignore Genesis 1 which clearly states both were created equal—and what's more, in God's image. Genesis 2 is more

---

[471] Betty Lehan Harragan. *Games Mother Never Taught You, Corporate Gamesmanship for Women.* (New York: Warner Bros. 1977), 48.
[472] For a complete explanation of why this is so, see Harragan, 37—65.

concerned with the why of sin, the why of marriage, why things are the way they are, according to Lange.[473]

Paul said that man prays with his head uncovered out of respect for his Lord and master, Christ, and because he, the man, is lord and master over the woman. In 1 Cor. 11: 7, "A man should certainly not cover his head, since he is the image of God and reflects God's glory; but woman is the reflection of man's glory." What Paul has done is juggle the verses from the two creation accounts. Mankind as reflection of God's image does not appear in the account in Genesis 2, but in Genesis 1, which emphasizes simultaneous creation.

The impression that woman was not made in God's image was not just a Pauline philosophy; that thought lasted well into church history. For instance, 1100 years after Corinthians, in Gratin's First Codification of the Law, Paul's statement is used as the model: "It is the natural order among humans that women be subject to their husbands . . . because it is only right . . . . that the lesser serve the greater . . . . woman was not made in God's image."[474] On the other hand, in 1 Cor. 15: 20-26, Paul says, " . . . . Death came through a man; hence the resurrection of the dead comes through a man also."

Since Paul so frequently says in his letters that everyone is equal in Christ, in fairness, the fact that he says woman is not made in God's image is probably not his true understanding, either. This is another example of his personal conflict between his understanding of the full extent of freedom through Christian Baptism and adjustment to traditional concepts. We can dismiss some of the inconsistency in Paul's epistles because we know they generally were dictated "off the cuff" in response to particular questions in particular churches. They were dictated to one or another of Paul's colleagues and then signed by Paul with a short personal greeting. "Although some of the passages were obviously written after long and careful thought," the *Jerusalem Bible* said, "more often the style suggests spontaneity

---

[473]   Lange, 160.
[474]   As quoted in McGrath, 54, "Gratian, C. 122, CXXXIII, q. 5."

and urgency."[475] Unfortunately, the translator and the reader do not know which is which.

The orthodox Jewish notion of Yahweh was of God-as-filling-the-whole-universe, without shape or form. Mankind is like God in the capacity for goodness and creativeness, in God's delegated power for human dominion over creatures.[476]

Paul's denial of power and dominion of the woman, by using Genesis 2 as the creation model, is a denial of Genesis 1. In that God tells both Ish and Ishah, the male and the female, they have dominion and authority for it is only together that they, (mankind/humankind) constitute the image of God. After all, Ish recognizes Ishah as his other self: "This at last is bone of my bones and flesh of my flesh." (Gen. 2:23).

For full clarity of the passage in Genesis, we should read it as saying, "God said, 'Let *us (Elohim) make man* (mankind/humankind, adamah, the plural collective noun) *in our own image,* in the likeness of *ourselves,* and *let them be masters* of the fish of the sea, the birds of heaven, the cattle, all the wild beasts and all the reptiles that crawl upon the earth.'" (Gen. 1:26).

That command is often overlooked in favor of the statement in Gen. 3:16, "your yearning shall be for your husband and he will lord over you." For instance, that quote and not the joint-dominion quote from Gen. 1 is stressed in a popular home-study course about headship and submission and the joys of being a good homemaker, "The Philosophy of Christian Womanhood."[477]

In that course the authors use Genesis 1:25 and 28 and Genesis 2:15 literally as the basis of the characteristics of the male ego. Genesis 2:15 says, "Yahweh (God) took the man and settled him in the Garden of Eden to cultivate and take care of it," the course says. The characteristics of the male ego are these: to exercise dominion

---

[475]   *Jerusalem Bible,* "Introduction to the Letters of St. Paul," 194.

[476]   McGrath, 55.

[477]   Dorothy McGuire, Carol Lewis and Alvena Blachley, "The Philosophy of Christian Womanhood, Tri-R Associates, Inc (Denver, CO, 1970), lesson 1, "The Male Ego," and Workbook, 1-18, Tape 1.

(Gen 1:26) to subdue and to multiply (Gen 1:28), to tend and to guard. (Gen 2:15)

"The Philosophy of Christian Womanhood" course says a woman is not to usurp the man's authority because the man was given the drive to exercise dominion and authority.[478] "Men feel resentment when women are in authority over them. This comes naturally; they feel this is competition for their God-given authority. Men want to go as high as they can; promotions at work are the name of the game. It means a lot to a man to keep getting ahead, to keep getting enough prestige to exercise dominion," explains the female narrator of the "Philosophy of Christian Womanhood" tape.[479]

The course suggests that a man must keep advancing until he gains all the authority he can handle: the more responsibility for him, the better. Anything short of utilizing his total ability will eat into his ego. At home, when the woman usurps his God-given authority, there is the real competition. The course says when that happens, the man withdraws into a shell, just to keep peace, and allows the woman to run the household.

The course explains a man's desire to subdue things is exemplified by attempts to put the forces of nature under control. That is evident, the course said, in the man's ability to adapt challenges and "not to let things get him down." It is this drive that enables the man to do things that have never been attempted, the course said.

The drive to multiply and fill the earth is the sex drive. The drive to attend and care means a territory he can care for, be totally responsible for, i.e., his home, the castle, and even its lawn.[480]

That's why any infringement on his territory, for instance, the woman mowing the lawn, "robs' him of his God-given drives and makes him feel "set upon," according to the course. Although the oven and the bathroom are part of the territory, part of the "castle,' the course does not say he is responsible for cleaning them. The course distinguishes between maintenance—his territory—and cleaning.

---

478   Ibid.
479   Ibid.
480   Ibid.

If I interpret the course correctly, that's an area of territoriality he readily "relinquishes."

The drive to keep and protect, the tape suggested, was best exemplified through chivalry and is destroyed by a woman's air of independence. (Chivalry is understood here in the romantic notion of 'pedestalization' and not its reality of the powerlessness of women) that is, when the woman competes with a man in matters of leadership and strength, she "destroys" him, or rather his macho self.

Many women claim to have been extraordinarily blessed through this particular course but I found its interpretation of Scripture to be haphazard and fundamental. You don't hear much about the course in the 21st century. Obviously, the writers of the course did not know that the "man" of the first creation story was a collective noun (adamah) meaning mankind/humankind and not just the male, *Ish*. The course does not say, as Genesis 1:26-31 does, that it was simultaneous creation and simultaneous appropriation of authority and drives. The course ignores that the ego and sex drives were given also to the woman. The same drives were given to both. For a woman not to utilize these drives, ingrained in human nature, is as self-destructive as when the man avoids or ignores them, it seems to me.

For instance, with the sex-drive, the course makes it appear as if only men, normally, had this rather than both men and women. According to the course, part of the sex drive for the male is "the desire to see response and complete satisfaction in the wife." It is through this satisfaction that "the woman receives benefits both physically and emotionally."

That explanation makes the woman dependent upon a man's happiness for her own. That infers that she does not experience anything unless he, in effect, wills it for her. Any benefit for her is a by-product of his. This philosophy is brought out in the made-for-television movie from the bestseller "The Woman's Room." Newlyweds of several months, Mira and her husband are discussing her unhappiness at not experiencing anything in their sex life. Turning away from her to go to sleep, he says, "That's okay. It's nice for me."

However, that attitude and philosophy seem to be a contradiction to the principle of Christian marriage: "Thus the two shall become one," where that "one" is a new entity, an amalgam of two persons. It is their unification and not the total eclipsing of one by another.

Christian Baptism and Galatians 3:28

Perhaps, more significantly, what that realm of thinking about women ignores is the emphasis of Christianity—that in Christ, through Baptism, all sins are washed away. The original order is restored. In Baptism, women no longer are under the thinking "that your husband will lord it over you."

Lange and Cushing explain: "It is only after the Fall that woman's role is seen as submissive to man. This submission is clearly the result of sin. It is part of the curse that 'your urge shall be for your husband, and he shall be your master.' (Gen. 2:16) Therefore, female submission, like sickness, hatred, and death, is not part of God's perfect will for us; rather, it is seen as one of the effects of man's (mankind/humankind's) sin."[481]

Galatians and Romans (which is an amplification of the material first handled in Galatians) were written between 57 and 58 A.D. The subject matter is how Judaism and Christianity relate to one another. Paul is speaking to Jewish-Christians who lived in Galatia and Rome. He is talking about being one in faith, regardless of sex or social status. He is reiterating that being baptized in Christ is an equalizer. Baptism, through faith, is the entrée into the Body of Christ, in which no one part has greater or less significance than any other. (See 1 Cor. 12:12-27.)

This message of synthesis into Christ is repeated at least as frequently, if not more, than the passages about order for women. Colossians 3: 10-12 is almost identical. "You have stripped off your old behavior with your old self, and you have put on a new self, which will progress toward true knowledge, the more it is renewed in the image

---

[481] Lange, 158.

of its creator. In that image there is no room for distinction between Greek and Jew, between the circumcised or the uncircumcised, or between barbarian and Scythian, slave or freeman. There is only one Christ, He is everything and He is in everything."

When Paul refers to the Greeks, he is speaking of the inhabitants of the entire Hellenic world, including the Romans, especially when he uses the word in contrast to barbarians. When he uses the word "Greeks" in contrast to the Jews, he means pagans in general, according to the *Jerusalem Bible*.[482]

The message of oneness in Christ is repeated frequently throughout the New Testament. First of all, there are Jesus' own words in the Gospel of John (17:21): "May they all be one, Father, may they be one in us, as you are in me and I am in you, so that the world may believe it was you who sent me."

Paul repeats it several times, including: "For I am not ashamed of the Good News; it is the power of God saving all who have faith— Jews first, but Greeks as well—since this is what reveals the justice of God to us: it shows how faith leads to faith, or as Scripture says: 'The upright man finds life through faith." (Romans 1: 16-17) Scripture says in Romans 10:11-13, "Those who believe in Him will have no cause for shame; it makes no distinction between Jew and Greek. All belong to the same Lord who is rich enough, however many ask for His help, 'for everyone who calls on the name of the Lord will be saved.'"

Also, Christians are told by the Spirit to look to faith for those rewards that righteousness hopes for, since in Christ Jesus whether you are circumcised or not makes no difference—what matters is faith that makes its power felt through love. (Gal. 5:6)

In fact, one of the times Paul repeats that message is just one chapter away from his statement (in Cor. 11:10) that woman was created for the sake of man. In Cor. 12:13 he says, "In one Spirit we were all baptized, Jews as well as Greeks, slaves as well as citizens, and one spirit was given to us all to drink." This contradicts the suggestion of basic inequality for woman—that she was created for

---

[482] *Jerusalem Bible*, Romans 1, footnote #1a.

man's "use"—with the statement of equal creation for sanctification through Baptism and life in the Spirit.

Galatians 3:28 is called the "great Pauline doctrinal proclamation of equality." It is believed to have been part of a baptismal formula, Carroll said,[483] and it certainly appears so from its context in Galatians 3. Perhaps it is also a little dig at them. Paul seems to be reminding the converts who they are—new Christians—and where they came from—the patriarchal chauvinism that said "male, Jewish and freeman" were better than anyone else. Paul is suggesting they are supposed to be different now that they are living the love of Christianity. He is reminding them to shape up and be conformed to the example of Christ.

> The exclusion of women from ministry does not derive from the example of Jesus. There is one saying of Jesus which is most consistently quoted in the Gospels and the writings of Paul: the "great commandment "or the "love command." Both Paul and the Evangelists attempted to show the growth and development of the early church as evidence of the Christian community's effort to interpret the love command. Fidelity to this command provided the criterion for solving new disputes as the Church confronted new issues. Paul demonstrated a prophetic understanding of the role on this mandate when he challenged Peter and the other Jewish Christian authorities for their refusal to allow the Gentiles free entrance into the church. Paul chastises Peter for submitting to convention and thus failing to apply the lesson of Jesus' central teaching. This confrontation and its settlement emphasized the love command as the absolute criterion for settling disputes in the Christian Church. As such it presents a meaningful model for resolving the question of the role of women in the Church, both as to ways of proceeding and as to content.[484]

---

[483] Carroll, 84.
[484] Lange, 158, 162.

"There is neither Jew nor Greek, there is neither slave nor free, there is neither male nor female; for you are all one in Christ Jesus" (Gal. 3:28), was not merely coincidental in its phrasing and its analogies. L. Swidler called the verse an obvious contradiction of the daily rabbinic prayer of Thanksgiving. "Praised be God that He has not created me a Gentile; praised be God that He has not created me a woman; praised be God that he has not created me an ignorant man."[485] Conservative and Orthodox Jewish men in our day still recite that prayer. As mentioned above, it is not supposed to be anti-female but refers to man's responsibility under God's law, explained a Jewish friend who is a professor of Sociology at Rutgers University.

"There is a moral as well as historical prophecy contained in the words to the Galatians. In a political and social sense, these words contain a charter of liberation for all humanity," Kolbenschlag said.[486] She continued, "In a psychological and moral sense, the words suggest that Jesus unites in His personality all aspects of the human condition, as a principle on convergence that is the supreme design of the universe . . . . The Pauline message anticipates the coming kingdom: in the evolutionary sense that the early church hoped for and in the interior sense that Jesus constantly reiterated."[487]

Double Salvation Required For Women

In Paul's First Letter to Timothy (Ch. 2, verses 9-15), he reiterates some of the directives from Corinthians—which again contradicts most of the rest of the message contained in his pastoral letters. "During instruction, a woman should be quiet and respectful. I am not giving permission for a woman to teach or to tell a man what to do. A woman ought not to speak because Adam was formed first and Eve afterward and it was not Adam who was led astray but the woman who was led astray and fell into sin. Nevertheless, she will

---

[485] L. Swidler, "Jesus Was a Feminist," 178.
[486] Kolbenschlag, 131.
[487] Ibid.

be saved by childbearing, provided she lives a modest life and is constant in faith and love and holiness." (1 Tim. 2:11-15).

As it happens, Scripture scholars believe that the letters to Timothy and Titus were not authentically Pauline but rather written by an ancillary disciple, sometime after Paul's death, who used Paul's teaching and name to give it credibility. That was a routine practice in those times and not considered plagiarism but accepted as if it had been Paul's. So, whomever "wrote" the letters to Timothy was using the more socially-accepted ideas, not Paul's complete thinking: that humans were created equal.

In that childbearing sentence above, Paul (allegedly) denies the substance of the message he was sent to proclaim—that it is salvation based on faith which saves, not good works. Certainly, we must be just and merciful and be concerned for the poor, the ill and underprivileged. But the writer here makes distinction between salvation for men and for women, it seems to me. Men may be saved through faith but a woman requires "double salvation": faith and childbearing. Since Paul advocates his personal preference of non-marriage as the most acceptable spiritual lifestyle (1Cor. 7:8-9), what happens to the woman who dies and is not married or who didn't have any children? The writer doesn't answer. Is she saved or not? If you interpret the section literally—then apparently not.

Margaret Clarkson in her book, *So You're Single!,* said the state of being single is a consequence of sin and not the order established in Eden.[488] Early Christian female martyrs and religious sisters throughout history would probably deny that statement. Jesus purposely did not marry so he could belong to all families and Paul chose not to—both contrary to the regular practice of their times. Maybe a lot of women today do not marry because of circumstances—that is, no one asked, the guys were the wrong person to marry, or a fiancé died abruptly—rather than from a choice for singleness. But that doesn't make them sinners because they're not married.

---

[488] Margaret Clarkson, *So* You're Single! (Wheaton, IL: Harold Shaw Publishers, 1978).

The ghost writer, in that verse, is also contradicting Paul's own words in Romans:

> So far then we have seen that, through our Lord Jesus Christ, by faith we are judged righteous and at peace with God, since it is by faith and through Jesus that we have entered this state of grace in which we can boast about looking forward to God's glory. (Verses 1-3)

Also:

> Sin entered the world through one man and through sin, death, and thus death has through the whole human race because everyone has sinned. If it is certain that death reigned over everyone as the consequence of one man's fall, it is even more certain that one man, Jesus Christ, will cause everyone to reign in life who receives the free gift that he does not deserve, of being made righteous. Again, as one man's fall brought condemnation on everyone, so the good act of one man brings everyone life and makes them justified. As by one man's disobedience many were made sinners, so by one man's obedience many will be made righteous. (Verses 12-12, 17-21)

That seems to indicate the woman was exonerated; she was not responsible at all—just the man. That, in fact, is not any more true than saying she was solely responsible. Why is it that that verse is never interpreted literally?

Paul knew he was being a bit un-Christian in his comments about women's place, McGrath said. "Possibly he recognizes in his line of reasoning the rabbinic despising of women, rather than the Christian teaching in regard to them. He badly weakens his own argument by admitting: 'However, though woman cannot do without man, neither can man do without woman in the Lord; woman may come from man, but man is born of woman—both come from God.'" (1 Cor. 11:11-12)[489]

---

[489] McGrath, 52.

Interpolations

Nowadays Paul is labeled as a woman-hater and a classic male chauvinist. But, in truth, he is unjustly blamed for a lot of the discrimination against women in the church and in society from his day to ours. Why? First of all, for every text that refers to the inequality and subordination of women in society, there is a counter text. Secondly, and more importantly, Paul *did not write* many of the texts in question. That may be a surprising fact, but it's true. Many of the texts were inserted as late as the second century *after* the letters to Corinthians and Timothy were written.

Biblical scholars say the 'be quiet' verses (to lump them together) were later insertions, which Morris called, "The work of antifeminist scribes."[490] In particular, 1 Cor.14:34-36 is seen as an interpolation, which is "an insert to a discourse in order to falsify a text."

The questionable passage is "as in all the churches of the saints, women are to remain quiet at meetings since they have no permission to speak; they must keep in the background as the law itself lays down. If they have any questions to ask, they should ask their husbands at home: it does not seem right for a woman to raise her voice at meetings." Morris explained in Biblical versions earlier than the Latin Vulgate, those verses appear at the end of the passage as verses 39 and 40. "The very fact that they were moved makes it much more likely that they were interpolation," Morris said.[491]

Another scholar who disputes the authenticity of the passage is Fr. Raymond Brown, one of the foremost Scripture scholars in the U.S. "It is frequently argued that 1 Cor. 14:34-36 is not genuinely Pauline," he said.[492] "The section is to be regarded as an interpolation," Brown quoted from H. Conzelmmann's book, 1 <u>Corithinians</u> (p.246).[493]

The groups which are most likely to interpret and practice the headship and submission passages, such as Charismatics and

---

[490] Morris, 123.

[491] Ibid.

[492] Brown, "Roles of Women in the Fourth Gospel," *Women: New Dimensions,* Footnote 3, 113.

[493] Ibid, 121.

Pentecostal Christians, are also very deeply rooted in the Bible and study it intensely. In another apparent contradiction, they are overwhelmingly unaware of the fraudulence of these passages.

The contradictory counter texts to the headship and submission passages are never fully explained neither in any of the books on this topic I studied, nor in the "Philosophy of Christian Womanhood" course. Examples of these counter-tests are:

- While Ephesians 5:24 states that wives must be subject in everything to their husbands, Eph. 5:21 states, "Be subject to one another."
- 1Cor. 11:7 says that "the man is made in the image and glory of God while woman is the glory of man." Gen. 1:27 says both male and female were made in the image of God.
- 1Cor. 14:34 states women should keep silence in churches. 1Cor. 11-5 recognizes women do pray and prophesy, with prophesy as the charism ranking second after apostleship. (1 Cor. 12:28). Eph. 2:20 clearly states that apostles and (New Testament) prophets are the foundation of the church, with Christ as the cornerstone. There is also 1 Cor. 14:26 which says, "Let everyone be ready with a psalm or sermon."

FUNDAMENTAL INTERPRETATION OF SCRIPTURE

We also have to consider the aspect of fundamental or literal interpretation of the Bible, regardless of the particular passage. The Bible is God's instrument, divinely inspired, but not dedicated by the Holy Spirit to the Old Testament prophets sitting in a cave somewhere using a typewriter or an iPad.® The Bible is God's divine message to human persons of diverse times and culture. It is studied by still different humans of other languages and society. For hundreds of years before it was written down, the material from the Old Testament particularly, was oral history, which is often elaborated or stylized to get the point across.

To "write the Bible" God used human language with all its innuendoes and construction and human people with their unique personalities and prejudices. The late Cardinal Huberto S. Medeiros of Boston once told a meeting of the Catholic Biblical Association that it is always vital to remember that when studying the Bible, "It is the very words of God in the words of men."

Denial of the fact that God can use the human to express divinity is a denial of Incarnation, the central doctrine of Christianity—that is, that Jesus, God, became man. Christian faith is based on the fact that God chose the human to reveal himself—through the human Jesus and the human word. That's according to Catholic Theologian, the Rev. George MacRae, who permanently held the Charles Chauncey Stillman Chair of Roman Catholic Studies at Harvard University Divinity School.[494]

> That attitude toward the Bible, which sees it as God speaking His own language, a superhuman language which comes into the world from outside of itself, that kind of an attitude comes down to denying the seriousness of God's plan to make Himself known in the world of human beings as a human being. And that is a major charge . . . . The fundamentalist doesn't recognize it as God's work in human words but treats it as a non-human product, a kind of magic document.

> The Bible is full of contradictions, and if they refuse to study it as a human document, then God is all mixed up and that is not our image of God. What it is is that different words have different meanings . . . . The fundamentalist can't cope with that. When you say that is God speaking on His own, that assumes an attitude that makes God contradict Himself, confuse Himself and us, and that's not the way we want to look at that book.

---

[494] Excerpt from a talk by Fr. George MacRae to the Massachuttes Charismatic Leaders Conference, Boston University, June 1978, and reprinted in "Missing the Word," *Catholic Charismatic Magazine*, Vol. 3, No. 5, Dec./Jan. 1979, 15.

Only an understanding of the Bible as human language makes it possible for us to reconcile the discrepancies we find in it . . . . Fundamentalism denies that the Bible should be interpreted. It is of the essence of the fundamentalist attitude to say you don't have to interpret God when He's talking to you, just listen. The fundamentalists' refusal to get involved in interpretation eventually results in private interpretation, that each person is his or her own interpreter.

That comes down to say that the Bible will mean what I choose it to mean at any given time and that's terribly arrogant and dangerous. They deny the basic thing they say they want to preserve—preserve the idea that the Bible is so important that it's God speaking. But if I interpret it for myself, I am denying that it's God speaking. It's me speaking.[495]

Are Paul's guidelines on order in marriage revealed universal laws for all Christians for all times, or are they not? Some Christians say yes—that these directives are divinely inspired and they appear in the Word of God, and are repeated several times, so, yes, they are for all time. Other Christians say no. They contend these household order directives were specific guidelines for those localized churches in that era and that society. As society changed, and the Christian message of equality in God's sight became more prevalent, and correspondingly society's evaluation of women improved, it is no longer necessary to adhere to cultural mandates from the first century.

Pros and Cons

The debate will probably never end. There are actually no right or wrong answers to the question, though proponents on each side might (and usually do) disagree.

---

[495]   Ibid.

There are Christians in all major denomination who practice the principles of headship and submission. Others do not. Some have never even heard of them. As far as I'm aware, none of the major mainline Christian denominations, such as Lutheran, Episcopalian or Catholic mandate these principles for their married couples. Some Baptists teach that the man is the head of the household.

As far as liturgical services go, the Protestant denominations have utilized women's gifts for years as preachers, presbyters, acolytes, ordained deacons, ministers and priests. Although the first ordination of women into the Episcopal priesthood was in 1975, women have been allowed to be ordained as ministers in the Methodist and Lutheran churches, among others, for many years. American women were first ordained as deacons in the Episcopal Church in 1845.[496]

Women in the Catholic Church are increasingly involved in liturgical functions, except for the deaconate and priesthood, especially through Lay Ecclesial Ministry (LEM) training.

Even in Pentecostal groups, women have been leaders in the manifestation of the gifts of the Holy Spirit. With strict interpretation of the headship guidelines, women have not always been allowed to be "elders," nor teach co-ed Bible School. In the Charismatic branches of mainline churches, there is increasingly less emphasis on the practice than a few years ago. Many denominations have adapted the Catholic-initiated Pre-Cana or Marriage Encounter weekends for their engaged or married couples.

In her book, *How to Be Happy in NO Man's Land,* ordained minister Iverna Tompkins, who is also a divorcee and mother, wrote headship refers "to authority, not superiority. It is positional, not qualitative. It doesn't mean that we're less than man, inferior to him."[497] She explained that without proper submission in our (marital) relationship, women are open to deception, especially in the Spiritual realm.[498]

---

[496] Alla Bozarth-Campbell, *Womanpriest, a Personal Odyssey,* Paulist Press (New York, NY, 1978.) 105.
[497] Tompkins, 54.
[498] Ibid.

Gladys Hunt in her book, *Ms. Means Myself,* said a man's headship is merely fulfilling his responsibility as leader of the household. "It does not necessarily mean that he has superior intelligence, wisdom or ability; it simply means he is responsible to God for the family. A good leader is not a dictator," she said. Submission comes out of love and does not negate the woman's capabilities for responsibility or leadership, Hunt said.

Marabel Morgan, the author of controversial books, *The Total Woman* and *Total Joy,* described submission as "adapting" to her husband's way. She explained that eliminated the problems of two egos battling in the marriage. Submission is voluntary but must be predetermined, she said.[499] "If a woman adapts only for an ulterior motive," Morgan said, "she is not adapting, she is manipulating."[500]

The submissive woman has an obligation to express her opinion and ideas but acquiesces to her husband's view, proponents explain, unless he proposes doing something immoral or illegal. Simply stated, submission is "giving in" out of love for Christ first, and for the husband as head of the household under Christ, second. It is also belief/faith that God will use the husband's decision for divine glory, even if it appears to be the "wrong" decision initially.

Proponents of headship and submission say it is wonderfully freeing. They claim they are happier than ever before and, after incorporating its principles, their marriages have been transformed for the better. Frequently, "unsaved" family members, particularly husbands, who are recalcitrant about going to church, come into a personal relationship with Christ after the wife practices submission. Proponents claim there is a direct correlation between the two but it is probably more from the living out of love of Christianity than the actual acquiescing or adapting to the husband's wishes which prompts the "unsaved" member to seek Christ.

Proponents say people frequently get the wrong impression of submission and proselytize that submission to the husband's wishes

---

[499]   Marabel Morgan, *Total Joy*, Spire Books, Fleming H. Revell Company (Old Tappan, NJ, 1976), 68.

[500]   Ibid.

is not the same as being a doormat. It does not mean "being stepped on," or that the woman has no opinions. Often, proponents say, submission and headship open up new avenues of conversation and love in the husband-wife relationship, particularly, if it was waneing. It shows each partner the value of loving service instead of personal selfish goals. Children show new respect, and not indifference to their fathers, who assume the disciplinary role, proponents claim. The husband is responsible also for the financial direction of the family, a role which frequently was delegated to the wife since she was at home, running the house.

"You thought it was a liability but you'll discover it's a privilege," said Elizabeth Rice Handford, in her book about the topic, *Me? Obey Him?* "You have the freedom from having to take the consequences of making decisions."[501]

Opponents of submission disagree with that very idea, saying submission is a denial of Christian Baptism and keeps women's position as that of a "minor child." They contend vigorously that it uses Scripture out of context and deliberately to denigrate women.

Submission appears to be geared for the homemaker, whatever else she may do. In the first century, when it began, most women didn't do anything else. I found no literature about submission and the working woman. No one needs the advisory that your boss is not your spouse. Trying to submit to an unjust boss may not be appropriate in the workplace. Recent statistics show more than 51 percent of the women in the U.S. *double* as workers and homemakers. The majority of all women who work do so out of economic necessity. That includes a lot of Christian women, of course.

Women Who Work

In the middle of the 2009 recession, American women surpassed working men for the first time in American history, said Catherine

---

[501]   Elizabeth Rice Handord, *Me? Obey Him?*, Sword of the Lord Publisher, (Murfreesboro, TN, 1972) 55.

Pampbell in *The New York Times On Line.*[502] That was due to the large numbers of men laid off, particularly in manufacturing and farming jobs. At the peak of women's working in 2000, 77 percent of women between ages 25 and 54 were in the workforce.[503] Women who work make 80 cents for every dollar a man makes, according to the Bureau of Labor Statistics. (It used to be 69 cents in the 1980s. Women's worth gained 11 cents in 30 years.)

Women tend to work more part-time jobs and have less health insurance. Studies found women who work outside the home have more time for childcare and housework, since their partners also tend to pitch in more at home. However, fewer mothers prefer full-time work as of poll results from Feb. 12, 2007.

In Sept 2007 a Gallup Poll of 1,000 individuals showed women prefer to work outside the home, 58 to 37 percent, not quite two to one. Three percent said they wanted to do both and two percent had no opinion. Two years previously, in 2005, only 54 per cent of women said they preferred working outside jobs. The last time a substantial number of women preferred staying at home was 1974.

Men preferred outside work by 68 percent, which is almost three-quarters of those queried. Twenty-nine percent wanted to stay home, one percent wanted to do both and two percent had no opinion.

Having children changed the results somewhat. Among mothers, 58 percent said they wanted to stay home and so did 35 percent of dads. The poll has a three percent margin of error.[504]

Don't forget, a number of working women today include women in parish ministry or other parish jobs or working in lay ecclesial ministry.

On the other side of the headship issue, opponents believe it fosters what men already believe about women because of cultural influences: that women are incapable of making important decisions.

[502] Catherine Pampbell, "As Layoffs Surge, Women May Pass Men in Job Force," New York Times On Line, Feb. 5, 2009.
[503] Eduardo Porter, "Women in Workplace—Trend Is Reversing,"
[504] Miranda Hitti, "Women Prefer Working Outside the Home," *WebMD Health News On Line*, Sept, 6, 2007.

Opponents say submission keeps women from decision-making in the home and in the church.

Opponents believe statements like Handford's quoted above—that headship and submission free a woman from taking responsibility—undermine that women are adults who must take the responsibility for, and face the consequences, of their own decisions. That is maturity. Her remark sounds very immature in this day and age.

Opponents believe submission has been twisted by many men "to lord it over their wives." Instead of interpreting their responsibility in it—to love their wives as Christ loves the church, unto death (Eph. 5:21-32), they have used it to make her a non-assertive house slave. In some cases, that attitude has wrecked the woman's emotional stability and even the marriage.

Opponents say submission is not done out of love by many women—especially initially—but is done as a barter system with God, to "insure" salvation for their husbands and family, and that's putting God in a box. "If I do this, then you, God, have to do that." It doesn't work that way; in case you haven't learned it yet, human beings are not in a position to tell God what to do.

Opponents say submission keeps women from decision making in the home and in church structures. Opponents claim that, worst of all, as a denial of Christian Baptism, submission denies the talents, abilities, gifts and new life in Christ that are given to all who are baptized.

The only area of the Roman Catholic Church where the principles of headship and submission were practiced was in the Charismatic Renewal, said James A. O'Brien, the founding director of the Upper Room Spiritual Center, New Monmouth, NJ. O'Brien believed, if any question was divisive enough to ever split the renewal in the Catholic Church, it was this. He said people were so divided on the question, that if a split ever did happen, it would be schismatic. That is, the very fundamental interpreters would form a splinter church.[505] O'Brien, who was an outspoken critic of the practice, was at that time Diocesan Liaison to the Bishop of Trenton, N.J., for the Charismatic

---

[505] Personal Interview with James A. O'Brien, 1979.

Renewal in the diocese. Today there increasingly is less emphasis on the practice in the Renewal than there was in the 1970s and 80s. Leadership by women is very much a part of the New Covenant.

Also, this trend away from it may be in greater conformity to the Documents of Vatican II, which sets the formal direction for the Roman Catholic Church in modern times. The documents discuss the goals of Christian marriage but contain no mention of headship or submission. "This does not mean that the Council (the Second Vatican Council) thinks it is wrong." Lange and Cushing explain.

> But rather that it was not important enough to mention in a relatively brief article. The Council did say things such as: 'Christian husbands and wives are cooperators in grace' and 'It (marriage) needs the kindly communion of minds and joint deliberation of spouses.' If not the letter, then at least the spirit of the Council, indicates something broader than male headship. And if male headship were the revealed core of what Christian marriage is about, I would certainly have expected the headship of the Church to have discerned this explicitly."[506]

Lange and Cushing also explain female submission to male authority is one in a hierarchy of obediences listed: the submission of slaves, children and citizens. They were the prevalent social norm in first century Rome and are stoic virtues. Similar lists are found in Epictetus and Seneca.[507]

Opponents of modern-day conformity to these New Testament social-role models of headship and submission cite another reason why this practice "seemed to predominate" in the homes of Catholic Charismatics in the earlier days of the Renewal. When it started in the Catholic Church in 1969, the only base to emulate was Pentecostal Protestantism, which supports these directives almost as universal Christian principles. It was presented as "part of the package." That

---

[506] Lange., 162-3.
[507] Ibid., 162.

is, if you accepted the infilling of the Holy Spirit through adult recommitment (rebirth) in Christ, and if you exercised the gifts of the Holy Spirit, then you also followed the literal interpretation of the Bible on these passages and directives.

Increasing numbers of lay and clerical Catholic Charismatic leaders have concluded after much prayer, research on the Scriptures, and the living out of love in Christian marriages and communities, that it isn't necessarily so. Two of the Charismatic leaders who agree with the last premise are Lange and Cushing. "We are faced with a dilemma. How can Paul urge women to be submissive to the husband if 'all are one in Christ?' God wants us to live in the New Covenant. People may follow these codes if they wish, but they will not bring salvation and are not necessary for all Christians."[508]

If these principles work for your family and in your marriage, fine.

In the 21st Century, the Catholic position is that "shared leadership" is a long standing position of the Catholic Church. For example, some of the greatest mystics in church history were women—Teresa of Avila, Catherine of Siena, Julian of Norwich, and Theresa of Liseux.

Catherine is especially interesting from the female perspective for shared leadership. For 70 years, in the 1300s, the popes resided in Avignon, France, and that, accordingly, was known as the Avignon Papacy, and to some historians, as "The Babylonian Captivity." In 1377, the papacy returned to Rome under Gregory XI. Upon his death, Urban VI was chosen as the successor on the promise that he would stay in Rome. The French cardinals refused to accept his election and chose their own pope, Clement VII. For almost 40 years, the two pontiffs claimed the spiritual powers of St. Peter, and each was convinced of his own legitimacy. That was called "The Great Schism."

Catherine was told by the Lord in a vision to heal the Great Schism. But even she was skeptical as she related in her diary: "How shall it be done with me as Thou hast said? For my sex is an obstacle

---

[508] Lange, 181.

as Thou knowest, Lord . . . because it is contemptible in men's eyes . . . . But the Lord answered, 'I pour out the favour of my spirit on whom I will. There is neither male nor female, plebian or noble. All are equal before me. Therefore, my daughter, it is my will that thou appear before the public.'" [509]

Catherine of Siena publicly rebuked the pope and he followed her advice. The papacy has been headquartered in Rome ever since.

Two centuries later, Teresa of Avila was attacked by the papal nuncio in the 1500s, who growled she was "a disobedient, contumacious woman who promulgates pernicious doctrine under the pretense of devotion; is ambitious and teaches theology as though she were a Doctor of the Church, in contempt of the teaching of St. Paul, who commanded women not to teach."[510]

The role of the prophet is never easy.

The irony of that nuncio's statement above is that the church subsequently discerned that Teresa of Avila, Theresa of Liseux and Catherine of Siena *are* Doctors of the Church! That means they are officially teachers of the whole church. Doctor of the Church is a title conferred on ecclesiastical writers of eminent learning and a high degree of sanctity, who have distinguished themselves by their defense, exposition and preservation of the doctrine of the church. Lange and Cushing comment that these women as Doctors of the Church are "quite a way from Paul's advice that women not be allowed to teach."[511]

---

[509] McGrath, 154.

[510] Ibid. Also, at one point there was even a third pope, a soldier of fortune named Baldassare Cossa, who took the name John XXIII. Cossa was elected by a splinter group, the Conciliarists, in 1408. Subsequently, on the death of Pope Pius XII in 1958, a man named Angelo Giuseppe Roncalli was chosen by the College of Cardinals as the new pontiff. He chose the name John XXIII to prove the man, Cossa, was not a legitimate successor to St. Peter. John XXIII became the best loved pope of the 20th century and initiated the Second Vatican Council. From: *A History of the Western World*, D.C. Heath and Company (Boston MA, 1964), 186-289 and *Maryknoll Catholic Dictionary*, Appendix VI, "Popes of the Catholic Church," 667.

[511] Lange, 181.

McGrath said:

> Three passages from I Corinthians (with some later passages in I Timothy) have served for 1900 years to bar women from any effective participation in the decision-making processes of the church. Worse, they have closed to her the study of the sacred sciences—of what use to study what you were forbidden to impart? As a consequence, they have played no small part in depriving women through the ages of all but the most elementary education, to the frustration and impoverishment of the women, and very probably also of the church and the world. [512]

Does headship and submission reflect the example of Jesus toward women? Whether inadvertent or not, we'll never know, but it seems that Jesus' encouragement of women to speak up in an age when they could not speak publicly; His use of women to spread His message at the well, at the cross, at the tomb; His use of their faith as examples to the men; and His radical concern for equalized thinking about women—was subverted. His male disciples apparently could not fully understand His intent. It has affected the ministry of women in the church ever since.

---

[512] McGrath,154.

CHAPTER 22

What Now?

What roles do women in the church have today at the dawning of the 21st century—the third millennium after Jesus Christ was born and died? What can we do? The answer is simple: everything, except the sacramental roles reserved to the ordained. At this time in the Church, that is for men only.

Although public attention on ministry is usually on the sacramental functions performed by a priest or deacon, church ministry isn't just sacramental.[513] It is way more than that—but we often don't see it, especially when the role is almost exclusively done by women, such as today's Directors of Religious Education (DRE). Now a member of the parish staff, DREs prepare children for reception of the sacraments, or instruct them in the Catholic faith—often with thousands of pupils in one parish and in one year.

People see that women's ordination to the priesthood or deaconate hasn't happened, so they say, "What changes?" There are many. "Everything" includes a wide variety of ministries which

---

[513] There are seven sacraments: Baptism, Confirmation, Reconciliation (previously popularly called Confession or Penance), Eucharist, Marriage, Holy Orders (ordination), and Healing (also called Sacrament of the Sick and previously known as Extreme Unction but popularly called "The Last Rites".) They are, as the Baltimore Catechism said to us baby-boomers in parochial school or religious education, "an outward sign instituted by Christ to give grace." The modern day definition in the Catechism of the Catholic Church (1994) section 775, is, "The seven sacraments are the sign and instruments by which the Holy Spirit spreads the grace of Christ, the head, through to the whole church, which is his body."

women are doing in the church today, most of which were not allowed—or even thought of—20, 30, or 40 years ago! These range from altar girls serving at liturgy (that is Mass or Eucharist)—official in 1994!—Lectors, Eucharistic Ministers (See Canon Law §230.3), parish ministries, hospital chaplains, prison ministry, all the way to female appointments as chancellor and vice-chancellor of dioceses. Those are the highest administrative positions in a diocese—formerly areas of male exclusivity. Since 1983, Canon law, code 228, specifically states that women may be appointed to chancery positions. Out of 398 chancellors, about 25 percent were women in 2009.

The current focus of the Roman Catholic Church is two-fold: toward evangelization and with the involvement and ministry of the laity. Evangelization is the mission of the church, its heart—to spread the gospel of Jesus Christ. That will be done, significantly, through the ministerial role of the laity, its future. Naturally, this includes women. This book is all about how women's history/roles have changed in the Catholic Church from scriptural days to the present. And it is about the remarkable contributions women have made to church life.

Catholic women have realized significant strides from the traditional roles in which they were placed historically by society and by the male-oriented institutional church, itself. Amazing changes really—considering the centuries-long milieu of patriarchy and misogamy (and, unfortunately, under which most women throughout the world still live, in one form or another).

There are three major recent innovations which are dynamic and exciting changes for women. One is the ministry of **Parish Life Coordinator (PLC);** the second is the **Emerging Models of Pastoral Leadership Project (Emerging Models or EMP);** and the third is the growth of **Lay Ministry**.

Zeni Fox in *New Ecclesial Ministry: Lay Professionals Serving the Church*, explains the term lay ministry has two meanings: "Lay Ministry refers both to the universal call to holiness which flows from baptism and the gift of the Spirit, and to non-ordained persons who are serving in designated roles in ministry."[514]

Perhaps the most exciting innovation of all is the **1. Parish Life Coordinator (PLC) (sometimes called Pastoral Life Coordinator).** That's where a person, either lay or religious, or a committee, runs the parish when there is no resident pastor. This is under supervision of a priest—who usually isn't in residence—or, as in the Midwest, where he has many PLC parishes to coordinate. The use of PLCs is widespread in the U.S., and in South America, in the early part of the 21st century. Canon Law was changed in 1983, less than 20 years ago, to allow PLCs. Canon 517, Section 2, states:

> If because of a shortage of priests, the diocesan Bishop has judged that a deacon or some other person who is not a priest, or a community of persons, should be entrusted with a share in the exercise of the pastoral care of a parish, he is to appoint some priest who, with the power and faculties of parish priest, will direct the pastoral care.[515]

The majority of PLCs in the U.S. at this time are women—whether lay or religious. This is obviously a revolutionary change in church life, pastoring roles, and for its effect on women's ministries!

One woman's experience pastoring a Midwestern church for four years was recently the front page cover story in *America Magazine,* a monthly Jesuit publication, on March 9, 2009.[516] In the story entitled, "Exceptional Pastoring," Mary M. Foley wrote:

> I have had the rare, joyful and privileged opportunity to pastor a Catholic parish as a laywoman . . . My last assignment

---

[514] Zeni Fox, *New Ecclesial Ministry: Lay Professionals Serving the Church,* (Franklin, WI: Sheed & Ward, 2002), 118.
[515] As quoted in Kathleen Egan-Bittner, J.D., LLM, paper in pastoring course for ILEM, 2008. From the Code of Canon Law, Canon 517, Section 2.
[516] Mary M. Foley, "Exceptional Pastoring: Women in Parish Leadership," *America,* Vol. 200, No 8, March 9, 2009, 11-13.

in ministry was especially challenging, because I was the only person serving in such a role within four dioceses in the state, and people were generally unprepared for such a change. In spite of the challenges, this was a ministry full of joy and one in which I felt most fully alive. In a word, it is a ministry for which I was made. Pastoring is my vocation. I deeply love my church, and I am thankful for every ministry opportunity I have had; but I am especially grateful for having had the opportunity to serve the church as a Pastoral Life Coordinator.[517]

Ms. Foley said the ministry is still rare—only 500 men and women served as pastoral leaders of parishes without a resident pastor at that time, according to research by the Center for Applied Research in the Apostolate (CARA).[518] Ms. Foley served in a variety of parish ministries for more than 20 years. Her position as PLC was at a Midwestern suburban parish of 935 families.[519] The Bishop told her she was to attend cluster meetings with the diocesan priests. Initially, some of these priests protested and had a minor revolt. The issue was resolved. Over time collegial relationships developed with some of the same priests who had objected at first to her presence.[520]

Some people fear ministries such as hers, and think by encouraging lay ecclesial ministry, they are devaluing the priesthood and the need for more vocations to it and to the Religious Life. Ms. Foley disagrees. "Religious vocations are God-given, and the task of anyone pastoring within the church (bishop, priest, or Pastoral Life Coordinator) is to recognize, affirm, encourage, nurture and support all the gifts God had given to the community of faith," she explained.

The second significant development is **2. The Emerging Models for Pastoral Leadership Project** in the American Churches (Emerging Models Project). It is the cutting edge today of social

---

[517] Ibid.
[518] Ibid.
[519] Ibid.
[520] Ibid.

research, planning for, tracking parish ministries and pastoring. Its very successful Phase I ran from 2003 to 2009, and its on-going Phase II is slated for 2009 to 2012.[521]

Coordinated by the Center for the Applied Research in the Apostolate (CARA) at Georgetown University, Washington, D.C., the Emerging Models Project is a joint venture by five national ministerial associations[522] and is funded by them with generous outside grants, totaling millions of dollars, including those by Lilly Endowment, Inc. However, many average Catholics, even a friend who is a deacon, don't even know about the Emerging Models Project, what it does and how important it is for the future in our changing church.

The Project's goals are to provide solid research on the emerging models of parish pastoral leadership; to stimulate a national conversation on creating vibrant parishes and to explore ways in which its member associations can collaborate to serve the church.[523] One of its tasks is to track PLCs and other pastoral leaders. According to its data, the Northeastern U.S. had the fewest number of PLCs because 1) it is where a majority of people who identify themselves as Catholics live; 2) where most priests and deacons are located; and 3) the geographical areas to cover are smaller, parishes are closer and more numerous.[524]

The rest of the country faces a serious shortage of male priests and deacons plus vast amounts of territory to cover in each parish

---

[521] The Emerging Models Project, Phase I, was headed by a woman, Marti R. Jewell, who holds a Masters in Divinity, and who left the Project in 2009 to accept a university teaching position. By August 2009, no replacement had yet been named. Phase II's total implementation may be delayed because of that gap.

[522] There were six organizational partners originally, one subsequently dropped out: National Association of Lay Ministries (NALM), the Conference for Pastor Planning and Council Development (CPPCD), the National Association of Church Personnel Administrators (NACPA), the National Association of Diaconate Directors (NADD), the National Catholic Young Adult Ministry Association (NCYAMA), and the National Federation of Findings of the Emerging Models Project," Marti R. Jewell, April 21, 2008, 1.

[523] Jewell.

[524] Jewell.

and diocese, so PLCs are more numerous. In Alaska for instance, the U.S.'s largest but least populated state, the average parish's geographic area is 4,000 miles, compared to seven miles in the Northeast.

EMP conducted mega amounts of focused research,[525] in its initial years. What it discovered is "that the Spirit is inviting us into an unanticipated future."[526] It found: "Structures are changing, leadership roles are evolving and pastoring practices are being adapted . . . . and something new is emerging."[527] They learned, "Parish life as we know it is changed. And what is emerging is very hopeful."[528]

The third major change is **3. The emerging role of the laity.** That means all of us who are not ordained nor are vowed religious. Women are an integral part of this—from PLCs, to pastoral associates or assistants (the titles changed but the functions are similar), to other forms of lay ministers.

During Vatican II, which ended in 1965, there was a great emphasis on collegiality, restoring the office of deacon, and the role of the laity. The Vatican II documents on *the Church*, the *Church in the Modern World*, and on *the Laity*, are the most quoted ecclesiastical documents of recent time, according to Leonard Doohan in *The Lay-Centered Church*.[529] These documents challenge all members of the Church to a new awareness of what it means to be Church.[530] Priests and religious are called to facilitate the development of lay ministry and shared ministry.

---

[525] EMP research included: 11 symposiums with 800 people; 3100 online surveys; extensive written and phone surveys; focus groups of bishops and diocesan consultations; 12 diocesan resource and lay ministry consultations; hundreds of interviews with young adults, Bishops, priests, deacons, and lay ministers. EMP, Marti R. Jewel, "Keynote Address: Major Findings," National Ministry Summit, April 21, 2008, 1-2, Accessed on-line 2009.

[526] Ibid, 1.

[527] EMP, Marti R. Jewel, "Keynote Address: Major Findings," National Ministry Summit, April 21, 2008, 1-2, Accessed on-line 2009., 1.

[528] Ibid., 2.

[529] Doohan, Leonard. The Lay-Centered Church. (Minneapolis, MN: Winston Press, Inc., 1984), 26.

[530] Ibid.

As Vatican II stated, all approaches are partial without a shared responsibility in ministry, lay people working along with the hierarchy.[531] What some people don't realize is "the laity are not a bridge between Church and the world; the laity *are* church."[532] In fact, "The laity are the church's presence to the world."[533] They are not merely an extension of the hierarchy, nor did Jesus entrust the Church's mission solely to the hierarchy.

The laity is *church*, and in ministerial roles, it also *serves the church*.

Since Vatican II, three popes—Paul VI, John Paul II, and Benedict XVI—and the U.S. Conference of Catholic Bishops (USCCB)—have issued numerous documents and pastoral letters on the importance of the laity and various ministerial functions. One of the most important changes for laity happened in 1971, when the deaconate was restored as a permanent office in the church. "That was the beginning of the restructuring of all the ministries in the Catholic Church," Fox said.[534]

Another important step was on Aug. 15, 1972, when Pope Paul VI issued *Ministeria Quaedam*. In this document the "minor orders of acolyte, reader and others, were a) opened to lay men; b) these functions or roles were not called "ministries;" and c) no longer were these ministries reserved to candidates for the Sacrament of Orders.[535] Canon 228 in the Revised Code of Canon Law allows

---

[531] Ibid. 47.

[532] Ibid. 24.

[533] Ibid., 9.

[534] Fox, 120.

[535] Ibid., 255. When I was growing up in the "Baby boomer" generation, women lectors weren't allowed—since lectors were considered a "minor order," enroute to the priesthood. The function of a lector is simple: to proclaim the gospel, not just read Scriptural passages. We understand today how silly it was for women to be prevented from that role but, nevertheless, it was the standard practice. Now, in liturgy, women lectors abound, as do women serving as Special Ministers of the Eucharist (EM), Music Ministers, cantors and leaders of song, even ushers. When women, often nuns, started serving as Eucharistic Ministers, distributing Holy Communion at liturgy, people would cross from one communion line to another to deliberately avoid the female EM. Some wise pastor solved a lot of those early resentments by making the most critical women into EM themselves! After 20 or more years

laypersons to assume ecclesial office and functions and to serve as advisors and experts to pastors.[536] It was up to the diocesan bishop to implement these changes, as local needs warranted.

"Ministry, grounded in Baptism, is the building up of the body of Christ for the mission of the Church. Ministry not only serves the internal needs of the church but enables the Church to pursue its mission of the transformation of the world," Fox said.[537]

In many dioceses there is specific training program for lay people who want to work in church ministry professionally, called the Institute for Lay Ecclesial Ministry (ILEM). Participants graduate with a graduate degree in Theology. ILEM is the acronym used by the U.S. Conference of Catholic Bishops (USCCB) and is a national title. The Diocese of Trenton, N.J.,[538] for example, has one of the highest concentrations of Catholics in the country, despite its small four-county geographic size. It began its three-year Institute for Lay

---

of female EMs, some cross-over still happens but mostly it doesn't. Rooted tradition dies hard. I became a lector in 1973 because as the priest in charge, Fr. Bradley, repeatedly announced from the altar during Sunday Mass, "This is the largest parish in uptown Manhattan and there aren't enough people to be lectors." When I applied, he said, "but you're a woman." I replied, "I'm a people . . . and you said there weren't enough people to be lectors." I got the job . . . (I also think no one else applied.) I was finished college and graduate school. I was interested in a career in journalism; I was not attempting to make a radical feminist statement in the church or have a coup d'état—just to do some volunteer work. Some of my female friends followed and became lectors, also. They asked me after a while if I would wear a choir robe—I said, "Yes, if the male lectors wear them too." I just wanted it to be fair. I never heard about it again. I was the first female lector in Good Shepherd's main church on 211th and Isham Streets in the Inwood section of northern Manhattan. Yes, the judge's wife read at the Folk Mass in the school auditorium, but the pastor didn't even acknowledge that Mass existed!

[536] Fox, 182.

[537] Ibid.

[538] The Trenton Diocese is relatively small in geographical size—just four counties in Central New Jersey—Mercer, Monmouth, Ocean and Burlington—but it has one of the most densely Catholic populations in the entire country. In 2006, its 125th anniversary year, Trenton was the 20th largest diocese in the country with more than 750,000 Catholics, according to dioceseoftrenton. org, "History" and "The Monitor."

Ecclesial Ministries (ILEM) program in 2002, with the first graduates commissioned in 2004. Since its founding, more than 150 men and women have trained as lay ecclesial ministers in the acclaimed program, according to Jo-Lynn Krempecki, administrator of ILEM, and Associate Director of the Office of Catholic Education.[539] Research and investigations of other dioceses' similar lay training programs started in the 1990s, she explained. The program is "continually being tweaked," Krempecki said, to make it the best possible.

In Jan. 2010, 35 more individuals started the ILEM program. At that time, the diocese was lead by Bishop John M. Smith, who was committed to "having all of his pastoral leaders well-formed," Ms. Krempecki said.[540] He was succeeded by Bishop David O'Connell, who was consecrated in August 2010 as the Co-Adjudicator Bishop. Bishop O'Connell formerly was the head of Catholic University. Of the 132 plus ILEM people who are trained, or will begin the program, the majority was women (it was 111 to 21 males in 2009) Ms. Krempecki said. "Most participants are women," Krempecki said, "We welcome more men."

Lay leaders have a significant responsibility in the church, she explained. They are formed (trained), then authorized for ministry in an official ceremony. It is ministry which is for regular service to the community or parish, not just occasionally. Most of the LEMs are already working in ministry, either as volunteers or as paid members of parish staffs, before taking the program, she explained. Some, especially men with families to support, also have a secular job since salaries are poor. This is an issue the whole church is facing. Acceptance and perception by pastors towards the ILEM graduates had been very open and increasingly welcoming, she said.

Some of the roles women LEMs in the Trenton diocese are doing are: Pastoral Associates, which is usually being next in command of a parish with only one or two priests; retreat directors; business manager; hospice ministry; DREs; university chaplains; working

---

[539] For more information about ILEM contact your local diocese or Ms. Krempecki at 609-403-7130 or jkremp@dioceseoftrentonorg.
[540] Conversation with Jo-Lynn Krempecki, August, 2009.

with Catechumens; diocesan officials like the Associate Director of the Hispanic Apostolate; the Director of Pastoral Care; Director of Family Life; and the Director of Pastoral Planning to name a few, according to Krempecki.

The training is intensive and concentrates on 10 areas to gain the Masters in Theology: Introduction to Theology, New Testament, Hebrew Scripture, Church Ecclesiology, ministry, morality, pastoral care, religious formation, canon law and the sacraments. Some of the courses are given at the local Catholic university. Each diocese's program for formation of LEM is unique, according to Krempecki, and differs slightly. Just one of the several high ranking programs is Chicago's, she said. Just a few of the other dioceses with an ILEM program are Winona, MN.; Allentown, PA.; and San Jose, CA.

Back to the Emerging Models Project. Its data incorporates the ministries women are doing and what's in store as new ministries evolve to meet the changing needs. EMP asked what makes a parish spiritually vital and alive. The answer: welcoming, Eucharistic communities. EMPs major findings as detailed in Marti R. Jewel's "Keynote Address: Major Findings," at the National Ministry Summit, April 21, 2008. They are:

- There are more than 18,000 parishes in the U.S., serving a population of 64 million Catholics, or 22% of the U.S. population. There are 195 dioceses and Archdioceses in both the Latin and Eastern Catholic traditions across the country.
- The U.S. Catholic population is growing—and moving south and west. The majority is under age 50. Half of the Catholics under age 30 are Hispanic. Changing demographics and diversity are the realities today.
- There are approximately 20,000 diocesan priests, 70% of whom are over age 55. Two-thirds of the dioceses have more parishes than diocesan priests.[541]

---

[541] EMP, Ibid.

- Diocesan and religious priests together total 41,489, as of June 3, 2009, according to the U.S. Conference of Catholic Bishops. There are one billion Catholics worldwide.[542]
- Mega parishes are growing in the Southern Tier, California, and on the Atlantic seaboard. Some parishes have more than 10,000 families.
- Spanish-speaking people have moved into every diocese, as well as other cultural minorities. And many parishes have multiple language bases. The dioceses of Los Angeles, CA, and Newark, NJ, each celebrate Sunday liturgy in more than 60 different languages.
- Where populations are diminishing, as in the Northeast, parishes are being closed, merged or clustered, with each option offering new pastoral challenges. For instance, long-standing parishioners are often fearful and anxious that they will be ignored and neglected when their parish is merged, according to *The Monitor,* newspaper of the Diocese of Trenton, N.J.
- Parishes in small towns and rural areas often share a pastor, have small staffs or none, or are being led by parishioners.
- The primary strategies used by bishops to deal with the diminishing number of priests are clustering parishes, using deacons, or multiple parish pastoring. Nearly half of the U.S. parishes share their pastor with one or more parishes or missions. Some of these circuit priests only reach a parish once or twice a month. Some pastors lead three, four or more parishes.
- Multiple-parish pastoring involves unique, identifiable skills and capabilities that cannot be reduced to just providing the same ministry in more places. Yet, few dioceses are providing formal training for this emerging form of leadership. Yes, multiple pastoring is hard on the individuals doing it—but many pastors are highly creative and energized by the challenges of multiple-parish settings.

---

[542] USCCS, on-line Press Release, June 3, 2009.

- These emerging models have a significant impact on human resources, and cause an increased awareness of legal and civil implications, including employment law, and of the church being employer. Adequate salaries and healthcare are issues in the church as well as everywhere else.
- The growing presence of laity in leadership roles calls for appropriate and adequate education and formation. (Further, formation of parishioners is the area most lacking in Catholic parishes.) Parishes are moving from a solely clergy based system to a system based in partnership.
- Being ethical and being collaborative are the marks of leaders themselves. Social justice is part of the very fabric of pastoral leaders. The key questions are: how do we work together as a team? How do men and women work together, or how do the ordained and professional staffs work together?
- Communities of the future will be vibrant and welcoming with smaller faith-based communities; total ministering communities with increased lay leadership; mission-focused, justice-based communities and inclusive of diverse peoples and forms of leadership.
- Excitingly, the next generation of leaders is active in the church today. In a nationwide study of college students and young adults in their 20s and 30s, 1,600 said they are interested in lay ministry. Overall, the young people said they wanted to know more about their faith. Yet, no one had mentioned to them the possibility of working in lay ministry or becoming a priest or religious.
- Importantly, the pastoral leaders confirmed in the EMP research that Catholics want Eucharistic, sacramental communities. This is core to their identity as pastoral leaders. People are concerned if they can be a "Eucharistic people" if they only have access to the Eucharist once a month, once a week, on days other than Saturday or Sunday. Pastoral leaders don't want to lose access to the Eucharist, and want it presided over the by the ordained. They know the church is

being invited into a larger understanding of what it means to be a Eucharistic People.[543]

Following up on some of those facts cited above, new ministries for women will develop just from the data gleaned by the Emerging Models Project. For example,

- If the issues in a parish concern language and citizenship, as they must with immigrant populations, lay ministers could teach civics and citizenship, or English as a Second Language (ESL) to minorities in the parish, or faith formation programs in the other languages.
- They could hold interactive seminars or courses for children or young people about their faith or prepare them to work in lay ministry.
- They could publish a parish bulletin insert in the other language talking about faith formation in the particular parish. Ministry should be about what's needed in the parish and should be limited only by the imagination and resources to achieve it.
- In the weeks preceding Christmas, the most accessed internet websites are those about Christmas carols, said Theresa Boucher, an artist, author, and active lay minister serving in the Diocese of Trenton, NJ. She and her husband, John Boucher, hold Master's Degrees in Religious Education and have been involved in catechist training and adult faith formation for more than 36 years. John is the Director of the Diocese's Office of Evangelization and Parish Development.

Theresa and John recently created a popular program to tap into this seasonal interest in Christmas. Called the "Christmas Carol Festival," it is where "unchurched," that is, inactive Catholics, are invited back, with their children in tow, to experience the message of Christmas through the songs and hymns and pageantry of the season.

---

[543]   Ibid., 1-6.

There's no scolding or recriminations: just the joy of Christmas. There may be witnesses by lay people, group discussions about Christmas, and refreshments. It awakens the participants interested in the church once again and invites them to keep coming back. It was just a simple idea and now is a widely-used method of evangelization. The "Christmas Carol Festival," and its training workshop and guidebook, won the "New Wineskins" Award for best new ministry in 2010.[544] It is wildly popular! More than 4,000 people participated in the first three years. Mr. Boucher said each parish committee goes through training and then they decide what they want to present in its own presentation of the festival. Generally, there is a lot of music, he noted.

- Every three months, the Office of Evangelization in the Trenton Diocese mails (or e-mails) copies of "Vibrant Parish Life," a multi-page list of diocesan announcements, upcoming workshops and training courses, and other parish development. It offers thousands of residents, evangelization course alums, catechists, Lay Ecclesial Ministers, and others, ways they can increase their individual spirituality. It's a simple yet effective tool to keep residents informed about what's going on regarding offerings in the diocese and furthers the evangelization role of every Catholic. Mailing will be discontinued in early 2012 and only e-mail used.
- Several parishes, including St. Veronica, Howell, NJ, use "Social Media" sites, such as Facebook, to inform their "friends" about parish activities, such as retreats, the Christmas Carol Festival, and other parish outreaches, even homily messages. The Archdiocese of Philadelphia has used some of these techniques to contact participants as well. The Diocese of Trenton has its own website to further enlighten Catholics, especially young people who are devotees of

---

[544] For more information about the Christmas Carol program, contact Mrs. Boucher at www.Christkey.org. For the Office of Evangelization and Parish development, call 609-406-7400, ext. 5605.

electronic media. It even uses radio programs for Black Catholics and diocesan produced cable television shows for teenagers, and others for seniors.

The Emerging Models data spells out what's needed in the church in the U.S. at this moment in history. All parish ministers and staff have to do is build on it. As Zeni Fox said in *New Ecclesial Ministry*," "Ministry is not envisioned as power over, but rather is an action from within the very network of relationships which constitute the life of the community."

CHAPTER 23

Forty Plus Years of Controversy

This chapter deals with the last 40 years of controversy in the Catholic Church. First, is the issue of women's possible ordination to the Ministerial Priesthood and /or to the Ministerial Deaconate and, second, are there some ancillary topics that connect to the issue of Women's Ordination.

Some people, who think only of the church's official stance on ordination at this time, "No," would argue this is the end of the chapter: two sentences. Other people say it is women's *probable* ordination, not *possible* ordination. When I started this research, I was told repeatedly that women's ordination to the priesthood was "inevitable." I was told this by women, both lay and religious sisters, and by men, including priests. Over and over again.

The Church hierarchy has steadfastly denied that this is even possible through the *Declaration on Women's Admission to the Ministerial Priesthood (Inter Insignoires),* issued by the Sacred Congregation for the Doctrine of the Faith, on Oct 15, 1976 under Pope Paul VI,[545] and 18 years later, in Pope John Paul II's *Apostolic Letter on Reserving Priestly Ordination to Men Alone (Ordinatio Sacerdolatis),* issued May 24, 1994.

---

[545] Oct 15 is the feast day of St. Teresa of Avila. While I'm sure it was not a coincidence that the Declaration was released on that date but more like a Vatican "dig" at the contradiction, a few years later, she was named "Doctor of the Church" by Pope Paul VI.

Will this ever change in the future? Only the Holy Spirit knows. Remember our idea of timing is not the same as God's.

The Sacraments are the center of church life and generate attention—families invite company to help celebrate Baptism, First Communion, Confirmation, Marriage, and Ordination. Eucharistic Liturgy is celebrated daily at "Mass," where congregants may receive Holy Communion (Eucharist). Much has changed in the Catholic Church in the past 40 years but onlookers don't recognize these differences because what they see are priestly celibacy and women in non-ministerial functions, no women officiating. They don't *see* anything different.

So what's different? Virtually everything is after the miracle of Vatican II. We now see women Lectors, Eucharistic Ministers, leaders of song, and altar servers at Liturgy, which we didn't see years ago! Congregations have adapted to many changes—Mass is said in the vernacular and facing the congregation, and Catholics can receive Communion in the hand or on the tongue, for 40 years. Women serve as PLCs (Parish Life Coordinators, mostly in the West and Midwest) and as Pastoral Associates. As important as they are—and they are—they are still ancillary positions.

"The Emerging Models Project of the American Church," as mentioned above, is a multi-year project initiated by the bishops to document the current status of the church in America and to forecast areas of need for future decades. Its statistics on the church in American are alarming regarding the exclusively male priesthood.

Alarming Statistics

- The Emerging Models Project said the church in the U.S. is experiencing a serious crisis in the lack of male vocations to the priesthood. There is a present dearth of priests and deacons in three-quarters of the country. Only in the Northeast of the U.S. is there sufficient clergy at this time. Mandatory celibacy and a desire to earn a more substantial income are the two most frequently cited reasons for the drop in male priestly vocations.

- 70 percent of the approximately 20,000 diocesan priests are over age 55.
- Many parishes have no staff, or are led by parishioners. Two-thirds of dioceses have more parishes than priests.
- Parishes are being merged, closed or clustered. In the southern tier, in California and on the Atlantic Seaboard, individual "mega-parishes' are serving more than 10,000 families.
- There is the unavoidable aging of priests, deacons and religious sisters. Many religious orders do not have current classes of novices. That means there is no one to take their places.
- The question is frequently asked: due to the shortage of priests who can consecrate the bread and wine, can the church stay as a Eucharistic-centered church if consecration of the Holy Eucharist, is only done periodically, say once a month or even less often, and not daily, or every Saturday and Sunday?[546]
- The new and emerging roles of the Laity are still evolving. How do these roles change with fewer priests?

"Maleness of Christ" Argument

The Church's main argument against women's ordination in the 1976 Declaration was "the maleness of Christ." Women cannot be priests, it stated, because Jesus was a man and women can never replicate

---

[546] FYI, Deacons can't consecrate the bread and wine; they are ministers of service at the Liturgy and lead other functions, such as baptisms, marriages and funerals, even counseling, formerly only performed by a priest. Extraordinary Ministers of Eucharist can't—theirs is distributing ministry at mass, to the sick and homebound. When a priest is not available to celebrate liturgy, a "Communion or Eucharistic Service" may be held, using hosts pre-consecrated at a previous Liturgy. It may be lead by a deacon or a lay person. Unlike the Liturgy or Mass, it contains fewer prayers and, of course, no consecration. Some people think it's just a "shorter mass," since some of the prayers are the same, but that's inaccurate—it's different, not Mass.

that. The term "maleness" is a polite euphemism for biology—having a penis—not masculine traits like broad shoulders or a beard. The Declaration stated maleness is integral for the ministry of priesthood.

It seems odd that a physical body part—or not having one—should be the criterion for church ministry. A wonderful monsignor I know has the autoimmune disease, Lupus, and he can no longer stand or walk as he used to; he must sit when delivering a homily, but having a disease, which negatively affects his body, doesn't make him less of a presbyter. It is his brain, spirit, training, vocation and his ministry which matter, not his legs or stamina.

I know many Catholic women who are "everyday, ordinary Catholics"—wives and mothers, divorced or unmarried, many of them active in church ministries, like my long time friend Annie, all of whom have no interest in ordination for themselves. Her real name is used with permission. Women uniformly find the "maleness line of reasoning" to be flat out "insulting" to women everywhere. Annie is also regular tither—that is, she donates 10% of her income to church ministries. The "maleness" contention infuriates her so: she believes it indicates women and their ministries are ignored and belittled by the hierarchy. If women, who are the mainstay of the church, stopped going or contributing, what would become of it? I'm sure the clerics who devised the "maleness" argument never considered that as a consequence!

Whatever else the church says about a priest's role—many people believe the main function of a priest is as a leader of worship. If so, it isn't necessary that only a male could do that, a religious sister told me years ago. She had a Ph.D. in a technical chemical field and worked a professional job for a Fortune 500 Company.[547] "Women can lead worship too," she said.

Many people presume that women who support women's ordination do so because they personally want to be ordained; that's

---

[547] Sisters often work for corporations today, especially to use their salaries for their communities, to help pay expenses for older sisters and so forth. Besides, they often earn more salary than they would in more traditional jobs, like teaching children, sadly.

totally untrue. Support for this expression of ministry is much wider than those who actually believe they have the vocation for the office. In every recent poll of U.S. Catholics, both men and women favor Women's Ordination.

What happens to the Bread and Wine at Eucharist? At the consecration, a great mystery occurs, according the Church; it is called "Transubstantiation." The Catholic Catechism, Section 1376, explains, "By the consecration of the bread and wine there takes place a change of the whole substance of the bread into the substance of the body of Christ our Lord, and of the whole substance of the wine into the substance of His blood," and from Section 1377, "Christ is present whole and entire in each of the species and whole and entire in each of their parts, in such a way that the breaking of the bread does not divide Christ."[548] The word Transubstantiation was first used to describe this religious mystery in the 11th century and confirmed at the Council of Trent in the 1500's.

Christ is unrepeatable, so if the bread and wine are transubstantiated into His Body and Blood, why does the person initiating this have to be male? It may be my simplistic understanding of the process but if the bread and wine turn into Jesus' Body and Blood, it doesn't turn into the priest's body, whomever that may be. The Church says the priest represents Christ.

One of my deacon friends explained that, "The priest does not become Christ. He's merely the figuration or symbol of Christ." In Wickipedia it says, "The Catholic Church holds that when the bread is changed into his body, not only his body is present, but *Christ as a whole is present* (i.e, body and blood, soul and divinity). The same holds for the wine changed into his blood. This belief goes beyond the Doctrine of Transubstantiation, which directly concerns only the transformation of the bread and wine into the body and blood of Christ."[549]

Yes, Jesus was male because His mission, as Davidic king, required that the saving Lamb must be an unblemished male—that is,

---

[548] *Catechism of the Catholic Church*, (New York: Image Books/Doubleday, 1994), Sections 1376 and 1377, 384-5.
[549] Explanation by Deacon Ralph Hammock, 2010. Also, Wikipedia, 2010.

sinless. Jesus came to fulfill the Law and it stipulated the sin offering had to be sacrificed alive in a blood sacrifice. It is the blood which made the sacrifice redemptive. The Messiah had to be a Jewish male from the line of David, because the gentiles had no theological status in Israel; women and slaves even less. Therefore, none of them could literally fulfill the law. Jesus did. There are 333 prophesies about the Messiah in the Old Testament and Jesus fulfills everyone. No one else even comes close, nor ever did or could.

It wasn't even until after the Resurrection that "the Twelve" disciples came to be called Apostles, or even differentiated as "The Twelve." Paul and Barnabas were known as "Apostles" in the early church but they did not belong to the Twelve. Many Scriptural passages show other disciples, besides the "Faithful 11," also saw the Resurrected Jesus. According to the *Ignatius Catholic Study Bible*, the term "all the apostles" indicates a wider circle than the Twelve, as in Acts 14:14 and 2 Cor. 8:23.[550] Luke 24:33 says, "The eleven and those with them." Paul in 1 Cor. 15: 3-8 lists a series of different believers who saw the Risen Lord including: "Peter, 'the Twelve'; 500 brethren; James; 'all of the Apostles'; and last of all himself."

Paul somehow forgot to mention that Mary Magdalene saw Jesus before Peter did. We've been conditioned to think the term "Apostles" means the "Twelve," that they are synonymous descriptions. Rather, that's just a convenient way of looking at it. The larger group of Disciples/Apostles certainly did include women; only the men subsequently called "The Twelve" did not. When Paul mentioned "500 brethren" he's talking about a rather large crowd of believers who saw the Risen Christ and who basically had traveled in ministry with Him. Was that a composite "brethren" of men and women—or just men, as in the Multiplication of the Bread stories? If men and women, that means way more than 500 saw the Resurrected Christ. Five hundred people are considered a large crowd today—back then it was considered enormous.

Women now can be Pastoral Associates (also called Pastoral Assistants), helping to run the parish and its activities, something

---

[550] *Ignatius Catholic Study Bible*, 306.

unheard of years ago. One female Pastoral Associate in New Jersey is about as much of an "insider" as an un-ordained, married woman can be in the early 21st century male-dominated church. She serves on many diocesan boards and represents the diocese at other meetings, so she asked not to be identified here. She is educated, has a strong personal faith, and is a great person.

In her work-parish, there is just the pastor, her and secretaries. She and her husband live in a separate parish. As Pastoral Associate she is responsible for everything the pastor doesn't handle; that is overseeing and initiating many outreaches and ministries within the parish. She is an integral part of what the military calls, "the Command Structure" in her parish, which consists of several thousand families and individuals.

She said in an interview in 2009 that the women's ordination issue is a "dead horse," that is, nothing can change or revive it. She said, "The higher-ups don't want to even hear about it." They think it's behind them, dead. "Worse," she said, "if women's ordination did happen, it would be schismatic for the church"—meaning it would split the church in two. She criticized women seeking ordination as in a struggle "for power and control" and believes these women "don't want to be told what to do." Her reaction sounds harsh and frightened but she is an insider and that's the hierarchy's attitude.

People arguing for women's ordination claim *not allowing* it is a denial of the privileges granted under Baptism and that deprives a woman from receiving the grace from the Sacrament of Orders. They refute the argument that they want to be in charge, saying they are *not* seeking power and control, that ministry is to be a *servant* to the people of God. They maintain they definitely have a vocation, or call, to ministry, and that it is God-given, like any vocation. They say that they are willing to work within the church structure. Most of all, advocates for women's ordination contend this is a movement of the Holy Spirit, which cannot be denied.

The church's traditionally answers that reception of the sacraments and/or serving in Sacramental ministry are privileges, not rights. It holds that no one has an inherent right to do so, not even men. It says not everyone can or will receive all seven sacraments—that the Church is not a democracy with "entitlements." Most of all, the hierarchy says, it is upholding tradition passed down from the Apostles—not to ordain females.

Right now, yes, a man could receive all seven sacraments if circumstances allowed. Women can receive six. Men can be widowers and become priests, or leave the priesthood and then marry. Today, women can't receive Holy Orders, nor can Deacons, if married. Men can't receive Orders if screened out as unqualified, or psychologically unfit. Priests and single people don't receive Matrimony. Children who die won't receive all the sacraments. People who die in emergencies like a car or plane crash, or in war from a car bomb in Iraq and Afghanistan, called an Improvised Explosive Device (IED), often don't have priests nearby to offer the Sacrament of the Sick.[551] Or, perhaps the body is so badly destroyed, anointing isn't possible, as in many deaths at the World Trade Center, on September 11, 2001.

Regarding women's ordination, I don't know if a schism could or would happen, or if that's just an argument to give the possibility of women's ordination "the worst possible scenario." The same prediction was made in the 1970's when the Episcopal Church first ordained women. That never happened. The same prediction was made about the issue of Headship and Submission. That never happened either.

What did happen is the male priests who did not agree with women's ordination in the Anglican Communion banded together and petitioned the pope for them to become Roman Catholic priests. Eventually, this request was permitted. It happened in 2009, and a second wave of an additional 100 clerics, happened in 2010.

---

[551] The Sacrament of the Sick was formerly called Extreme Unction, though commonly known as the "Last Rites." It was so called, not because it was administered at the end of life, though it often was, but because it was the last sacrament listed which used chrism or Holy Oil for anointing: Baptism, Confirmation, Holy Orders and Extreme Unction. The oil represents the Holy Spirit. The other three sacraments are Eucharist, Matrimony, and Reconciliation (formerly called Penance, and commonly known as "Confession")—no oil is administered in reception of these.

The Episcopal male priests who did not disagree with the female ordinations continued in their ministry in the Episcopal Church.

These men and their priestly vows—and their wives and families—were accepted "lock, stock and barrel," with some minor arrangements to fit with their Anglican backgrounds. These Episcopalian priests say they switched because they are more in line with the hierarchical authority structure of the Roman church—power vested in the top in the pope, which then is delegated to cardinals and bishops. They say the Episcopalian decision-making isn't as clear-cut; that in the Catholic Church the pope has the final authority, not a group of elders.[552] The Church claims that's the reason for their switch, not women's ordination. Was that an Episcopal /Anglican schism or just a splintering? Now these men minister in Roman parishes as Roman Catholic—and some are married—priests.

It seems to me that the two, seemingly unrelated questions—women's ordination and a married clergy—are linked as never before, especially after Episcopal priests who opposed women's ordination in their church, and who were mostly married, were accepted as priests in the Roman Catholic Church.

This effort to align with the Catholic Church started in the 1970s when Rev. Canon Alfred J. DuBois headed the Pro-(Temporary) Diocese of St. Augustine of Canterbury, an Episcopalian community, headquartered in Burbank, CA. He and his colleagues disagreed with the Episcopal Church's ordination of women and petitioned the Vatican to be reconciled with the Roman Catholic Church and to come under the authority of the pope. The USCCB and the Vatican granted permission in 1980.[553]

---

[552] In addition to the two groups of Episcopalian priests accepted recently in the Catholic Church by the pope, a friend told me that the late NYC Cardinal John O'Connor had also accepted married Episcopalian priests into the fold. Again, the priests had petitioned him with their request.

[553] DuBois also said the male priest reflects "the creative activity of God the Father" because "the male has the initiative in creation." If the words sound familiar, they are—it's the same argument and vocabulary from Aristotle, Augustine and Aquinas.

If the same situation happened that Episcopal priests wanted to join the Roman Catholic Church but for another root cause, I wonder if the Catholic Church would have accepted their Episcopal colleagues so readily? Despite ecumenism efforts, I think not. Regarding ecumenism, the Catholic Church's closest ecumenical ties today are with the Lutheran Church, not its nearer cousin, the Episcopalians, according to a priest who headed a diocese's Ecumenical efforts for many years.

When Bishop Timothy Dolan was named head of the New York Archdiocese by Pope Benedict XVI in 2009, the perennial questions arose from the media about the clergy being able to marry and women's ordination both to the priesthood and the deaconate.* Church commentators say the New York Archdiocese is considered to be the nearest to the Vatican for Catholic orthodoxy—its "spokes-diocese," if that were grammatically possible. *(Dolan was made cardinal in 2012.)

The new archbishop said the question of a married clergy had to be revisited. The Vatican interpreters said that meant Dolan wasn't speaking for himself alone but that his statement was made with papal assent—not just off the cuff in response to reporter's questions. It indicated that the Vatican wants the issue to be revisited.

If the Vatican wishes to readdress the question of priestly celibacy, it will—if not immediately. The hierarchy d e l i b e r a t e s and that takes time. If Pope John XXIII had put the question of having an Ecumenical Council, the first in 100 years, to a committee, they might still be debating whether to do it! Inspired by the Holy Spirit, he announced it, surprising everyone.

Regarding women's ordination to the priesthood, it appears the hierarchy is not in a hurry to revisit this question quickly at this moment. Although they are separate issues, women's ordination to the Ministerial Deaconate is classified in the minds of clerics with priestly ordination, so it seems that this topic might not be studied too readily, either. Of course, as the widely publicized advertisement for betting on one state's lottery—hinting of the possibility of winning millions—reminds us, "you never know!"

Non-Celibate Clergy

What the Catholic Church has now is not a celibate clergy. Rather, it is a mixed marital status clergy, including celibates and married. Yes, there are also homosexual priests; that's been known for many, many years and probably was true throughout the history of the church. Most of them proceed with their Christian mission with no disruption to the church community; it has been said the male-only environment of priesthood was a draw to some homosexual men. Apparently, vocations are non-discriminatory for sexual orientation.[554] In the recent priest scandals of the 1990's and 2000's, the child abuse offenders were often homosexual men, said one confidential source.

---

[554] Some well-known homosexual priests in our time include the wonderful priest and servant of God, the late Bishop Emerson Moore. He was the first black appointed to become a Bishop in the Archdiocese of New York. As a bishop, he lived at Holy Family parish on East 46th Street, New York City, and subsequently died of AIDS. Franciscan Father Mychal Judge, was a chaplain of the New York Firefighters for years before his untimely death at the World Trade Center on 9/11/2001. He was administering the Sacrament of the Sick to those injured in the blast when a ceiling of the building fell, killing him instantly. Also, a successful fundraiser for a large diocese is gay and it doesn't diminish his capabilities as a priest or fundraiser. He was mentioned, anonymously, in a story about gay priests in *National Catholic Reporter* newspaper years ago, so his sexual orientation is known in the wider community. In between being an archdiocesan fundraiser the first time, and a return to it years later, he was the pastor in the parish where I lived. In another case, a gay priest in a suburban diocese has an active Prison ministry, and on and on. Unless he told us at the retreat he was leading, as he did, how would we know? While people disagree about the homosexual lifestyle and find it either abhorrent or acceptable—the gay men and women, called lesbians, insist they were born this way and that it is not a 'developmental' issue. Many of them struggle with celibacy issues in programs like the Catholic Dignity, where gays promise to be sexually inactive. The fact is gays are in the world, the church and, yes, the U.S. military and the priesthood. For years, the Jesuits in one of their NYC parishes had a monthly Mass for the gay and Lesbian communities. Under the late Cardinal O'Connor that was eliminated. Many of the regular attendees at that Mass probably were struggling to be "inactive." For eliminating that Mass, O'Connor was soundly criticized as being a bigot. However, at the same time, compassionately, Cardinal O'Connor was an active supporter of several AIDS ministries, and visited AIDS patients in hospitals or hospice programs at least once a week.

Most of the victims were at puberty or older. The fact that these perpetrators were known homosexuals was neglected by the media for whatever reason.

If Catholic priests were free to choose celibacy that would be one thing—but to have it imposed is another. Especially, while at the same time, in the Latin Rite, having formerly Episcopalian married priests is allowed. (Their priestly vows were accepted and they are now Roman Catholic priests.) Also, priests in the Byzantine Rite under the pope's aegis many marry if they do not wish to go on to be appointed bishops. This was always allowed. Clearly having a part celibate and a part married clergy gives a very disparate message.

Why were Roman Catholic priests who left to get married, or were "laicized" to do so, not invited back into ministry? Why are these men and their families ignored and looked on as traitors? Why is there a double standard? If all these men came back, would there still be as severe a priest-shortage? Rev. Brendan Williams, pastor of St. Veronica's Church, Howell, NJ, said in 2011 that a survey was done of those men who left the priesthood and married. The response was they didn't want to return. Fr. Williams believes that's because their individual priestly ministries were dead before they left the priesthood. If that's true, leaving really didn't have to do with the marriage question. Fr. Williams also said without the power of Jesus and the Holy Spirit in priestly ministry, it can die.

You don't hear anything about the families of the Episcopalians-turned-Catholic priests. One New Jersey priest I asked in 2010 said, "That's the way they want it." I thought that meant the higher-ups, but it may also be the families themselves. How are these families surviving on a priest's minimal salary? Did the married priests get a raise? Where do they live—certainly not in the rectory with the other priests? Who provides the majority of child care? Who pays for college and health care? Did the whole family willfully "turn Catholic" or just the priests? Isn't it psychologically difficult for the families who for years identified themselves as one denomination, then suddenly, they are another? The priests made a choice to convert—the families didn't necessarily. Assuming the wives go along, are the families resentful of their Dad's choice?

And what about the ancient argument against a married clergy—that being married would distract the priest from his duties to God and the church? What about the ancient arguments that when a married priest dies, who inherits his property—the family or the church? That's one of the main reasons celibacy was imposed in the first place in the 1100's.

As the recent sex scandals in the church made us too aware, some men who are priests do not imitate Christ. He is all good; they are pedophiles or other sexual abusers, criminals, fallen. While most priests are virtuous and maintain their vows—*only one percent of the active clergy was involved in the sex scandals*—and that's still one percent too many—there are those who do not keep their celibacy vow—by having sex with men or with women. It had been ever thus. It's been true in Latin America and Africa for years. In the Middle Ages having papal mistresses was commonplace. One pope, who was known for great nepotism toward his family members, was Pope Paul III in the 1500's; he had a grandson, Ottario Farnese, Duke of Parma.[555] And, one pope was the grandson of a preceding pope![556] It seems like many of these clerics in the Middle Ages—*after* celibacy

---

[555] Wikipedia on the "Papacy."

[556] Here are examples: Accessed from Wikipedia in 2010 for sites for Rome, Popes, Sexually Active Popes, Rodrigue Borgia, St. Francis Borgia, and Pope Alexander VI, among others.

Pope Felix III (483-492) was the great, great grandfather of Pope Gregory the Great. Celibacy was not required then.

Pope John XII (955-964) was known for great debauchery.

Benedict IX in the early 10th century also had children. Extremely corrupt, Benedict IX allegedly sold the Papacy to get married. He served and was ousted as pope three times; he was a youth, age 20 or younger, the first time, when his family bought the chair of Peter for him.

The 15th century was known for widespread papal corruption.

Pope Paul III (1534-1549) had children. Many popes fathered children either before or during their papal reigns. It was one of the reasons leading up to the Protestant Reformation.

Pope Alexander VI (Rodrigue Borgia), who became pope in 1492, is classified as the most corrupt pope ever. He had four children: one was son, Giovanni Borgia; his daughter was the notorious Lucretzia Borgia, who headed the Papal Court when Alexander was away. Yet his grandson was a saint, St. Francis Borgia.

was mandated—were more concerned about earthly desires than their churchly ministries.

John Paul II's Apostolic Letter: *"Ordinatio Sacerdolatis"*

Women have certainly been discriminated in many ways over time by the Church; no one honestly can refute that. While prohibiting women from priesthood and the deaconate appears to be further forms of discrimination, Pope John Paul II (JPII), who was a great supporter of women in general and for their contributions to the Church, claimed—*"no, it isn't."* The Vatican Declaration, issued in 1976, generated much controversy; Pope John Paul II decided to reemphasize its basic premise in his letter, *Ordinatio Sacerdolatis,* and in it he tried to address some of the issues which were raised following the Declaration.

The Apostolic Letter *"On Reserving Priestly Ordination to Men Alone" (Ordinatio Sacerdolatis),* was released on May 22, 1994, 18 years after the Vatican Declaration was issued. Pope John Paul II stated when the question of women's ordination arose in the Anglican Communion in the 1970's, Pope Paul VI was "safeguarding the Apostolic tradition" and "removing a possible barrier to Christian unity" by issuing the declaration. (Oddly enough, women's ordination in the Episcopal Church, and in other Protestant denominations, and the Catholic Church's steadfast refusal to do so, has become a barrier to Christian unity. Other denominations thought it haughty of the Catholics to proclaim that *only* it was listening to the true voice of God.)

John Paul II said Paul VI was following the "constant tradition of the church of Jesus choosing only men." He states, "The exclusion of women from the priesthood is in accord with God's plan for his church."[557] Jesus' action choosing only male disciples "shows clearly that Christ's way of acting did not proceed from sociological or

---

[557] Pope John Paul II, "Apostolic Letter on Reserving Priestly Ordination to Men Alone," (*Ordinatio Sacerdolatis*), May 22, 1994, paragraph two.

cultural motives peculiar to his time," John Paul stated.[558] This was "in union with God's eternal plan: Christ chose those whom he willed," JPII said.[559] "The Apostles did the same when they choose fellow workers, those who would succeed them in their ministry."[560] At the conclusion of his letter the pope wrote, "I declare that the church has no authority whatsoever to confer priestly ordination on women and that this judgment is to be definitely held by all the church's faithful."[561]

Even after *Ordinatio Sacerdolatis*, controversy, disagreement and discussion continued. So the Congregation for the Doctrine of the Faith (CDF) released *Responsum ad Dubium* (Reply to a Doubt) in Oct. 1995, approved by JPII. It stated under the "ordinary magisterium," the teaching of *Ordinatio* is: "the church did not possess the authority to ordain women" was to be held definitely. In 1998, the term "ordinary magisterium" was clarified. One of the problems is that not every Bishop and Cardinal agree on this issue, so it's not uniform within the magisterium. Apparently, there is no consensus. Of course, the church consistently maintains the issue is doctrinal not disciplinary.

Additionally, on the other hand, the Pope said, **"The presence and the role of women in the life and mission of the church,** although not linked to the ministerial priesthood, **remain absolutely necessary and irreplaceable."**[562]

Yes, Jesus chose the Twelve—all males and all from Galilee, there were no Gentiles. So, if the priesthood has to represent that model, where would the church be today? The Roman Curia is largely Italian. The Irish were the mainstay of the priesthood for generations. Today, America is considered a missionary country with many priests from Africa and India. Jesus conformed to the mores of His time when necessary and didn't when they were hurtful to His followers. With due respect to the late pope and his opinion, it has to be pointed out that statement about Jesus' cultural motives factually

---

[558] Ibid., paragraph four.
[559] Ibid.
[560] Ibid.
[561] Ibid., paragraph 12.
[562] Ibid.

is inaccurate. John Paul overlooks the facts that the Bible says that women did indeed travel in ministry with Jesus and provided for Him out of their own resources. Angels and women were the only ones who ministered to Jesus' needs (Mk 1:13; Lk. 23:49).

Jesus also **chose** Mary Magdalene to go and tell the male disciples that He was alive. Mary Magdalene was called "the Apostle to the Apostles" in the Church Liturgy for centuries. She went and proclaimed "Jesus lives" when the male disciples were cringing in fear in the Upper Room, afraid they too would be arrested and murdered, as He had been. Her job was *evangelista*. Besides Mary of Magdala, there were other women who witnessed to women in the Early Church, women who were leaders in the early church community; it's a fact also that the church grew rapidly among both men and women.

Neither Jesus nor the male disciples were priests in the Jewish priestly caste, or even from the priestly Tribe of Levi. Neither did Jesus ordain anyone, male or female. Nope, not one. The pope didn't mention that. Nor did Jesus appoint any deacons. Yes, the Apostles chose their fellow workers, but *since women weren't allowed to talk to men in public,* whom could the Apostles pick except men to evangelize and minister to men? Even deacons in the early church could not address women. John Paul II's statements seem to be what lawyers frequently argue in court about a litigant's liability, *"He knew or should have known."* Besides, I'm a lay person and if I know it—and now you do too, if you didn't before—the pope *certainly must have known* that the ordained priesthood evolved several centuries later, *not at the time of the Apostles,* specifically in the 3rd Century. That's at least 300 years without an ordained priesthood. The servers chosen by the apostles were long dead by the time the priesthood was instituted. Did John Paul suppose no one else already knew that information in 1994? This is not the period after the Council of Trent when its results were not publicized for centuries. The Internet and 24-hour news cycles give us answers in seconds.

The media "spin" on political happenings around the world, explaining the behind the scenes rationale for those happenings and legal analysis, has given us a critical eye. Knowing what we know now about the culture and mores of Jesus' and early church times regarding women, it seems "like Vatican spin" to say that the exclusion of women "had nothing to do with sociological or cultural motives peculiar to Jesus' time." Politicians often say what they want us to hear, not necessarily, a direct answer to the question. John Paul II was certainly an adept politician, as well as pope, humanitarian, playwright, skier and priest. He was dogmatically anti-Communist in the Cold War era, which contributed to his political savvy.[563] Pope John Paul II had many gifts and personal charisma but he was also very conservative and doctrinaire about Catholic tradition and teaching. He was far more open and liberal in his dealing with people. Like "poetic license," I believe he used "papal license" to say "prohibiting women from the priesthood was in accord with God's plan," for the following reasons:

1. We don't know the mind of God, nor the future. Not even the pope does. Prayer certainly helps, as does the Holy Spirit's guidance and insight. God does speak to us but He also doesn't do unnecessary things. Physically blinding us, as happened to St. Paul in the New Testament, doesn't usually happen to get us to change our minds or opinions today.

2. We have no information from any of his writings or statements that John Paul II received a revelation from God about this topic. The Apostolic letter itself doesn't mention such a thing. Maybe it happened, or perhaps not. I think that if it had occurred, the pope certainly would have included that in his letter. We do know, however, that the pope personally was opposed to the idea of women's ordination; *Ordinatio Sacerdolatis* reflects this.

---

[563] John Paul II is up for future canonization based on his entire papacy. On Jan 14, 2011, John Paul II was "Beatified;" Pope Benedict named JPII to the category, "Blessed," on the road to sainthood. He was previously named to the "fast track" for this honor. One significant healing—of a religious sister with Parkinson's disease—was attributed to JPII's intercession. Another significant healing must be proven before sainthood can be achieved. As it happened, JPII was also in poor health in 1994, which may have motivated him to write the letter. According to *Time*'s story on the "Person of the Year" in 1994, his left hand shook from the previous assassination attempt and injuries; he hobbled with a cane because of bone replacement surgery; and some doctors thought he was depressed or despondent. The actual Beautification ceremony was held in May 2011.

3. Papal infallibility was used only once—in 1950, when Pope Pius XII declared Mary's Assumption into Heaven. The pope is infallible only in matters of faith or morals, "not in church policy, discipline or the pope's private opinion," according to *The Maryknoll Catholic Dictionary.*[564]

Yes, Jesus chose male disciples to be the founders of the church, but as mentioned above, it was the prophets and prophetesses of the early Eucharistic commemorations who presided, according to the early Church order, the *Didache*, which was comparable to today's Canon Law. We already know that women did hold prophetic office in the early church. It was only when there were insufficient prophets and teachers from the lay community that bishops and deacons were selected. The Bishops and deacons became the "ordinary ministers of the Eucharist" because of heresies like Gnosticism and a growing suspicion of prophesy, McGrath noted. That lead to the suppression of the prophets in the church, she said, except for canonized saints, and until more recent times.

Women had no role in their society at that time—so how could they have been the organizers at the dawn of this crucial endeavor? One point in creating the church was to make it viable to survive until the end times—it wouldn't have gotten off the ground if people couldn't talk to one another.

Pope John Paul mentions the Blessed Mother in his letter. He had great personal devotion to her—"that she did neither receive the mission proper to the Apostles nor the ministerial priesthood clearly shows the non-admission of women to priestly ordination cannot mean that women are of lesser dignity, nor can it be construed as a discrimination against them."[565]

Mary's role was to bring Christ to us; that is still her role centuries later. She didn't have "to do" anything else. The fact that Mary wasn't a priest doesn't really pertain to the issue that women are prohibited from being ordained. People who oppose women's ordination often say, "If Jesus wanted women to be priests, he would have ordained his mother." Pardon me but that's just malarkey. Remember Jesus didn't

---

[564]   Maryknoll Catholic Dictionary, 293.
[565]   JPII, paragraph 7.

ordain anyone. The Apostles didn't give birth to Jesus. That was not their role; it was Mary's unique place. Mary was filled with the Holy Spirit when the angel came initially on the Annunciation, and when she went to visit Elizabeth. She was refilled on Pentecost. Do you think she sat home and just sewed? I bet she talked to everyone she ever met about her lord and savior, who happened also to be her son. He is foremost her redeemer. (Coincidentally, redeemer in Hebrew means relative.) And, I bet, she was a dynamo talking about him! Besides, she's a Jewish mother talking about her only son! She is also evangelista, a forerunner of what every Christian is called to be today, an evangelist for the kingdom. And in the frequency cited term, "the priesthood of all believers", then Mary was indeed a priest and Mary Magdalene was too. The "Priesthood of all believers" is based on a person's Baptism and Confirmation and living a good Christian life. For the two Marys, it was their belief in Jesus as Messiah, since they predated Christian sacraments.

Like the accommodations of the early church to the cultural mores of its time, regarding women speaking and prophesying in Church assemblies, the "founders" of the church had to be men for its culture and society. *Not because* Jesus was male or chose men to follow him. The amount of freedom granted to the women in the churches was way beyond what they received in the outside pagan community. The women were saved and baptized just as the men were, as we are reminded in Gal. 3:28, "There is neither Jew nor Greek, there is neither slave nor free, there is neither male nor female; for you are all one in Jesus Christ."

Galatians 3: 27-28

Gal. 3:27-28 fascinates Christian women by its "vision of equality, wholeness and freedom," said theologian Elizabeth Schusser Fiorenza. She said the verses were affirmed by Vatican II in The Constitution on the Church (No. 32): "Hence there is in Christ and in the church no inequality on the basis of race nor nationality, social condition or sex, because there is 'neither Jew nor Greek . . . (Gal. 3: 28).'" She continued:

Yet this vision was never completely realized by the Christian Church through its history. The context of the conciliar statement reflects the discriminatory praxis* of the church, insofar as it maintains the equality for all Christians in respect to salvation, hope and charity but not with respect to church structures and ecclesial office.[566]

Fiorenza said the church's failure to see the vision of Gal. 3:28 in its own institutions resulted in its long sexist history which attempted to justify inequality and to suppress the vision of Gal. 3:28 and its call of freedom and equality within the church.[567]

In the Vatican II document, Decree on the Apostolate of the Laity, the bishops said, "Since in our time, women have an ever more active share in the whole life of society, it is very important that they participate more widely, also, in the various fields of the church's apostolate."[568] Also, the council said of its own constituent purpose, "In this assembly, under the guidance of the Holy Spirit, we wish to inquire how we ought to renew ourselves, so that we may be found increasingly faithful to the gospel of Christ."[569]

The Gospel of Christ includes Gal. 3:28, of course.[570]

---

[566] Elizabeth Schusser Fiorenza, "Feminist Theology as a Critical Theology of Liberation," *Women: New Dimensions,* 43. *Praxis is the practical application of rules, accepted as habitual practice or custom.

[567] Ibid.

[568] Walter M. Abbott, S.J., ed., *Documents of Vatican II.* "Decree on the Apostolate of the Laity," Chapter III, "The Various Fields of the Apostolate, Section 9, 500.

[569] Abbott, "Message to Humanity," issued at the beginning of the Second Vatican Council by its Fathers, with the endorsement of the Supreme Pontiff, 3-4.

[570] By the way, women were present only as observers at the Council, *not* as participants. Pope John Paul II then Karol Cardinal Wojtyla, in Krakow, Poland, was prohibited by the communist Polish authorities from attending the Council, although he was involved by long-distance phone conversations and personal emissaries.

Similarly, the Synod of Bishops in 1971 said, "We also urge that women should have their own share of responsibility and participation in the community life of society and likewise in the church," as quoted in the report of the Vatican Study Commission on Women in Society and in the Church.[571]

Elsewhere in his *Ordinatio* Letter, John Paul II says, "**women are not less than men**," something he truly believed. Unfortunately, there are many who still believe we are. It is true in the first centuries of Christianity women were not corporate CEOs, nor church leaders, nor scientists, nor astronauts. And men weren't either. It's not known if women were altar servers then, but I would bet the long-established women's Altar-Rosary Societies, where initially the women washed and ironed altar cloths, arose from being sacristans of their day. The churches started in women's homes—who else to keep it neat?

Women and the Deaconate

The issue of women's ordination to the Deaconate, though often coupled with women's ordination to the Priesthood, is a separate question. There is an *irrefutable* tradition of women deaconesses in the Catholic Church. Also, a deacon does not celebrate Mass, nor consecrate the bread and wine, "so tradition is not being violated," as Edmond Cullinan said in *Worship* magazine in 1986, and explained by Zeni Fox in 2002.[572] The deacon just participates in different ministerial functions during the celebration. At one time in the 1970s deacons were compared to "being like big altar boys," now there are girl altar servers also. So, if you can have male deacons "taking over" for altar boys, why not have female deacons "taking over" for altar girls?[573]

---

[571] As quoted in Lange and Cushing, 157,. 24.
[572] As quoted in Zeni Fox, *New Ecclesial Ministry: Lay Professionals Serving the Church*, 120-121.
[573] In fact, before the regulation allowing girl servers, pastors used women to technically get around the rule of no girls. One said, "They do a beautiful job

The Church's reply is that women deaconesses were *only* in the *early* church; they "didn't last long" before the policy was removed; and that the early deaconate is unlike today's ministerial function. Basically, then it provided bread, other goods, and minimal nursing attention—not medical help, there was virtually none—to the early Christian communities. Those roles today are largely provided by social service agencies and the health care system.[574] Deacons did the same things for the men of the community and were forbidden from doing it for the women of the congregation. Someone did it though. Who could that have been?

According to the *Catholic Encyclopedia* on-line, "Deaconesses trace their roots from the time of Jesus through the 13th century."[575] Also, it is questionable if "formal recognition can be found in the New Testament, although Phebe (Phoebe) in Roman 16:1 is called *"diakonos"* . . . but there can be no question that before the middle of the fourth century women were permitted to exercise certain definite functions in the church and were known by the special name of *diakonoi* or *diakonissai*."[576] If the deaconesses existed until the 13th century in some locales—that was more than half of the life of the church, not a short time. Even if only to the fourth century, that's more than 400 years with women deaconesses.

"That in the early church (and still today in the Greek Orthodox Church), women were ordained as deacons, that women's roles have broadened in modern society, and that many women feel called to the deaconate," the Catholic Theological Society of America said in 1978, according to Fox. "Actual services being performed by

---

as you would expect. Some of the parishioners didn't like it at first but they got used to it." His diocese didn't permit females on the altar at the time.

[574] In the four counties of Diocese of Trenton, NJ, which though small geographically, has one of the most densely Catholic populations in the country, Catholic Charities is the largest welfare agency. It receives funding from the state because the state couldn't afford to provide all these services—food distribution, health services, AIDS ministries, housing, shelters for the homeless and for battered women, and on and on.

[575] The *Catholic Encyclopedia*, "Deaconesses" (Search was for "Deaconesses in the Early Catholic Church"), and Wikipedia.org/wiki/deaconesses.

[576] Ibid.

women, both secular and religious, could often be rendered more effectively if they were performed from within the office of deacon," Fox quoted.[577]

The ministry of the male deacon was eliminated for centuries and only brought back in its new form after Vatican II. Although approved at the Council in the 1960s, it wasn't put into practice until 1972. Prior to that, the Catholic Theological Society prepared a report for the U.S. Bishops on the restoration of the permanent diaconate in 1971. The writer stated, that along with collegiality, "The restoration of the deaconate as a permanent office in the Roman Catholic Church is the most significant structural innovation instituted by the Council (Vatican II) in regard to church office. In effect, it constituted the beginnings of a restructuring of all the Ministries in the Catholic Church."[578]

Hierarchy Ignores Advice of Advisors, Laity

Before the Vatican Declaration on Women was issued in 1976, Pope Paul had a commission study this controversial question for several years. Its conclusion: there was neither a valid nor a Scriptural reason why it was prohibited; it was merely tradition. The pope disagreed and said to advisors come up with a reason. "The Maleness of Christ" rational was the result. Were there any women on that panel of advisors? Probably not. It sounds like an all male decision to me. Remember, Aquinas said the conception of a female child was due to a defective mother, a defective seed from the male (never a defective man!) or a humid, wet wind.

Seminarians routinely are indoctrinated with Aquinas' philosophies and his attitudes are still pervasive in the church. Leaders in the church have long been taught surreptitiously to fear the presence of women, dating back to the negative "influence" of the blood taboos. It seems unconsciously they are afraid women in

---

[577] Fox, 120-121.
[578] Fox, 120.

leadership would take over the clergy and the hierarchy, in effect making a "gynecocracy" or rule by women, like the Amazon warriors. I don't think realistically that could ever happen! Besides, no one wants that.

Other advisory bodies ignored on this question were: the Vatican Committee on Women in Church and Society, the Secretariat for Christian Unity and the Pontifical Bible Commission. The Committee on Women in Church and Society was forbidden from even discussing the issue of women's ordination.

Within the laity at each subsequent poll the percentage of Americans who support women's ordination has increased. It's almost a two to one difference of supporters versus opponents. A joint CBS News/NY Times poll in May 2010 said 59% of American Catholics favored women's ordination in the Catholic Church versus 33% who were opposed. Seven similar polls were conducted by the two organizations between 1987 and 2010. The majority in each one favored women's ordination. That's today, despite JPII's letter. Other polls said more than 60% of American Catholics supported women's ordination.

Several times in the recent past other advisory panels to the papacy have also had their recommendations ignored. Besides the issue of women's ordination to the priesthood, the most notable of these is the decision on artificial birth control. The so-called "birth control" encyclical, "*Humanae Vitae*," or "*Of Human Life,*" was issued by Pope Paul VI on July 25, 1968. Beforehand, he had a top group of clergy, married couples, theologians, physicians, and others study the issue for a couple of years. The Catholic ban on artificial birth control was imposed by Pope Pius XII after the birth control pill was invented in the late 1950s. "The Papal Birth Control Commission," which sounds like an oxymoron today, was started initially by Pope John XXIII with only six theologians. Then Pope Paul expanded it to include many others. Cofounders of the Christian Family Movement, Patty and Pat Crowley of Chicago, and a Canadian couple, Laurent and Colette Potvin, were among the participants.

A majority of the Commission, 54 to 4, voted in 1966 to recommend relaxing the ban on artificial birth control. They favored a new approach—a more personal decision-making policy focused on the compelling spirituality of Christian marriage, as shared by the Crowleys and others. The report was presented to the formal commission of 15 bishops, whose majority agreed.[579]

When *Humanae Vitae* in its final form was issued two years later in 1968, it was, as the saying goes, as if "all hell broke loose." The dissent came from everywhere—clergy, couples, the laity, physicians, non-Catholics, theologians, educators, physicians, and the media. The hierarchy didn't know what hit, never anticipating such a furor. They expected the same old, same old—somewhat upset at first, and then acceptance from its constituents.

What happened to the report of the Birth Control Commission which the Crowleys, Potvins and others, including clergy men and bishops, had worked on so conscientiously for years? Did an evil enemy from another galaxy mysteriously take over? Was there a two-year PR blitz on the Vatican by the minority opinion folks to maintain the status quo? Did a powerful obstetricians lobby rise up to contend that birth control, or its euphemism, "Family Planning," would destroy their livelihoods? Why did the recommendations never make it to the final documents? The answer: it was just the pope's opinion. Was it due to fear of change? Fear of assassination?

Vatican II, in "the Constitution on the Church in the Modern World," promulgated in Dec. 1965, said the primary purpose of marriage was the mutual satisfaction of the partners—not the eons-long idea of procreation. The Papal Birth Control Commission concluded that there was no reason why artificial birth control should not be approved; to the Commission it was not a theological issue. Why was the advice of married couples ignored in a matter which concerned them? Why had the church for so long promulgated, indirectly, if not deliberately, that sexual sin is worse than other types of sin? Isn't sin, sin? Having advisory boards looks collegial—input from many—but if they are ignored, why do it? The report was

---

[579]   As it happened, the Crowleys and others had a significant impact on the Vatican II document, the Constitution on the Church in the Modern World, *Gaudium et Spes*, in its consideration of marriage.

revised—natural family planning, that is abstinence, was okay, but nothing else. They claimed it was a "natural law," meaning it was ever thus, not man-made, so it could not be changed. The idea "what was true in the past is true now" was the mantra of the whole episode.

In an article called, "*Humanae Vitae*: A Generation Later" by Janet Smith, a professor at the University of Dallas, who happens to be Catholic, and written in 2000, she explored the shock value over the encyclical:

> When *Humanae Vitae* was released, in July 1968, it went off like a bomb. Though there was much support for the encyclical, no document ever met with as much dissent, led to a real extent by Fr. Charles Curran and Fr. Bernard Haering. It was a historic and pivotal moment in church history. Dissent became the coin of the day. This had not been true prior to *Humanae Vitae*. Dissenting theologians had never before made such a public display of their position on any given issue. The open dissent to *Humanae Vitae* is a real watershed in the history of the Church. One can view the phenomenon as either a crystallization of something that had been bubbling under the surface for some time, or as a catalyst for everything that was yet to come. Soon theologians and eventually lay people were dissenting not only about contraception but also about homosexuality, masturbation, adultery, divorce and many other issues.[580]

Humanae Vitae caused such a furor over the alleged "outdatedness" of the church, particularly the hierarchy, to the modern world— notably in the U.S.—that many thousands of Catholics left the church completely. Or they became, what now is called, "unchurched." That is, they are nominally Catholic—but do not attend Mass, do not

---

[580] Janet Smith, "*Humanae Vitae: A Generation Later*," 2000. Accessed on-line 2010. Search was for Humanae Vitae.

practice the faith, or might only go to church on Christmas and Easter, and usually that's for their children's sake.[581]

Between 1968 and 2011, statistically, about one-third of Catholics left since *Humanae Vitae*. Some of those just dislike the hierarchy's dogmatism. Or they dislike having outside third parties tell them what to do especially regarding a private matter such as sex or marriage. Or they feel they don't need social services—so since they don't "get anything out of going to church"—why bother going? Many dislike the church's attitude toward gays, particularly gay men—while clerical garb, especially at Mass, still includes wearing vestments which work as "dresses," modeled after the Old Testament garments of the High Priest. Many married women dislike older celibate men telling them what to do. Many more dislike the sexual scandals and the hierarchy's reticence to admit they had been wrong by just transferring the guilty priest rather than rooting out the source of this seeming epidemic.

Pedophilia, which is sex with children under age 5, and sexual abuse of any minor, are serious crimes as well as psychological illnesses. These are not something to be pushed under the rug. Many dioceses became bankrupt or are on the verge of it after paying enormous civil compensation to victims. Two billion dollars has been paid out in U.S. dioceses so far by late 2010. And more suits are pending.[582] Apologizing isn't enough to compensate for destroyed lives. What happened to the integrity and values upon which Jesus formed the church?

A similar hue and cry resulted after the Vatican released the Declaration "On Women's Admission to the Ministerial Priesthood," in 1976. Considering what happened over both *Humanae Vitae*, and the Vatican Declaration, it should have come as no surprise

---

[581] These are the so-called "C & E" Catholics, for Christmas and Easter, compared to the "A & P" Catholics—who only go to church on Ash Wednesday or Palm Sunday—"to get something," i.e., palms or ashes. What these folks fail to realize is: "somethings" are given out "free" to participants every day at Mass—the Holy Eucharist and grace.
[582] Several articles on the priest-sex scandals accessed on-line 2010. Search for Catholic sex scandals 1990+.

to the hierarchy of the extensive criticism it received following the widespread sexual scandals of the 1990s and 2000s. When the allegations came to light, the hierarchy was seen as deliberately ignoring or overlooking the problem, or transferring the perpetrators to other parishes or other dioceses—instead of removing them from ministry altogether and sending these men to jail and also sending them for serious therapy. The trust of the lay people was seriously eroded.

What little was done was seen as too little, too late, in fact, it was seen as a cover-up. Huge monetary settlement for victims in the U.S. and in Europe, didn't even wake the hierarchy up that as the "shepherds," they are responsible for the activity of the staff, however disdainful and criminal. It was as if a memo went out telling the bishops to cover-up, overlook the allegations, then they will die out and go away. It didn't happen—and it won't. Why didn't the hierarchy take action when these events occurred? The old adage applies here, "There are none so blind as those who will not see."

Why is the church so slow to adjust? Apparently, that is its normal reaction mode. Non-disclosure is and was often the name of the game. The hierarchy apparently forgot any lessons learned at Pentecost and in the early church when things happened at lightning speed. It took hundreds of years before some of the findings of the Council of Trent, 1545-1563—which was in response to the Protestant Reformation—were finally made public. Protestantism was roughly 30 years old when Trent began. Some results were released immediately, but the others—hundreds of years. What it because most people couldn't read anyway? Could most priests? Was it from fear of further onslaught against the church by the new Protestant denominations?

The Council of Trent made some remarkable changes in eliminating the wide-spread corruption and in confirming the tenets of Catholicism, which had been under attack in the Reformation. Trent had 25 sessions over a number of papacies. European wars affected many of its participants—or those who chose not to participate. The next ecumenical council, Vatican I, was more than 300 years away, 1869-70.

In an on-line reading of the effects of Trent in 2010, one document suggested any change generated by the Council depended on its players. It stated, *"Any long term change in the Catholic Church depended on the attitude of the pope in power at one particular time. If there was no desire for change, there was no change!"*[583]

I think that is exactly the key behind the hierarchy's lack of interest in the topic of women's ordination today: there's no desire to change, regardless of the clergy shortage. It is impossible to judge what a negative impact the whole sex scandal epidemic has had on the church. From the abusers themselves and the cover-ups, it reminds me of the Watergate political scandals in the 1970s—orchestrated deviousness. The church dealt with internal sexual scandals previously in its 2,000 plus years but none were as far-reaching as this modern one—because of people's increased awareness of human rights for all, the horror of sexual abuse of children, and because of our constant updates of the news of the day reaching us on our iPads®, iPhones®, Blackberries®, telephones, mobile phones, Social Media, radio, television, cable, publications, computers and any other communication text or devises we now use.

As unlikely as it seems at first hearing, Pope Benedict XVI was apparently also part of the sex scandals, in the same way as many other bishops. According to a *Time Magazine* article about the persistent sex scandals in June 2010, then Bishop of Munich, Joseph Cardinal Ratzinger, knew of the molestation of a youth by one priest-perpetrator in 1980. He merely transferred the offender to another post instead of sending him to the German criminal justice system to pay for his crimes.* The article said Pope Benedict's knowledge and mismanagement of that sex abuse case, and possibly others, indicates the level of the church hierarchy's awareness of the scandals, years before they became public knowledge. The *Time* article states that mismanaging the assignment of that accused pedophile priest

---

[583] On-line search "How did the Council of Trent Change the Catholic Church" lead to Yahoo/Answers.com, History Learning Site, May 13, 2009, read in 2010.

under his charge was a revelation, and it lead to questions about his subsequent oversight of cases while a top Vatican official.[584]

* (Vatican: Standard treatment at the time.)

Pope Benedict apologized to the sexual abuse victims and their families on several occasions in the last few years for what happened to them. In a letter the pope wrote to Irish Catholics on March 19, 2010, apologizing for the devastating sex scandals there, he said:

> You have suffered grievously and I am truly sorry. I know that nothing can undo the wrong you have endured. Your trust has been betrayed and your dignity has been violated . . . . When you were courageous enough to speak of what happened to you, no one would listen . . . . It is understandable that you find it hard to forgive or be reconciled with the church. In her name, I openly express the shame and remorse we all feel.[585]

He has not apologized for his part in transferring the priest-violator in Munich. *Time* said Benedict's flock today—that is, the whole church—"want a very modern kind of accountability, not just mealy-mouthed declarations, buttressed by arcane religious philosophy."[586] That means no more hierarchal pushing of a negative issue under the rug, hoping it won't raise its ugly head again. "The Pope can cite theology and tradition in defense of the church, but with many Catholics wanting a very modern kind of accounting for the sex-abuse scandal, words and ritual may no longer be enough."[587] Benedict previously headed the hard-nosed Congregation for the Doctrine of the Faith (CDF), which in modern times succeeded the notorious Inquisition of the Middle Ages.

I think the same attitude is present regarding women in the church and ordination to the priesthood or deaconate. Push the questions under the rug and they're gone. Poof. It's magic. The two

---

[584] Israely, Jeff and Howard Chua-Eoan," The Trial of Benedict XVI", *Time*, Vol. 175, No 22, June 7, 2010, 38.

[585] Ibid., 39.

[586] Ibid., 38.

[587] Ibid.

issues of sex scandals and women's ordination had no connection, it seems, until the church recently aligned the two in a malevolent, but apparently unintentional, coupling. In July 2010, the Congregation for the Doctrine of the Faith (CDF) reissued Vatican norms on classifications of serious offenses, *Normae de Gravioribus Delictis,* or grave crimes. The top of the list dealt with the sex scandal culprits. The new norms said the first response should be to report the person to the local police authorities. Also, the Statute of Limitations for filing abuse cases was extended from the victim's 18th birthday, adding an additional 20 years. The same penalties for sex abuse of minors are to be applied to any abuse of developmentally disabled adults. These and other regulations, which were first devised in 2001, then revised in 2007, were basically a tightening and strengthening of current practices of dealing with serious crimes. These norms were under the category dealing with criminal activity, "for a moral crime."

Another update in the norms was under the category of administration of a sacrament for a grave crime, *Delicta Graviora,* or "a sacramental crime." It stated any cleric who "attempted the ordination of a woman," both he and she would be excommunicated and he could be dismissed from the priesthood.

When the norms were publicized it "appeared" as though the church was comparing sexual abuse of a minor with a woman's desire to become a priest. The first is a crime—against God and humanity. The latter, for now, is an aspiration to receive a sacrament. It turned out to be a public relations disaster for the Church. Again, a lot of ordinary Catholic women were offended. Women were furious at the thought the two could even be considered together. They objected strenuously. It is not a crime to want to receive a sacrament.

Generally, the media coupled them when reporting the story, since they were grouped as "norms." That was even though they were announced separately—but on the same day. A *National Catholic Reporter (NCR) Story,* "PR Win Slips Away from Vatican: Calling Women's Ordination a 'Grave Crime'" distracts from tougher abuse policies, explained John L. Allen. In his on-line column on July 16,

2010, the day after the norms were issued, Senior NCR Correspondent Allen wrote, "On a day when it should have had a clear PR win— 'Church tightens rules on sex abuse,' the Vatican managed, according to many media watchers, to step on its own story once again."[588] It would have been easier all around if the ordination norms were issued a few days after the scandal ones.

Yes, you can find lists online of women who claim to have been authentically ordained in and for the Catholic Church, and women who claim to be bishops, too. The women in question believe they were authentic ordinations and they now follow in the Apostolic line. They believe they are at the forefront of what's coming in the Catholic Church. These women say they are tired of waiting. They apparently believe it is better to go ahead with an unauthorized ordination than none at all. They work in splintered off groups of Catholics, or from their homes, according to on-line lists.

The church considers these to be rogue ordinations and invalid. The ordaining priests, as well as the women, apparently are excommunicated. They call it self-excommunication.

The latest in the continuing saga was from one-third of the Germanic theologians and scholars from Catholic Universities in Germany, Austria, and Switzerland in early Feb. 2011. Here, 143 theologians out of the 400 in the region signed a manifesto calling for radical changes in the Catholic Church. It appeared in *Suddeutsche Zeitung*, a German daily newspaper. The theologians called for the ordination of women, married priesthood, acceptance of gay marriage, and popular election of bishops.

The German Catholic bishops said they would study the document at its March 2011 meeting. Nothing was heard of those results, if anything happened. Obviously, several of the proposals contradict current church policies. The letter marked the strongest internal criticism of the church in Germany since the "Cologne Declaration" of 1989 in which more than 200 German-speaking theologians attacked

---

[588] *National Catholic Reporter*, "PR win slips away from Vatican: Calling Women's Ordination a 'Grave Crime'," August 3, 2010 and accessed on-line, January 2011.

the conservative teachings of Pope John Paul II. According to this recent document, when Benedict was still Cardinal Ratzinger in 1970 he joined eight other German theologians, who wrote to German bishops, and questioned whether the practice of celibacy was still relevant. Benedict is a theologian who retains a chair at Regensburg University. "The church needs married priests and women in church ministry," the document said. "The liturgy cannot be frozen in traditionalism."[589] Pope Benedict visited his homeland Sept. 22-25, 2011, in honor of the 60th anniversary of his ordination to the priesthood.

Catholic News Service (CNS) reported the theologians' appeal was in response to the widespread clerical sexual and physical abuse scandals in Germany last year. These cases involved hundreds of youngsters. The signers of the manifesto said they could no longer remain silent in the face of a lingering crisis in the Catholic Church. The statement was issued, they said, to open a discussion about the future of the church. "We have the responsibility to contribute to a new start," the statement said. Two-thirds of all parishes will be without a priest by 2020, according to the document, and there is an attempt to merge parishes in Germany,[590] similar to what is occurring in the U.S. at the present time.

The theologians said Germany had suffered "an unprecedented crisis" in 2010 and that "2011 must be a year of departure for the church." The reasons: there are fewer young men choosing the priesthood, many churches will have one or no priest within a few years, and revenues are way down in the wealthy German church, said the Associated Press.[591]

Will this criticism lead to any change in Vatican thinking? Stay tuned. As the pope probably realizes it is very different from endorsing an intellectual argument 20 plus years ago, even as a bishop, to making decisions for the more than one billion Catholics worldwide.

---

[589] Bartillas, Martin. "German Catholic Theologians Call For Radical Changes," *Enerpub*, Feb 4, 2011, 1-2. Accessed-on-line 2011.

[590] Catholic News Service, as reported in *The Catholic Sun* on-line, Feb. 4, 2011.

[591] Baetz, Juergen, "German Theologians Call for End to Celibacy." Associate Press, as reported in Yahoo! News on-line, Feb. 4, 2011.

I know also that things *do change* and *have changed* in the church. Except for central dogma and the full truth of the gospel, which this issue isn't, things have changed in the Church for 2,000 plus years. Of course, things have changed. Even "tradition" has changed. As mentioned in various chapters in this book, we've seen many changes in the church, specifically some for the good and some not quite as significant. Some of these changes are:

- **Slavery,** since the 19th century, it is no longer acceptable. It is found throughout the Bible. Paul cautions slave-believers to be faithful to their masters.
- The **Inquisition**, originally a tribunal for the discovery and punishment of heresy, was started in Rome by Pope Innocent III (1198-1216). It spread all over Europe and even to some Spanish colonies. The Inquisition was marked by severity of questioning, physical torture, extreme punishment, no civil rights for the accused, and often execution. It lasted until the 17th and 18th centuries in some places. Thousands were killed based on little or no evidence.
- **Intinction**, or dipping the host into the chalice, allegedly used in the time of the great horrific plagues in Europe to prevent sipping from the cup to avoid possible contamination. For several reasons, it came into disfavor, and, gradually the cup itself was no longer given at Mass to the congregants. Trent specified that Christ is entirely present in either form or species of the Eucharist, that is, in both wine and the bread and that it wasn't necessary to receive both species. Reception from the cup is back. Intinction may be done by the priest and given to the communicant; self-intinction is prohibited.
- **Copernicus,** once excommunicated for making outlandish claims about the solar system—that the earth was round not flat, was vindicated and received a long-overdue apology. Plus reinstatement.
- **The Shroud of Turin** was declared a fake after carbon dating tests showed it was from the Middle Ages, not the time of

Christ. How the images got to be on the Shroud is still a mystery.

- **New saints** have been named to the list of saints and **some long-standing names were removed** as being unsubstantiated.
- **Religious sisters** for the most part wear modern day clothing, depending on their ministry, not outfits stemming from the past, which were current when the order was founded, as in the Middle Ages or 16th or 17th centuries.
- The powerful **Medieval Abbesses**, who held ecclesial rank and the jurisdiction of bishops, are no longer in church service. Most Americans today never even heard of them. Europeans probably have heard about them but may not know the extent of their authority. Some of the abbeys still function and others are mostly tourist spots.
- Baby boomers and older folks certainly remember **not eating meat on Fridays and Christmas Eve.** Now, abstinence is only on Fridays in Lent. However, what started as a religious penance has become a great Italian (and some other cultures) tradition of having a variety of fish meals on Christmas Eve.
- And remember **having to fast 12 hours before receiving Holy Communion?** Now the communicant must wait one hour. Lenten fasting is only on Ash Wednesday and Good Friday and the recommendations say "only one main meal"—not all day without hardly any food. Instead, the church recommends doing something good for people who need help.
- The well-remembered **Baltimore Catechism** is kaput. A new Catechism of the Catholic Church was issued in 1994. Liturgical music has changed.
- After Vatican II, the **deaconate** was resurrected after being dormant for centuries.
- **Celibacy and the clergy**: It was a married clergy until the 1100's, then the hierarchy enforced celibacy and it is proclaimed today as if it had always been so, for the interim at least, its status is assorted—with both celibates and some married clergy. Are more married clerics coming in the future? If so,

and the rule is changed, will it be a universal rule applying to Byzantine and Latin rites and former Episcopalians alike?

- **Mass is said now facing the congregation and in the vernacular.**
- **Communion** can be received in the hand or on the tongue.
- **Offering the cup at Communion time** has come back into use.
- **Women no longer need to wear head coverings in church**, nor do they need to be "churched," or blessed,[592] after the birth of a baby. In fact, mothers can now be present for the baby's baptism where years ago it was only the god-mother.
- **Women are serving** as Lectors, Eucharistic Ministers, and serve in parish positions, on parish boards and in chancery offices. As well, there are **women serving as Parish Life Coordinators (PLCs), Pastoral Associates and even as girl altar servers**, as well as every sort of ministry from religious education to music ministry.
- **The first person named** to the prestigious title of "Doctor of the Church" in the 21st Century, is a woman.

Theophany

Pentecost was when "the Spirit's compelling energy announced a new moment in God's plan of salvation."[593] Pentecost, often called the "Birthday of the Church," was a "Theophany," that is, a manifestation of God. I believe the acceptance of women in liturgical roles in the

---

[592] "Churching" stemmed from the Jewish tradition that women had to wait seven days after the birth of a male child and 14 days after a female birth, as in her monthly period, a time called niddah or the nidus state, when she was sexually separated from her husband. She had to wait 33 days for a male child or 66 days for a female before taking her purifying bath or mikveh. This was based on Lev. 12:2. No reason was given in Leviticus for the double amount of time after a girl's birth.

[593] Adapted from sentences in *Workbook for Lectors, Gospel Readers and Proclaimers of the Word*, Year C, 2010, Pentecost Sunday, May 23, 2010, Liturgy Training Publications, 2009, Archdiocese of Chicago.

church should be the "newest moment" in God's plan of salvation. I believe it would be another Theophany or manifestation of God. There is no way God intended half of his creation to be left out of Divine plans and grace. That's just not our understanding of God.

If the male priesthood has given us scandal, bigotry, and delay for 2000+ years, why not try a new approach? Tradition dies hard but it is not insurmountable. In World War II, while the U.S men were overseas fighting, the U.S. women were doing formerly all male jobs in factories, building fighter jets and machinery and so forth, and then *flying them to the front*. The war would not have been won without the contributions of both men and women.

I believe as Catholics we have to pray for this new Theophany to happen. I believe the spirit has to motivate entrenched clerics to be willing to let go of lifelong assumptions. It would take an extraordinarily brave pope, willing to take risks and face present and future condemnation by conservatives, the media, lay Catholics, by virtually everyone and anyone, to do so. Popes do have an astonishing amount of things to be concerned over; maybe even more than the U.S. president. I can see why they might like to have one issue set aside and never to raise its head again. But that's not going to happen in our 21st century world anymore.

I was a journalist working as a reporter when I started this book. Women's ordination was just a news story to me. I had no opinion about it. As a "cradle Catholic," that is, a baby born into a Catholic family, I knew women weren't permitted to be ordained in the Catholic Church; I thought there had to be a valid, legitimate reason why not. After extensive research, including serious study of the Scriptures and how Jesus treated women, I totally changed my opinion. I deliberately didn't start out reading secular feminists and Christian feminist theologians because I didn't want to be influenced. Countless people shared their ideas and thoughts with me, some very conservative, some not. I attended many workshops to hear different points of view, including hearing Mother Teresa who was sponsored by an ultra-conservative group of Catholic women. She talked about Jesus and love, never touching on its agenda.

I believe as part of this Theophany, this movement by the Holy Spirit, women will be ordained eventually, primarily to preserve our most important tradition—our Eucharistic church. As an active Catholic laywoman, I know this is contrary to the current teaching of the church. I hope this book, which is a new way of looking at things Catholic, will become part of the dialogue for new issues within the church.

Yes, change is difficult but not impossible. God is not static. The Church shouldn't be either.

Bibliography

Scripture:

The Jerusalem Bible, Reader's Edition. Garden City, NY: Doubleday & Co., 1966.

King James Bible.

The Way, The Living Bible. Catholic Edition. Wheaton, IL: Tyndale House Publishers, 1971.

Ignatius Catholic Research Bible. "New Testament." San Francisco, CA: Ignatius Press, 1996.

Print:

"A Bad Time for Women," *New York Times*. Vol. CXXX, No. 44,966. June 1, 1981: A 16.

Abbott, Walter M., S.J., Editor. *The Documents of Vatican II.* New York, NY: The American Press, 1966.

Ali, Ayaan Hirsi. *The Caged Virgin: An Emancipation Proclamation for Women and Islam.* New York, NY: Free Press, a division of Simon & Schuster, 2006.

Andrews, Gini. *Your Half of the Apple: God and the Single Girl.* Grand Rapids, MI.: Zondervan Publishing House, 1972.

"Back Off Buddy: A New Hite Report Stirs Up a Furor Over Sex and Love in the 80's," *Time*, Vol. 130, No. 15. Oct. 12, 1987: 68-73.

Baetz, Juergen. "German theologians Call for End to Celibacy." *Associated Press,* as reported in Y*ahoo! News.* Accessed Feb. 4, 2011.

Bartillas, Martin. "German Catholic theologians call for radical changes," *Enerpub,* Feb. 4, 2011: 1-2. Accessed on line.

Beckham, Joanne Lamphere. "Scholar Says Apostles Were Sometimes Women," *Religious News Service,* Nov. 16, 1979: 4-5.

Bettelheim, Bruno. *The Uses of Enchantment: The Meaning and Importance of Fairy Tales.* New York: Alfred A. Knopf, 1977.

Bird, Joseph and Lois. *The Freedom of Sexual Love.* Garden City, NY: Image Books, 1967.

Bittner, Kathleen Egan. "The Emerging Role of the Parish Life Coordinator." Final paper for Canon Law Course, Institute for Lay Ecclesial Ministry (ILEM), Diocese of Trenton, NJ, 2008.

—"Presentation: Priest Shortage." Paper in Pastoral Theology Course, ILEM, Diocese of Trenton, NJ, 2007.

Blanuies, Harry. *Words Made Flesh: God Speaks to Us in Ordinary Things of Life.* Ann Arbor, MI: Servant Books, 1985.

Bozarth-Campbell, Alla. *Womanpriest, A Personal Odyssey.* New York: Paulist Press, 1978.

Blum, Susan W., *The Ministry of Evangelization.* Collegeville, MN: The Liturgical Press, 1988.

Briggs, Kenneth A., "Catholic Bishops Vote to Drop 'Men' from the Liturgy," *New York Times.* Vol CXXX, No. 44,766, Nov. 13, 1980: A 21.

Brody, Jane E., "Sperm Found Especially Vulnerable to Environment," *New York Times.* Mar. 10, 1981: C1, 3.

Brown, Dan. *The Da Vinci Code, A Novel.* New York: Random House, 2003.

Brown, Raymond E., and Donfried, Karl P., ed., *Mary in the New Testament.* Fortress Press, Philadelphia, PA, and Paulist Press, New York and Ramsey, NJ, 1978.

Bruns, J. Edgar. *God as Woman, Woman as God.* New York: Paulist Press, 1973.

Burghardt, Walter J., S.J., ed., *Women New Dimensions: Theological Studies.* New York: Paulist Press, 1975, 1977.

Burke, Mary P., *"Reaching for Justice: The Women's Movement,"* Washington, D.C.: Center for Concern, 1980.

Burns, David D., M.D., *Feeling Good.* New York: A Signet Book, New American Library, 1981.

—*Intimate Connections.* New York: William Morrow & Co., Inc., 1985.

Buscaglia, Leo. *Love.* New York: Fawcett Crest, 1978.

Cahill, Lisa Sowle. *Between the Sexes: Foundations for a Christian Ethics of Sexuality.* New York: Fortress Press, Paulist Press, 1985.

"Canon Lawyers Back Equal Rights for Women in Both Church, State," Religious News Service, Oct. 18, 1979: 4.

Caprio, Elizabeth. *The Woman Sealed in a Tower: A Psychological Approach to Feminine Spirituality,* New York, NY and Ramsey, NJ: Paulist Press, 1982.

Carpenter, Teresa. *"Courage and Pain: Women Who Love God and Deny their Churches," Redbook.* April 1980, Vol. 154, No. 6: 19, 151, 153, 155-6.

"Case of Women Trouble, Episcopal Church (Priests)" Time. Vol. 110, No. 80, Oct. 17, 1977.

Catechism of the Catholic Church, New York: Image Books/ Doubleday, 1994.

Catholic Charismatic. Vol. 1, No. 6, Feb/Mar, 1977.

Catholic Charismatic. Vol. 3, No. 5, Dec 78/Jan 1979.

Catoir, John Fr. *"Coping with the Church's Human Element," Catholic News Service. The Monitor,* Trenton, NJ, July 4, 2002: 7.

Chittister, Joan D., O.S.B., *"Brotherly Love in Today's Church,"* (originally appeared in *America*) reprinted in *New Woman, New Church.* Vol. 3, No. 2, Mar. 1980:8.

—*Job's Daughters: Women and Power.* The 1990 Madeleva Lecture in Spirituality. New York, NY and Mahwah, NJ: Paulist Press, 1990.

—*"The Ministry of Women," Catholic Charismatic.* April/May 1979: 26-29.

—*Women, Ministry and the Church.* New York, NY and Ramsey, NJ: Paulist Press, 1983.

Clark, Steve. *"Building a Christian Society,"* Part I, and *"Why Have Roles for Men and Women."* New Covenant, Vol. 10, No. 3, Sept. 1980: 13-17.

Clarkson, Margaret. *So You're Single!* Wheaton, IL: Harold Shaw Publishers, 1978.

"Clergywomen," *Time.* Vol. 11, No. 44, Apr. 3, 1978.

Collins, Mary. *Women at Prayer.* 1987 Madeleva Lecture in Spirituality. New York, NY and Mahwah, NJ: Paulist Press, 1987.

Cross, Donna Woolfolk. *Pope Joan, a Novel.* New York: Ballantine Books, 1996.

Cruden, Alexander. *Cruden's Complete Concordance to the Old and New Testament.* Grand Rapids, MI.: Zondervan Publishing House, 1975.

Darman, Jonathan. *The Mystery of Mary Magdalene, "An Inconvenient Woman."* Newsweek. Vol. CXLVII, No. 22. May 29, 2006: 42-51.

Delaney, Robert. *"Lay Ecclesial Ministry: Together in God's Service."* Article 5, *"Chancellors Have Neither Dull Moments Nor Clean Desks."* U.S. Conference of Catholic Bishops. Office of Media Relations. Department of Communications. Washington, D.C., 2010.

Delatiner, Barbara. "Priest without a Parish," *McCall's,* 105:20+ July, 1978.

DeRosis, Helen A., M.D., Pellegrino, Victoria Y., *The Book of Hope: How Women Can Overcome Depression,* New York: Bantam Books, 1976.

Diant, Anita. *The Red Tent, A Novel.* New York: Piscador USA, 1997.

Dobell, Elizabeth Rodgers, *"God and Women, the Hidden History,"* Redbook, March 1978: 37-44.

Doohan, Leonard. *The Lay-Centered Church: Theology & Spirituality.* Minneapolis, MN: Winston Press, 1984.

Dowling, Colette. *"The Cinderella Syndrome,"* NY Times Magazine, Mar. 22, 1981: 47-64.

Dragadze, Peter. *"Conversations with Pope John Paul II,"* Ladies
Home Journal, Vol. XCVII, No. 3, Mar. 1980: 93, 165-9.

Emerging Models of Pastoral Leadership: *About the Project.* National
Association for Lay Ministry, May 2009.

—*Discovering Leadership Models for Church.* May 2009.

*"European Catholic Theologians call for an end to celibacy, other
changes,"* Catholic News Service, as reported in *The Catholic
Sun.* Accessed on-line, Feb. 4, 2011.

Evans, Muriel. *"Ministries for Women: Old and New Testament
Examples of Women in Ministry,"* Aglow Bible Studies. Edmonds,
WA: Aglow Publications, 1975.

"'Father' Takes on New Meaning for Chicago Priest," NY Times,
July 8, 1981: C 20.

Feinsilber, Mike. "Americans want Male Dentists, Female
Hairdressers," Associated Press Dispatch, Jan. 7, 1981 (A023-
Women's Role).

Ferder, Fran. F.S.P.A., Ph. D., *Called to Break Bread? A Psychological
Investigation of 100 Women Who Feel Called to Priesthood in the
Catholic Church.* Mt. Ranier, MD: Quixote Center, Inc., 1978.

Filteau, Jerry. *"Pope Praises Women as Wives and Mothers,"* NC
Dispatch, Trenton, NJ: *The Monitor.* Vol. XXVII, No. 40, Nov.
13, 1980:6.

Foley, Mary M. *"Women in Parish Leadership: Exceptional
Pastoring."* America. Vol. 200, No. 8, March 9, 2009: 11-13.

Fox, Zeni, Ph.D. *New Ecclesial Ministry: Lay Professionals Serving
the Church.* Franklin, WI: Sheed & Ward, 2002.

Foxworth, Jo. *Boss Lady,* New York, NY: Warner Books, 1977.

Friday, Nancy. *My Mother, My Self: The Daughter's Search for
Identity.* New York, NY: Dell Publishing Co., Inc., 1977.

Furey, Richard G., C. S.S.R., *Mary's Way of the Cross.* Mystic, CT:
Twenty-third Publications/Bayard, 1984.

Gately, Edwina. *Rediscovering and Claiming the Feminine Soul.*
Trabuco Canyon, CA: Source Books.

Geaney, Dennis. *Emerging Lay Ministries.* Kansas City, MO:
Andrews and McNeel, Inc., 1979.

Gerding, Susan Blum, Ed.D. *Go and Make Disciples, a National Plan and Strategy for Catholic Evangelization in the United States, and Text Study Guide*. Washington, D.C.: NCCB, Bishops Committee on Evangelization, 1993.

Gerding, Susan Blum, Ed.D. and Frank DeSiano, C.S.P. *Lay Ministers, Lay Disciples: Evangelizing Power in the Parish*. New York and Mahwah, NJ: Paulist Press, 1999.

Goergen, Donald. *The Sexual Celibate*. New York, NY: A Crossroads Book, The Seabury Press, 1974.

Golden, Janet. *The Quite Possible She: Today's Christian Woman*. New York, NY: Herder and Herder, 1966.

Goldman, Ari I., *"A Sex Barrier for Cantors Is Broken: Conservative Jews Allow Women to Lead Services," NY Times*. Vol. CXXXVI, No. 47,042, Feb. 6, 1987: B 1, 3.

Grana, Janice, ed., *Images: Women in Transition*. Winona, MN: St. Mary's College Press, 1976.

Gray, Mark M., Ph.D., and Mary L. Gautier, Ph.D., *"Understanding the Experience: A Profile of Lay Ecclesial Ministers Serving as Parish Life Coordinators."* Washington, D.C.: Center for Applied Research in the Apostolate, National Association for Lay Ministry, May 2004.

—*"Understanding the Trends: Parishes Entrusted to Parish Life Coordinators."* Washington, D.C.: Center for Applied Research in the Apostolate, National Association for Lay Ministry, July 2004.

Groeschel, Benedict J., FFR, *Listening at Prayer*. New York, NY and Ramsey, NJ: Paulist Press, 1983.

Guentert, Kenneth. *"25 Things your Parish Can Do Before Starting a Singles Group," US Catholic,* April 1978: 30-32.

Handford, Elizabeth Rice. *Me? Obey Him?* Murfrusboro,TN: Sword of the Lord Publisher, 1972.

Harragan, Betty Lehan. *Games Mother Never Taught You: Corporate Gamesmanship for Women,* New York, NY: Warner Books, 1977.

Hart, Kathleen Fischer and Thomas N., *The First Two Years of Marriage: Foundations for a Life Together*. New York, NY and Ramsey, NJ: Paulist Press, 1983.

Heesacker-Kahn, Claire-Marie. *"Ordained Ministry and Women: An Approach,"* University of San Francisco, CA: Graduate Seminar Thesis, 1976.

Hellwig, Monika K. *Christian Woman in a Troubled World:* 1985 Madeleva Lecture in Spirituality. New York, NY and Mahwah, NJ: Paulist Press. 1985.

Hekker, Terry. *Ever Since Adam and Eve.* New York, NY: William. Morrow & Co., Inc., 1979.

Hennig, Margaret and Jardin, Anne. *The Managerial Woman.* New York, NY: Pocket Books, 1976.

Hewitt, Emily C. and Hiatt, Suzanne R., *Women Priests—Yes or No?* New York, NY: The Seabury Press, 1973.

Heyer, Robert J, ed., *Women and Orders.* New York, NY: Paulist Press, 1974.

Hitti, Miranda. *"Women Prefer Working Outside the Home,"* WebMD. Accessed on line, 2011.

Hunt, Gladys. *Ms. Means Myself.* Grand Rapids, MI: Zondervan Publishing House, 1972.

Hyatt, Carole. *The Woman's Selling Game.* New York, NY: Warner Books, 1979.

Hyer, Marjorie. *"Growing Catholic Church Losing Priests and Nuns."* *The Washington Post.* Vol. 104, No. 168, May 22, 1981: C2.

Inter Insigniores. The Vatican Declaration on Women's Admission to the Ministerial Priesthood. Sacred Congregation for the Doctrine of the Faith. Oct. 15, 1976.

Jewell, Marti, D. Min. *"Emerging Models: Where We Have Been and Where We Are Going: A Brief Summary of Phase I and Phase II.,"* Emerging Models of Pastoral Leadership Project. April 2009.

—*"Major Findings of the Emerging Models Project,"* National Ministry Summit, Emerging Models of Pastoral leadership Project. April 2009.

John Paul II. *"Letter of Pope John Paul II to Women",* June 29, 1995.

—*"On the Dignity and Vocation of Women."* (*Mutieris Dignitatum*). *Origins,* Vol. 18, No. 17, Oct. 6, 1988: 261—263 ff.

—*"On Reserving Priestly Ordination to Men Alone."* (*Ordinatio Sacerdolatis*), May 22, 1994.

Julian of Norwich. *The Life of the Soul, The Wisdom of Julian of Norwich.* Colledge, Edmund, O.S.A., and Walsh, James, S.J., translators. Mahwah, NJ: Paulist Press, 1966.

"Just How the Sexes Differ." Newsweek. May 18, 1981: 72-83, and *"Sex Research on the Bias."* 81.

Kates, Brian. *"U.S. Bishops Strike Sexist Language from Mass."* New York Daily News. Vol. 62, No. 121, Nov. 13, 1980:4.

Kolbenschlag, Madonna. *Kiss Sleeping Beauty Goodbye: Breaking the Spell of Feminine Myths and Models.* Garden City, NY; Doubleday & Co., 1979.

Kotker, Zane. *"The 'Feminine' Behavior of Powerless People."* Savvy. Vol. 1, No. 3, March 1980: 36-38, 42.

Lackey, Jim. *"NCCB Studying Admission of Married Episcopal Priests."* NC article. Trenton, NJ: *The Monitor*, Vol. XXVII, No. 28, Aug. 21, 1980: 1-2.

La Haye, Beverly, *The Spirit Controlled Woman.* Irvine, CA: Harvest House Publishers, 1976.

Landorf, Joyce. *The Fragrance of Beauty.* Wheaton, IL: Victor Books, 1973.

—*I Came to Love You Late.* Old Tappan, NJ: Fleming H. Revell Company, 1977.

Lange, Joseph, O.S. F.S., and Cushing, Anthony. *Called to Service.* Vol. IV. Living Christian Community Series. New York, NY: Paulist Press, 1976.

Lueke, Jane Marie, O.S.B., *"The Dominance Syndrome: Women's Subordination is the Model for all other Oppressive Structures."* Christian Century. 94:405-7, April 27, 1977.

McCaseland, David C., *"I Don't Feel Single Anymore!"* Presbyterian Journal. Oct. 17, 1979: 8-9.

McGarry, Michael, C.S.P., *"A Quality of Daring."* National Catholic Reporter. Oct. 12, 1979: 21.

McGrath, Sr. Albertus Magnus, O.P. *Women and the Church.* Garden City, NY: Image Books. Doubleday & Co., 1972. Thomas More Association, 1976.

McGuire, Dorothy; Lewis, Carol; and Blachley, Alvena. *The Philosophy of Christian Womanhood. A Practical Application of Scriptural Truth to a Woman's Daily Life.* Course book. Denver, CO: Tri-R Associates, Inc., 1970.

Mickelsen, Beverley and Alvera. *"Does Male Dominance Tarnish Our Translations?" Christianity Today.* Vol. XXII, No. 23, Oct. 5, 1979, 23-29.

Miller, William A. *Make Friends with Your Shadow: How to Accept & Use Positively the Negative Side of Your Personality.* Minneapolis, MN: Augsburg Publishing House, 1981.

Montague, Ashley. *The Natural Superiority of Women.* New York, NY: Macmillan Company, 1953.

Morgan, Marabel. *Total Joy.* Old Tappan, NJ: Spire Books, Fleming H. Revell Co., 1978.

Morris, Joan. *The Lady Was a Bishop: The Hidden History of Women with Clerical Ordination and the Jurisdiction of Bishops.* New York, NY: The Macmillan Company, 1973.

Murphy, Elly, Ed., *"The Single Experience: A Resource, Reflections and Models for Single Young Adulthood,"* U.S. Catholic Conference, Department of Education, Washington, D.C., 1979.

Naiifeh, Steven and Smith, Gregory White. *Why Can't Men Open Up?: Overcoming Men's Fear of Intimacy.* New York, NY: Clarkson N. Potter, Inc., 1984.

NCCB. *Strengthening the Bonds of Peace: A Pastoral Reflection on Women in the Church and Society,* U.S. Bishops Pastoral, 1995.

"New Approach Needed for Teaching on Contraception, says Archbishop." Trenton, NJ: *The Monitor,* Vol. XXVII, No. 34, Oct. 2, 1980: 7.

New Covenant Magazine. "The Christian Woman." Vol. 7, No. 12, June 1978.

—*"Questions Single Christians Face."* Vol. 5, No. 9, March 1976.

New Woman, New Church, Women's Ordination Conference, various individual issues.

Ohanneson, Joan. *Women Survivor in the Church.* Minneapolis, MN: Winston Press, 1980.

O'Reilly, Barbara. *"Breakaway Episcopal Group Seeks United Status with Roman Church." Religious News Service.* Sept. 28, 1979: 3-4.

—*"Bishops Attack 'Sin of Racism' But Fail in Assault on 'Sexism'." Religious News Service.* Nov. 16, 1979: 6-8.

—*"Bishops Fail to Gain Majority Needed to Remove Male References in Prayers." Religious News Service.* Nov. 15, 1979: 3-4.

—*"Catholic Biblical Scholars Claim Ban on Women Priests Not Logical." Religious News Service.* Nov. 20, 1979: 6-7.

—*"Christian Businessmen Gather to Worship and Fellowship." The Asbury Park Press.* Vol. 100, No. 124, May 25, 1979: A 19.

—*"Churches Are Mounting Special Ministries to Cope with the Needs of Single Persons." The Week in Religion. Religious News Service.* Nov. 2, 1979.

—*Contributing writer, Echo in the Heart, 125 years in the Diocese of Trenton, NJ, 1881-2006.* Trenton, NJ: 2007: 60—68, 71.

—*"Jesuit Who Advocates Women's Ordination Ordered to Give Up His Work, Be Silent." Religious News Service.* Nov. 23, 1979: 6-7.

—*Mary 'Greatest of Priests' Scripture Scholar Declares." Religious News Service.* Oct. 8, 1979: 9, and *"Scholar Says Mother Mary Was a Priest." The Washington Post,* Oct. 19, 1979: B14.

—*Nun Who Called for Women Priests Gets Heated Reaction—Pro and Con." Religious News Service.* Oct. 19, 1979: 12-14.

—*"Women Seminary Student Granted Scholarship by Catholic Bishop." Religious News Service.* Oct. 5, 1979: 9.

—*"Women 'Foot-Soldiers" in 'Quiet Revolution' in the Diocese." The Monitor.* Oct. 1, 1981: A 2-4.

Origins. The NC Documentary Series. National Catholic News Service. Washington, D.C.: Vol. 8, No. 45, includes *"Justice and the Roles of Women: Statement of the Bishops of Minnesota."* 709, 711-714.—*"Contemporary Women and the Church."* 715-718, and *"Local Implementation/Roles of Women."* 719-721.

—*"Partners in the Mystery of Redemption: A Pastoral Response to Women's Concerns for Church and Society."* Vol. 17, No. 45, April 21, 1988: 757-ff.

Pampbell, Catherine. *"As Layoffs Surge, Women May Pass Men in Job Force." New York Times.* Accessed on—line: Feb. 5, 2009.

Paternostro, Silvana. *In the Land of God and Man.* New York, NY: Plume, a Division of Penguin Books, 1998.

Paul VI. *Motu Proprio. Ministeria Quaedam.* Roman Rite.com. *Documents on the Liturgy 1963-1979.* MN: Liturgical Press, 1982: 908-911.

Pomerleau, Dolly, Fiedler, Maureen and Callahan, William R., *"Women Priests: a Research Report," America.* Nov. 17, 1979: 299-300.

Porter, Eduardo. *"Women in Workplace—Trend is Reversing," New York Times.* Accessed on line, 2011.

"The Roles of Men and Women in the Catholic Charismatic Renewal." Statement from the National Service Committee of the Catholic Charismatic Renewal in the U.S. *New Covenant.* March 1978: 18-19.

Ruether, Rosemary Radford. *"Women-Church: Neither Over Nor Under Men." National Catholic Reporter.* Vol. 23, No. 13, Jan. 23, 1987: 15.

Sacred Congregation for the Doctrine of the Faith. *Declaration on the Question of Women to the Ministerial Priesthood, with Commentary, Oct. 15, 1976.* U.S. Catholic Conference Publications Office, Washington, D.C, 1977.

Sanford, John A. *Between People: Communication One-to-One.* New York, NY and Ramsey, NJ: Paulist Press, 1982.

—*The Invisible Partners: How the Male and Female in Each of Us Affects Our Relationships.* Ramsey, NJ: Paulist Press, 1980.

Schaupp, Joan. *Women—Image of the Holy Spirit.* Denville, NJ: Dimension Books, 1975.

Schbeider, Sandra M. *Women and the Word, The Gender of God in the New Testament and the Spirituality of Women.* 1986 Madeleva Lecture in Spirituality, New York, NY and Mahwah, NJ: Paulist Press, 1986.

Schuller, Robert H. *"Love or Loneliness?" The Presbyterian Journal.* Oct. 17, 1979: 7.

Sekowsky, JoAnne. *A Christian Roadmap for Women Traveling Alone.* Edmonds, WA: Aglow Publications, 1975.

Shapiro, Howard. *The Birth Control Book.* New York, NY: Avon Books, 1978.

"Singles and the Church." The Presbyterian Journal. Oct. 17, 1979:10.

Smoke, Jim. *"Building Blocks for Growth," Solo Magazine for Positive Singles.* Vol. 3, No. 5, Oct. 1979:14.

Stephen, Beverly. *"The Struggle Between Faith and Feminism." New York Daily News.* Vol. 61, No. 184, Jan. 25, 1980: 34-35.

Steinem, Gloria. *"If Men Could Menstruate." MS. Magazine.* Reprinted in Kaufman, Gloria and Blakely, Mary Kay, editors. *Pulling Our Own Strings, Feminist Humor and Satire.* Bloomington, IN: Indiana Press, 1980: 25-6.

Stramara, Daniel F., Bro, O.S.B., *El Shaddai: A Feminine Aspect of God.* Pecos, NM: Dove Publications.

"Support for Women Priests Reported Growing Steadily." Religious News Service. Nov. 12, 1979: 17-18.

Swidler, Arlene. *Woman in a Man's Church: From Role to Person.* New York, NY: Paulist Press, 1972.

Swidler, Leonard. *"Jesus Was a Feminist." (New) Catholic World.* Vol. 212, No. 1270, January 1971.

Swidler, Leonard and Swidler, Arlene, eds., *Women Priests: A Catholic Commentary on the Vatican Declaration.* New York, NY: Paulist Press, 1977.

"Synod Speakers Highlight Family Life Problems." National Catholic Magazine. Trenton, NJ: *The Monitor.* Vol. XXVII, No. 34, Oct. 2, 1980: 1, 25.

Tavard, George H. *Women in Christian Tradition.* Notre Dame, IN: University of Notre Dame Press, 1973.

Tomczak, Larry. *Straightforward. Why Wait Till Marriage?* Plainfield, NJ: Logos International, 1978.

Tompkins, Iverna. *How to Be Happy in No Man's Land: A Book for Singles.* Plainfield, NJ: Logos International, 1975.

"Top Ten Stories." Religious Newswriters Top Religious Stories. Logoscope, Plainfield, NJ: Logos International, Vol. 3, No.2, 1979.

Trahey, Jane. *On Women and Power.* New York, NY: Avon Books, Hearst Corp, 1977.

"U.S. Bishops Nudge Rome for Review of Birth Control." Associated Press. New York Daily News. Vol. 62, No. 83, Sept. 30, 1980: 4.

*"U.S. Bishops Urging Rome to Re-examine Birth Control Issue." New York Times.*Vol. CXXX, No. 44,722, Sept. 30, 1980: A1, 6.

U.S. Conference of Catholic Bishops. *"The Catholic Church in the United States at a Glance."* Office of Media Relations. Department of Communications, Washington, D.C. 2007.

—*Co-Workers in the Vineyard of the Lord: A Resource for Guiding the Development of Lay Ecclesial Ministry."* Office of Media Relations. Department of Communications. Washington, D.C. Nov. 5, 2005.

—*From Words to Deeds: Continuing Reflections on the Role of Women in the Church."* Office of Media Relations. Department of Communications. Washington, D.C. Sept. 15, 1998.

—*Official Catholic Directory Statistics Show Catholics Still 22 Percent of U.S. Population."* Office of Media Relations. Department of Communications. Washington, D.C. News Release, June 3, 2009.

—*"Strengthening the Bonds of Peace: A Pastoral Reflection on Women in the Church and in Society."* Office of Media Relations. Department of Communications. Washington, D.C. Nov. 1994.

"Validity of Anglican Orders Remains an Issue." National Catholic Dispatch. Trenton, NJ: *The Monitor.* Vol. XXVII, No. 30, Sept. 4, 1980: 14.

Wahlberg, Rachael Conrad. *Jesus According to a Woman.* New York, NY: Paulist Press, 1975.

Wakin, Edward and Pantoga, Fritzie. *"How to Decide to Start/Stop Having Children." U.S. Catholic.* Vol. 43, No., 12, Dec 1978: 6-11.

Weaver, Mary Jo. *"Single Blessedness?" Commonweal.* Vol. CVI, No. 19, Oct. 26, 1979: 588-91.

Westenhaver, Edith. *"Bishops Reverse Themselves on Sexist Liturgical Words." Religious News Service.* Nov. 12, 1980: 1-2.

Wexler, Jacqueline Grennan. *"Conversations About the Pope." Ladies Home Journal.* Vol. XCVII, No. 4, April 1980: 78.

"Women and Ministry, A National Study of Roman Catholic Women."
Washington, D.C.: Center for Applied Research in the Church,
Progress Report, Aug. 15, 1979.

"Women and Priestly Ministry: The New Testament Evidence."
Catholic Biblical Quarterly. Vol. 41, Fall 1979: 608-613.

"Women of the Cloth, Episcopal Church." Newsweek. Oct. 24, 1977,
90:12+.

Wrightman, Paul. *Paul's Early Letters: from Hope through Faith to
Love.* Study Guide, New York, NY: Alba House, 1983.

Zagano, Phyllis. *"Catholic Women Deacons," America,* May 2009.

Other media and conferences:

"Spiritual Development." Two-year course given by Fr. Benedict
Groeshel and team for the New York Archdiocese's Center for
Spiritual Development.

The Healing School, Two-year course given by the Diocese of
Trenton, N.J.

"Women Moving Church." Three-day conference on the impact
of the women's movement on the Catholic Church in the U.S.
Washington, D.C.: Center of Concern, May 20-22, 1981.

Christian, Kathryn. *Ascension.* CD: 1998. P.O. Box 72, Williamsburg,
MI 49690.

Maloney, Fr. George. *"Mary: the Womb of God".* Eastern General
Conference, Tape No. 77EG25, Conference Cassettes, Ann Arbor,
MI., 1977.

O'Brien, Fr. William. *"Mary."* Eastern General Conference, Tape No.
78AC25, Ann Arbor, MI: Conference Cassettes, 1978.

On line:

The Catholic Encyclopedia. "Deaconesses." (Search was for
"Deaconesses in the Early Catholic Church"), http://www.

<u>new</u> advent.org/cathen/04651a.htm, and Wikipedia.org/wiki/ Deaconesses.

LaRue, Renee M. *"Church Ladies: Women in Leadership." U.S. Catholic.* Accessed on line, Dec. 16, 2010.

Other topics: Church sex scandals; *Humanae Vitae*; Priest shortage; USCCB documents, including pastoral on women; Vatican documents; Vatican norms 2010; Women Chancellors; Women Doctors of the Catholic Church; the Role of Women, Intermediate, Judaism.

Smith, Janet, Dr. *Humanae Vitae*: *A Generation Later.* 2000.

USCCB, Office of Media Relations, *"Ten Frequently Asked Questions About the Reservation of Priestly Ordination to Men."* 1998.

Walsh, Mary Ann, Sr., *"What Would Mary Do? Don't Ask Newsweek." The Monitor.* Accessed online, Feb. 23, 2011.

Wikipedia, the internet encyclopedia. Topics: "Julian of Norwich;" "Anchorite;" "Meister Eckhart and Medieval Mysticism;" "Ordination of Women". "Pope Paul III (Alexander Farnese)", "Pope who had grandsons," "Transubstantiation," "Catholic priests"

CPSIA information can be obtained at www.ICGtesting.com
Printed in the USA
BVOW020924170512

290408BV00002B/1/P